MELODY • LYRICS • CHORDS

2nd EDITION

FOR ALL "C" INSTRUMENTS

JUN 13 2003

CLASSIC ROCK FAKE BOOK

OVER 250 GREAT SONGS OF THE ROCK ERA

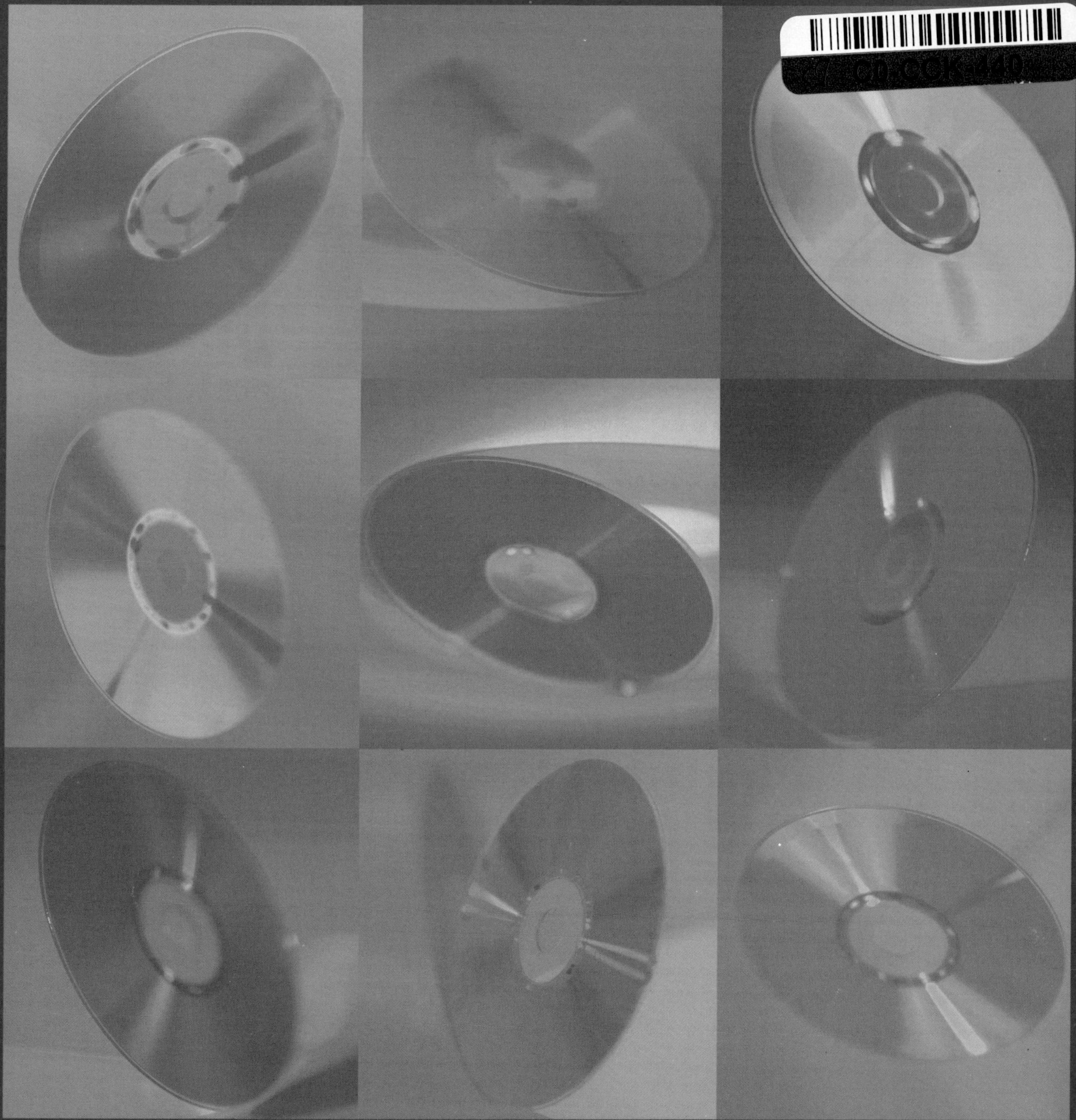

ISBN 0-7935-7856-6

HAL•LEONARD® CORPORATION
7777 W. BLUEMOUND RD. P.O. BOX 13819 MILWAUKEE, WI 53213

For all works contained herein:
Unauthorized copying, arranging, adapting, recording or public performance is an infringement of copyright.
Infringers are liable under the law.

Visit Hal Leonard Online at
www.halleonard.com

2nd EDITION

CLASSIC ROCK FAKE BOOK

CONTENTS

2nd EDITION

CLASSIC ROCK FAKE BOOK

ARTIST INDEX

THE AIR THAT I BREATHE

© 1972, 1973 (Renewed 2000, 2001) EMI APRIL MUSIC INC.

Words and Music by ALBERT HAMMOND
and MICHAEL HAZELWOOD

ALLENTOWN

© 1981, 1982 JOEL SONGS

Words and Music by
BILLY JOEL

AMANDA

Copyright © 1986 Hideaway Hits (ASCAP)

Words and Music by
TOM SCHOLZ

G C/G G Em Bm
So, it may be too soon, I know. The feel-in' takes so long to grow. If I
C G/B Am G D C/D
tell you to-day will you turn me a-way and let me go? I don't wan-na lose you. (Instrumental)
G/D D Bm Em Am7 D
Em Am7 D Em Am7
(End instrumental) I'm gon-na take you by sur-prise and make you re-al-ize, A-
D Em Am7 D
man-da. I'm gon-na tell you right a-way; I can't wait an-oth-er day, A-man-da. I'm gon-na
Em Am7 D E
say it like a man and make you un-der-stand, A-man-da. Oh, girl. Instrumental
Bm7 E Bm7 E
(End instrumental) You and I, I
Bm7 E Bm7
know that we can't wait. And I swear, I swear it's not a lie, girl. To-mor-row may be too late.
C D G D/F# Em Em/D C C/B Am Am/G
You, you and I, girl, we can share a life to-geth-er. It's now or nev-er, and to-mor-row may be too
D C/D G/D D G C/G
late. Oh. And feel-in' the way I
G Em Bm Am Am/G D
do. I don't wan-na wait my whole life through to say I'm in love with you.

AMERICAN WOMAN

© 1970 (Renewed 1998) SHILLELAGH MUSIC (BMI)/Administered by BUG MUSIC

Written by BURTON CUMMINGS, RANDY BACHMAN,
GARY PETERSON and JIM KALE

Additional Lyrics

2. American woman, get away from me
American woman, mama let me be
Don't wanna see your shadow no more
Colored lights can hypnotize
Sparkle someone else's eyes
Now woman, I said get away
American woman, listen what I say.

3. American woman, said get away
American woman, listen what I say
Don't come hangin' around my door
Don't wanna see your face no more
I don't need your war machines
I don't need your ghetto scenes
Colored lights can hypnotize
Sparkle someone else's eyes
Now woman, get away from me
American woman, mama let me be.

AND WHEN I DIE

© 1966 (Renewed 1994) EMI BLACKWOOD MUSIC INC.

Words and Music by
LAURA NYRO

Freely

N.C.

(Instrumental)

𝄋 Slow Two-Beat

A6 D6 A6 D6

(End instrumental)

A6 D6 A6 D6 A6 D6 A6 D6

I'm not scared of dy - in' and I don't real - ly care. If it's
Now trou - bles are man - y, they're as deep as a well. I can

A6 D6 A6 D6 Bm7/E D6 A6

peace you find in dy - in', well, then let the time be near. If it's
swear there ain't no heav - en but I pray there ain't no hell.

Faster

G D G D E7sus

peace you find in dy - in' and if dy - in' time is near, just
Swear there ain't no heav - en and I pray there ain't no hell. But I'll

Bm7 C♯m7 D D/E A D A D

bun - dle up my cof - fin 'cause it's cold way down there. I hear that it's
nev - er know by liv - ing, on - ly my dy - in' will tell. Yes, on - ly my

A D A Dmaj7 C♯m7 Bm7 D/E

cold way down there. Yeah. Cra - zy cold way down
dy - in' will tell. Yeah. On - ly my dy - in' will

A D A D A Bm7 C♯m7

there.
tell.

And when I die and when I'm

F♯m7 A7 N.C. Dmaj7 N.C. C♯m7 N.C. Bm7 D/E

gone, there'll be one child born in this

To Coda ⊕

A D A D

world to car - ry on, to car - ry on.

(Instrumental)

D.S. al Coda

A D A D A

CODA

⊕

A D A D A

on. Yeah, yeah.

(Instrumental)

Slow Two-Beat
A6 D6 A6 D6 A6 D6 A6 D6
Give me my free - dom for as long as I be.
A6 D6 A6 D6 Bm7/E D6 A6
All I ask of liv - in' is to have no chains on me.
Faster
G D G D E7sus
All I ask of liv - in' is to have no chains on me. And
Bm7 C#m7 D D/E A D A D
all I ask of dy - in' is to go nat - 'ral - ly. I on - ly wan - na
Half-tempo Rock
A D A A7
go nat - 'ral - ly. Here I go ha! Hey hey. Here comes the
dev - il right be - hind. (Spoken:) Look out, children! Here he come.
Here he come. Hey.
Two-Beat
A
Don't wan - na go by the dev - il. Don't wan - na go by the de - mon.
Don't wan - na go by Sa - tan. Don't wan - na die un - eas - y.
Freely
N.C.
Just let me go nat - 'ral - ly.
Slowly
Bm C#m
And when I die,
D/A E/G# F/A N.C. Bb/D F#/C# D
and when I'm dead, dead and gone, there'll be one child born in our
N.C.
world to car - ry on, to car - ry on.
Fast
A D A D
Yeah, yeah. (Instrumental)
A D A D A

ANGIE

© 1973 (Renewed 2001) EMI MUSIC PUBLISHING LTD.
All Rights for the U.S. and Canada Controlled and Administered by COLGEMS-EMI MUSIC INC.

Words and Music by MICK JAGGER
and KEITH RICHARDS

Am E7 G B♭ F C Dm C
(End instrumental) Oh, ___

G Dm Am C F G
An - gie, don't _ you weep, all your kiss - es still taste sweet, I hate that sad-ness in _ your eyes, ___ but

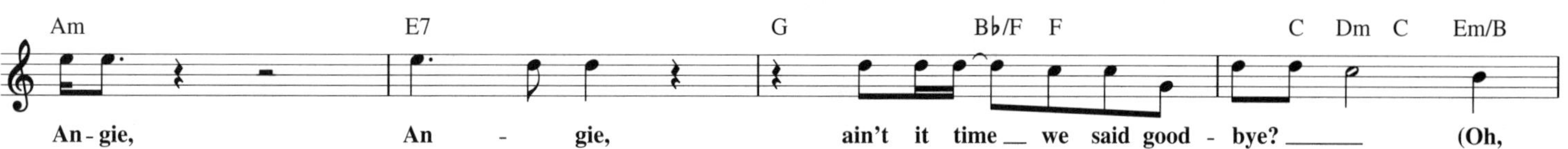
Am E7 G B♭/F F C Dm C Em/B
An-gie, An - gie, ain't it time _ we said good - bye? ___ (Oh,

Am E7 G B♭ F C Dm C
yes.) (Instrumental) (End instrumental) With no

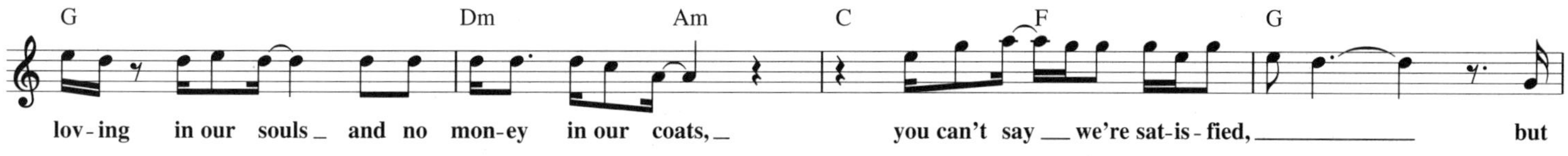
G Dm Am C F G
lov-ing in our souls _ and no mon-ey in our coats, _ you can't say _ we're sat-is-fied, ___ but

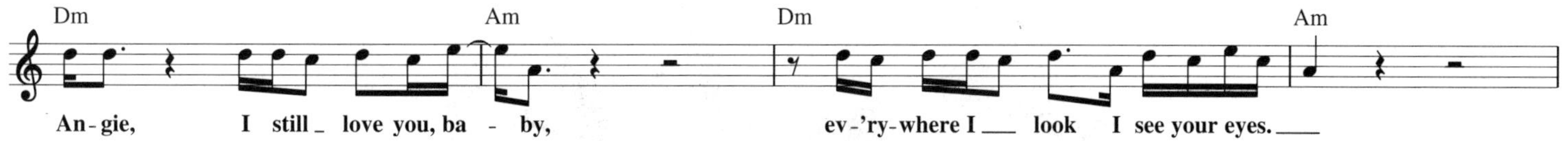
Dm Am Dm Am
An-gie, I still _ love you, ba - by, ev-'ry-where I _ look I see your eyes. ___

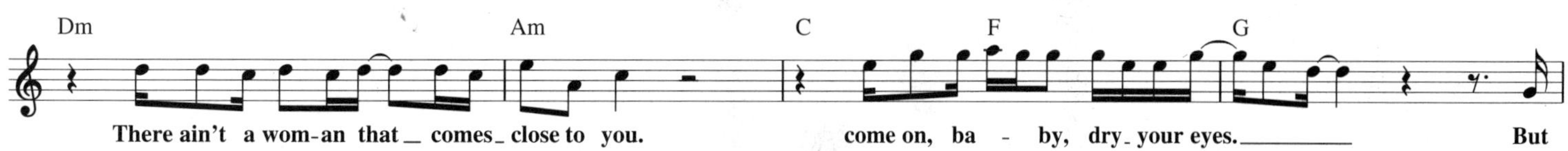
Dm Am C F G
There ain't a wom-an that _ comes _ close to you. come on, ba - by, dry _ your eyes. ___ But

Am E7 G B♭/F F C Dm C Em/B
An-gie, An - gie, ain't it good to be a - live? ___

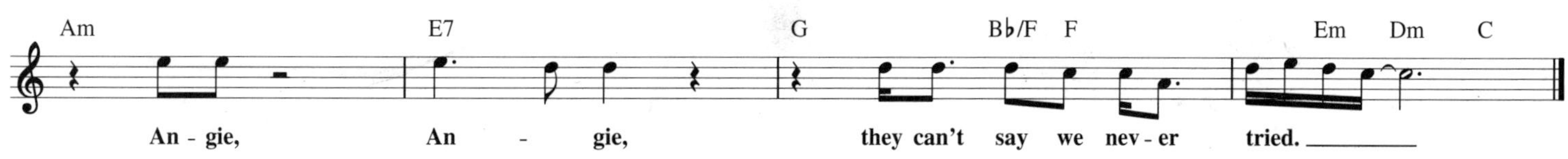
Am E7 G B♭/F F Em Dm C
An - gie, An - gie, they can't say we nev - er tried. ___

ANOTHER ONE BITES THE DUST

© 1980 QUEEN MUSIC LTD.
All Rights Controlled and Administered by BEECHWOOD MUSIC CORP.

Words and Music by
JOHN DEACON

ALL RIGHT NOW

Copyright © 1970 Blue Mountain Music, Ltd.
Copyright Renewed
All Rights for North and South America Controlled and Administered by Pubco
All Rights for the rest of the World Controlled and Administered by Rykomusic, Ltd.

Words and Music by PAUL RODGERS
and ANDY FRASER

ATLANTIS

Copyright © 1968 by Donovan (Music) Ltd.
Copyright Renewed
All Rights Administered by Peer International Corporation

Words and Music by
DONOVAN LEITCH

BABY, I LOVE YOUR WAY

Copyright © 1975 ALMO MUSIC CORP. and NUAGES ARTISTS MUSIC LTD.
All Rights Administered by ALMO MUSIC CORP.

Words and Music by
PETER FRAMPTON

Moderately

G G/F# Em Em/D C F7

Shad-ows grow so long before my eyes and they're mov-ing a-cross the page.
Sud-den-ly the day turns in-to night far a-way from the cit-y.
Moon ap-pears to shine and light the sky with the help of some fire-fly.
Won-der how they have the pow'r to shine. I can see them un-der the pine.

1,3 | 2,4

Bm E7 Am D7

But don't hes-i-tate 'cause your love won't wait.

To Coda

G D Am C

Ooh, ba-by, I love your way.
Wan-na tell you I love your way.
Wan-na be with you night and day.

Play 3 times

1 G G/F# Em Em/D C Bm Am Am7/D

(Instrumental solo ad lib.)

D.C. (take 3rd ending)

2 G G/F# Em Em/D C F7

(Instrumental solo ad lib.)

1 | 2

D.S. al Coda

But

CODA

G G/F# Em Em/D C F7

I can see the sun-set in your eyes, brown and gray and blue be-sides.

G G/F# Em C F7

Clouds are stalk-ing is-lands in the sun. I wish I could buy one out of sea-son.

Bm E7 Am D7

Don't hes-i-tate 'cause your love won't wait.

G D Am C

Repeat and Fade

Ooh, ba-by, I love your way.
Wan-na tell you I love your way.
Wan-na be with you night and day.

BACK IN THE U.S.S.R.

Copyright © 1968 Sony/ATV Songs LLC
Copyright Renewed
All Rights Adminstered by Sony/ATV Music Publishing, 8 Music Square West, Nashville, TN 37203

Words and Music by JOHN LENNON
and PAUL McCARTNEY

BACK IN THE SADDLE

Copyright © 1976 Daksel LLC
All Rights Administered by Sony/ATV Music Publishing, 8 Music Square West, Nashville, TN 37203

Words and Music by STEVEN TYLER
and JOE PERRY

Ab7 Db7 Ab7 Db7
I'm call-in' all the shots to-night, I'm like a load-ed gun. (Instrumental)
Bb7 Eb/Bb
Peel-in' off my boots and chaps, I'm sad-dle sore.
Bb7 Eb/Bb Bb7 Eb/Bb
Four bits gets you time in the rack; I scream for more. Fool's gold out of their mines,
Bb7 Eb/Bb
the girls are soak-in' wet. No tongue's dri-er than mine, I'll come when I get
Eb7
1
back. (Instrumental) I'm back in the sad-dle a-gain, (Instrumental) I'm
2
(Instrumental)
Absus Ab Bb/Ab EbmAb
I'm rid-in', I'm load-in' up my
I'm rid-in', I'm shin-in' up my
Bbm7 Ab Absus Ab Bb/Ab Ebm/Ab
pis-tol. I'm rid-in', I real-ly got a
sad-dle. I'm rid-in', the snake is gon-na
Bbm7
1 Ab
2 Ab
D.S. al Coda (with repeat)
fist-ful.
rat-tle.
I'm
CODA
Absus Ab Bb/Ab Ebm/Ab Bbm7
Rid-in' high.
1, 2 Ab
3 Ab
N.C.
(Instrumental)

BAD, BAD LEROY BROWN
Copyright © 1972 (Renewed) Time In A Bottle and Croce Publishing (ASCAP)
Words and Music by
JIM CROCE
Moderate Boogie-Rock tempo
G A7
Well, the South - side of Chi - ca - go is the bad - dest part of town,
- roy, he a gam - bler and he like his fan - cy clothes,
- day 'bout a week a - go, Le - roy shoot - in' dice
B7 C D7
and if you go down there you bet - ter just be - ware of a man name of Le - roy Brown.
and he like to wave his dia - mond rings in front of ev - 'ry - bod - y's nose.
and at the edge of the bar sat a girl name of Dor - is and oh, that girl looked nice.
G A7
Now Le - roy more than trou - ble, you see he stand 'bout six - foot - four. All the down -
He got a cus - tom Con - ti - nen - tal, he got a El - do - ra - do, too. He got a
Well, he cast his eyes up - on her, and the trou - ble soon be - gan, and Le -
B7 C D7 G
- town la - dies call him "tree - top lov - er," all the men just call him "Sir."
thir - ty - two gun in his pock - et for fun, he got a ra - zor in his shoe.
- roy Brown, he learned a les - son 'bout mess - in' with the wife of a jeal - ous man.
And he's bad,
G A7
bad Le - roy Brown, the bad - dest man in the whole damned town;
To Coda
1,2 3
B7 C D C G G
bad - der than old King Kong and mean - er than a junk - yard dog. Now, Le - Well, the two
Well, Fri -
A7
men took to fight - in', and when they pulled them from the floor
B7 C D7 G D.S. al Coda
Le - roy looked like a jig - saw puz - zle with a cou - ple of piec - es gone. And he's bad,
CODA
G B7 C D C G
Yes, you were bad - der than old King Kong, and mean - er than a junk - yard dog.
BEAST OF BURDEN
© 1978 EMI MUSIC PUBLISHING LTD.
All Rights for the U.S. and Canada Controlled and Administered by COLGEMS-EMI MUSIC INC.
Words and Music by MICK JAGGER
and KEITH RICHARDS
Slow beat
E B/D# C#m A E B/D# C#m A E B/D# C#m
I'll nev - er be your beast of bur - den. My back is broad, but it's a - hurt - ing. All I want is for
I'll nev - er be your beast of bur - den. I've walked for miles, my feet are hurt - ing. All I want is for
A E B/D# C#m 1 A 2 A
you to make love to me.
you to make love to me. Am I hard e - nough? Am I

E/G# A E/G# A B E B/D# C#m
rough e - nough?_ Am I rich e - nough?_ I'm not too blind _ to see ___ I'll nev - er be your beast_
A E B/D# C#m A E E/D# C#m A
__ of bur - den. So let's go home _ and draw the cur - tains, mu - sic on the ra - di - o. Come on, ba - by, make sweet love to me._
E B/D# C#m A E/G# A
Am I hard e - nough?_ Am I rough e - nough?_ Am I rich e - nough?_ I'm
E/G# A B E B/D# C#m A
not too blind _ to see. __ Oh, lit - tle sis - ter, ______ pret - ty, pret - ty, pret - ty, pret - ty girl._
E B/D# C#m A E B/D# C#m A E B/D# C#m A
(Instrumental)
You're a
(End instrumental)
E E/G# A E E/G# A E E/G#
pret - ty, pret - ty, pret - ty, pret - ty, pret - ty, pret - ty girl._ Pret - ty, pret - ty, such a pret - ty, pret - ty, pret - ty girl._ Come on, ba - by,
A E E/G# A (Spoken) E B/D# C#m A
please,_ please,_ please. I'll tell ya,_ you can put me out on the street.
E B/D# C#m A (Sung) E E/D# C#m A E B/D# C#m A
Put me out with no shoes on my feet, but put me out, put me out, put me out of mis - er - y, ___ yeah.
E B/D# C#m A E B/D# C#m A E B/D# C#m
All your sick - ness, I can suck it up. Throw it all at me, I can shrug it off. There's one thing that
A E E/G# A E B/D# C#m A
I don't un - der - stand. You keep on tell - ing me I ain't your kind of man._ Ain't I rough e - nough? Oh! Ain't I
E B/D# C#m A E B/D# C#m A E B/D# C#m A
tough e - nough? Ain't I rich e - nough, in love e - nough? Ooh, ooh ___ please. ___________
E E/G# A E A
I'll nev - er be your beast __ of bur - den. I'll nev - er be your beast_ of bur - den,
I'll nev - er be your beast __ of bur - den. I've walked for miles and my ___ feet are hurt - ing.
I won't need no beast __ of bur - den. I need no fuss - ing, I need no nurs - ing.
Repeat and Fade
E E/D# C#m A E B/D# C#m A A/B
Nev - er, nev - er, nev - er, nev - er, nev - er, nev - er, nev - er be. ____________
All I want is you to make love to me. ____________
Nev - er, nev - er, nev - er, nev - er, nev - er, nev - er, nev - er be. ____________

BAD MEDICINE

© 1988 EMI APRIL MUSIC INC., DESMOBILE MUSIC CO., INC., UNIVERSAL - POLYGRAM INTERNATIONAL PUBLISHING, INC., BON JOVI PUBLISHING and NEW JERSEY UNDERGROUND MUSIC INC.
All Rights for DESMOBILE MUSIC CO., INC. Controlled and Administered by EMI APRIL MUSIC INC.

Words and Music by DESMOND CHILD, RICHIE SAMBORA and JON BON JOVI

G5 F#5 E5 G5 E5 A5 G5 F#5 E5
what I need, whoa. Shake it up just like bad med - i - cine.
A5 G5 F#5 E5 Gmaj7 A
There ain't no doc - tor that can cure my dis - ease.
So let's play doc - tor, ba - by, cure my dis - ease.
Bad, bad
1 E(N.C.) 2 E5
med - i - cine. (Instrumental) I med - i - cine, is what I want.
Gmaj7 A E(N.C.)
Bad, bad med - i - cine. Oh it's what I need. I
need a res - pi - ra - tor 'cause I'm run - ning out of breath. You're an all night gen - er - a - tor wrapped in
B5
stock - ings and a dress. When you find your med - i - cine you take what you can get. 'Cause if there's
E N.C. E5
some - thing bet - ter ba - by, well, they have - n't found it yet, whoa. Your love is like
A5 G5 F#5 E5 A5 G5 F#5 E5
bad med - i - cine, bad med - i - cine, is what I need, whoa.
G5 E5 A5 G5 F#5 E5 A5
Shake it up just like bad med - i - cine.
There ain't no doc - tor that can
Your love's the po - tion that can
1 G5 F#5 E5 2 G5 F#5 E5 Gmaj7 A
cure my dis - ease. cure my dis - ease. Bad, bad
E(N.C.) Gmaj7 A E5
med - i - cine, is what I want. Bad, bad med - i - cine. (Instrumental)
Gmaj7 A N.C. G5 F#5 E5
Bad, bad med - i - cine.

BALLROOM BLITZ

Copyright © 1984 by BMG Songs, Inc.

Words and Music by MIKE CHAPMAN
and NICKY CHINN

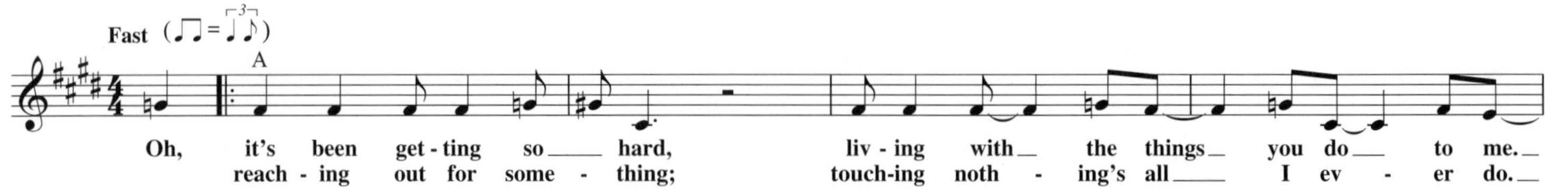
Fast
A
Oh, it's been get - ting so hard, liv - ing with the things you do to me.
reach - ing out for some - thing; touch-ing noth - ing's all I ev - er do.

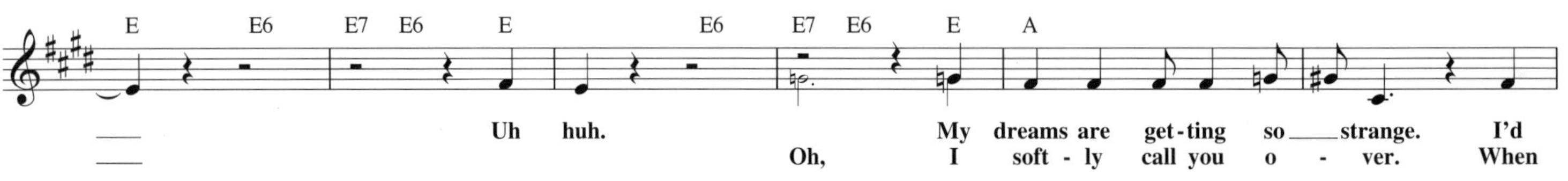
E E6 E7 E6 E E6 E7 E6 E A
Uh huh. My dreams are get - ting so strange. I'd
Oh, I soft - ly call you o - ver. When

E E6 E7 E6 E E6 E7 E6 E
like to tell you ev - 'ry - thing I see. Mm. Oh, I see a
you ap - pear, there's noth - ing left of you. Uh huh. Now a

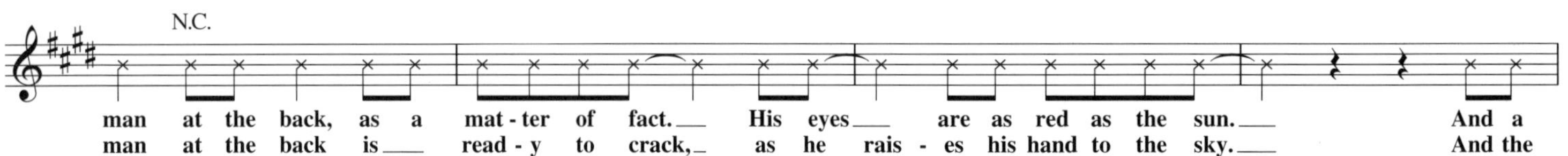
N.C.
man at the back, as a mat - ter of fact. His eyes are as red as the sun. And a
man at the back is read - y to crack, as he rais - es his hand to the sky. And the

girl in the cor - ner let no one ig - nore her, 'cause she thinks she's the pas -
girl in the cor - ner is ev - ry - one's mourn - er; she could kill you with a wink of her eye.

E F♯
- sion - ate one. Oh, yeah. It was like light - ning.
Oh, yeah. It was e - lec - tric,

A C
Ev - 'ry - bod - y was fright - 'ning and the mu - sic was sooth - ing
so fright - ful - ly hec - tic. And the band start - ed leap - ing

E
and they all start - ed groov - ing, yeah. Yeah, yeah, yeah, yeah. And the
'cause they all stopped breath - ing,
F♯ A B E
man at the back said, ev - 'ry - one at - tack, and it turned in - to a ball - room blitz. And the
To Coda
F♯ A B E D E♭
girl in the cor - ner said, boy I wan - na warn ya, it - 'll turn in - to a ball - room blitz, ball - room
1
E D E♭ E D E♭ E D E♭
blitz, ball - room blitz, ball - room blitz, ball - room
E E6 E7 E6 E E6 E7 E6 E
blitz. (Instrumental) I'm
2
E N.C./E N.C./D N.C./E D E♭ N.C./E D N.C./E
blitz. (Instrumental)
Play 3 times
D E♭ E
D.S. al Coda (Verse 1)
Oh, yeah. It was like
CODA
E D E♭ E E
Play 3 times
blitz, ball - room blitz, It's, it's a
Play 3 times
D E E6 E7 E6 E
Repeat and Fade
ball - room blitz. Yeah, it's a ball - room blitz. (Instrumental)

BARRACUDA

Copyright © 1977 by BMG Songs, Inc., Know Music, Strange Euphoria Music and Of The Roses Music

Words and Music by ROGER FISHER, NANCY WILSON, ANN WILSON and MICHAEL DEROSIER

Moderately fast
E5
C5
So this ain't the end, I saw you a - gain to - day. I had to

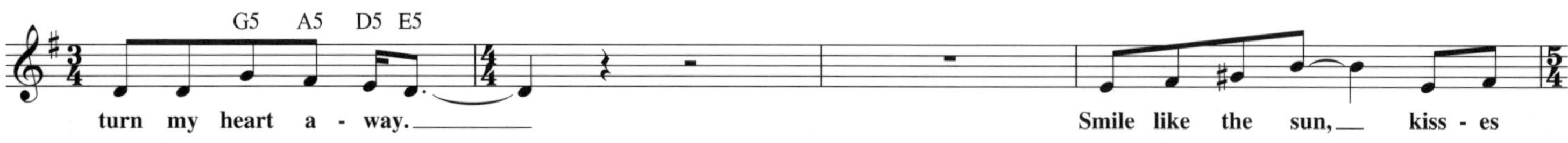
G5 A5 D5 E5
turn my heart a - way. Smile like the sun, kiss - es

C5
G5 A5 D5 E5
for ev - 'ry - one, and tales it nev - er fails.

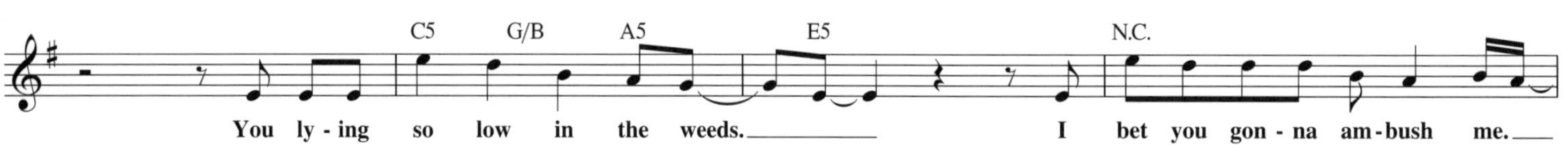
C5 G/B A5 E5
N.C.
You ly - ing so low in the weeds. I bet you gon - na am - bush me.

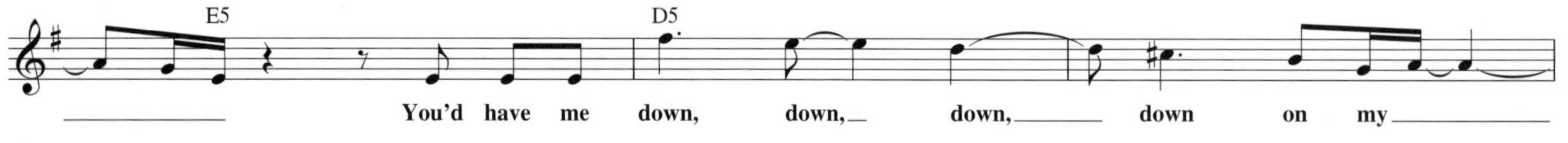
E5
D5
You'd have me down, down, down, down on my

A5
N.C.
E5
F♯5 G5
knees now would-n't ya, Bar - ra - cu - da? Oh! (Instrumental)

E5
F♯5 G5
E5
Back o - ver time we were

C5
G5 A5 D5 E5
all try - ing for free. You met the por-poise and me. Uh huh!

C5
G5 A5 D5 E5
No right, no wrong selling a song. A name
C5 G/B A5 E5
whisper game. And if the real thing don't do the trick you better
N.C. E5 D5
make up something quick You gonna burn, burn, burn, burn, burn to the wick
A5 To Coda N.C. E5 G5 A5 D5 E5
Ooh Barracuda. Oh yeah!
G5 A5 D5 E5 C5 A5
"Sell me, sell you," the porpoise said. Dive down, deep
E5 G5 A5 D5 E5 G5 A5 D5 E5
to save my head. You, I think that you got the blues too.
C5 A5
All that night and all the next swam without looking back. Made for the western
E5 F♯5 G5 A5 E5 D.S. al Coda F♯5 G5 A5
pools. Silly, silly fools. The
CODA
N.C. E5
Oh Barra, Barracuda. Yeah!

BELL BOTTOM BLUES

Copyright © 1970, 1971, 1978 by Throat Music Ltd.
Copyright Renewed
All Rights Administered by Unichappell Music Inc.

Words and Music by
ERIC CLAPTON

BEST OF MY LOVE

© 1974 EMI BLACKWOOD MUSIC INC., WOODY CREEK MUSIC and RED CLOUD MUSIC

Words and Music by JOHN DAVID SOUTHER, DON HENLEY and GLENN FREY

Moderately slow
C Dm7
Ev - er - y night I'm ly - in' in bed, hold - in' you close in my dreams;
Beau - ti - ful fac - es and loud emp - ty plac - es, look at the way that we live;
C Dm7
think - in' a - bout all the things that we said and com - in' a - part at the seams.
wast - in' our time on cheap talk and wine left us so lit - tle to give.
Em7 Dm7 Dm7/G Em7 F/G
We try to talk it o - ver but the words come out too rough; I
That same old crowd was like a cold dark cloud that we could nev - er rise a - bove; but
C Dm7 Dm7/G C 1 G7 2 G7
know you were try - in' to give me the best of your love.
here in my heart I give you the best of my love. Oh,
C Dm7 C
sweet dar - lin', you get the best of my love, oh, sweet dar -
Dm7 Fm7
- lin', you get the best of my love. I'm go - in' back in time and it's a
C Fm7 Dm Dm(add4)
sweet dream; it was a qui - et night and I would be all right if I could go on
G7 C Dm7
sleep - ing. But ev - 'ry morn - in' I wake up and wor - ry what's gon - na hap - pen to - day.
C Dm7
You see it your way and I see it mine, but we both see it slip - pin' a - way.
Em7 Dm7 Em7 Dm7 G7
You know we al - ways had each oth - er, ba - by, I guess that was - n't e - nough; oh, but
C Dm7 C G7
here in my heart I give you the best of my love. Oh,
Repeat and Fade
C Dm7 Dm7/G
sweet dar - lin', you get the best of my love. Oh,

BIRTHDAY

Copyright © 1968 Sony/ATV Songs LLC
Copyrght Renewed
All Rights Administered by Sony/ATV Music Publishing, 8 Music Square West, Nashville, TN 37203

Words and Music by JOHN LENNON
and PAUL McCARTNEY

THE BITCH IS BACK

Copyright © 1974 by Big Pig Music Ltd.
All Rights for the United States Administered by Intersong U.S.A., Inc.

Words and Music by ELTON JOHN
and BERNIE TAUPIN

With a driving beat

Ab Db/Ab Ab Db/Ab Ab
I was jus - ti - fied ___ when I was five, rais - in' cane, ___ I spit in

Eb7 Ab Gb Db Ab
your eye. Times are chang - in' now, the poor get ___ fat, ___ but the fev-er's gon-na catch you when the

Eb7 Ab Db/Ab Ab Db/Ab Ab Db/Ab Ab Db/A Ab Db/Ab
bitch gets back. ___ *(Instrumental)*

Ab Db/Ab Ab Db/Ab Ab Db/Ab Ab
(End instrumental) Eat meat on Fri - day that's ___ al - right, ___ I ev - en like ___ steak on a

Eb7 Ab Gb Db
Sat-ur-day night. I can bitch the best ___ at your so - cial do's, ___ I get

Db/Ab Ab Eb7 Ab Db/Ab Ab Db/Ab Ab
high in the eve-ning sniff-ing pots of glue. ___ *(Instrumental)* I'm a

𝄋 Eb7#9 Fm7 Db6
bitch, I'm a bitch, oh the bitch is ___ back; stone ___ cold so - ber as a mat-ter of fact. ___ I can

Eb7#9 Gb
bitch, I can bitch 'cause I'm bet - ter than you. It's the way that I move ___ and the

Eb7#9 Ab Absus
things that I do, ___ oh. ___ *(Instrumental)*

To Coda ⊕

Ab Absus Ab Db/Ab Ab
(End instrumental) I en - ter - tain ___ by pick-ing brains,

Db/Ab Ab Eb7 Ab Gb Db
sell my soul ___ by drop-ping names. I don't like those! ___ My God, ___ what's that! ___ Oh, its

Ab Eb7 Ab Db/Ab Ab Db/Ab Ab **D.S. al Coda**
full of nas - ty hab - its when the bitch gets back. ___ *(Instrumental)* I'm a

CODA ⊕

Absus Ab7 Gb Db Ab7
(End instrumental) Bitch, bitch, the bitch is ___ back. ___

Gb Db Ab7 Gb Db Ab Gb Db **Repeat and Fade**
(Instrumental) Bitch, bitch, the bitch is ___ back. ___ *(Instrumental)*

BLUE COLLAR MAN
(Long Nights)

Copyright © 1978 ALMO MUSIC CORP. and STYGIAN SONGS
All Rights Controlled and Administered by ALMO MUSIC CORP.

Words and Music by
TOMMY SHAW

Gm/D C/D Dm N.C.
all night, to be just who I am, well I'd rath - er be a blue col - lar man.
Dm C F/C C
Keep - ing my mind on a bet - ter life, where
Par - a - dise, can it be all I heard it was? I
B♭ 1 Dm N.C.
hap - pi - ness is on - ly a heart - beat a - way.
close my eyes and
(Instrumental)
2 Asus A Dm Gm/D
may - be I'm al - read - y there. I'll take those long nights, im -
C/D Dm B♭ C Dm Gm/D
pos - si - ble odds, keep - ing my back to the wall. If it takes all that, to be
C/D Dm N.C. B♭
just what I am, well I'm gon - na be a blue col - lar man.
C/B♭ B♭ 1-3 C/B♭ 4 C/B♭ Dm Gm/D
Do do do do do do do do. I'll take those long nights, im -
C/D Dm B♭ C Dm
pos - si - ble odds, keep - ing my eye on the key - hole. If it takes
Gm/D C/D Dm N.C.
all night, to be just who I am, well, I'd rath - er be a blue col - lar, got -
Dm
- ta be a blue col - lar, gon - na be a blue col - lar man.

BLUE SKY

Copyright © 1974 by Unichappell Music Inc. and F. R. Betts Music Co.
All Rights Administered by Unichappell Music Inc.

Words and Music by
DICKEY BETTS

BRAIN DAMAGE

TRO - © Copyright 1973 (Renewed) Hampshire House Publishing Corp., New York, NY

Words and Music by
ROGER WATERS

BREAKDOWN

Copyright © 1976 ALMO MUSIC CORP.

Words and Music by
TOM PETTY

Moderate Shuffle (♫ = ♩ ♪)

Am G Am G Am G Am G
It's all right if you love me. It's all right if you don't.
There is no sense in pre - tend - ing. Your eyes give you a - way.

Am G Am G Am G
I'm not a - fraid of you run - ning a - way hon - ey, I get the feel - ing you
Some - thing in - side you is feel - ing like I do. We've said all there is to

Fmaj7 G7/F Fmaj7 | 1 G7/F | 2 G7/F | 𝄋 Am G F G
won't.
say. Ba - by, break down. Go a-head give it to me.

Am G F G Am G
Break down, hon - ey take me through the night. Break down, now I'm

F G Am G Fmaj7 G7/F Fmaj7 G7/F
stand - in' here, can't you see? Break down, it's all right, it's all

Fmaj7 Am G **To Coda** 𝄌 Am G Am G **Play 5 times**
right, it's all right. *Solo ad. lib.*

F G7/F Fmaj7 G7/F **D.S. al Coda**

CODA 𝄌 **Repeat and Fade**
Am G Am G
Solo ad. lib.

BURNING FOR YOU

Copyright © 1981 Sony/ATV Tunes LLC
All Rights Administered by Sony/ATV Music Publishing, 8 Music Square West, Nashville, TN 37203

Words and Music by DONALD ROESER
and RICHARD MELTZER

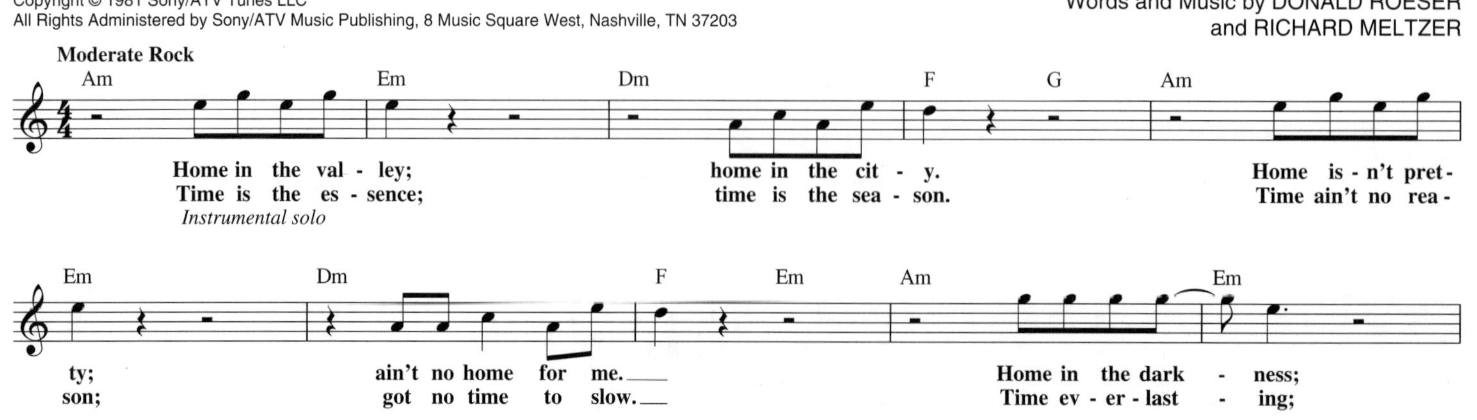

Dm
F
G
Am
Em
home on the high - way.
time to play "B" sides.
Home is - n't my way;
Time ain't on my side;
Dm
F
Em
A5 G#5 Am
G
F
G5
home I'll nev - er be.
time, I'll nev - er know.
Solo ends
Burn out the day;
burn out the night.
G5
C5
F5
(1.,3.) I can't see no rea - son to put up a fight.
(2.) I'm not the one to tell you what's wrong or what's right.
To Coda
G/B
N.C.
I'm liv - ing for giv - ing the dev - il his due.
I've seen suns that were freez - ing and lives that were through.
And
But
I'm burn - in', I'm burn - in', I'm burn - in' for you.
(Instrumental)
1
(D.C.)
2
D.C. al Coda
CODA
And I'm burn - in', I'm burn - in', I'm burn - in' for you.
Repeat and Fade

BUS STOP

Copyright © 1966 (Renewed) by Campbell Connelly, Inc., New York (ASCAP)

Words and Music by
GRAHAM GOULDMAN

Moderately

Em
Bus Stop wet day she's _ there I ___ say please share my um - brel - la. ___ Bus comes bus goes she _

G D Em
_ stays love _ grows un - der my um - brel - la. ___ All that sum-mer we ___ en - joyed _ it

C Bm Em
wind and rain and _ shine. ______ That um - brel - la we ___ em - ployed _ it by Au - gust she was mine. _

G F♯7 Bm A G
___ Ev - 'ry morn - ing I would see _ her wait - ing at the stop ___ some - times she'd

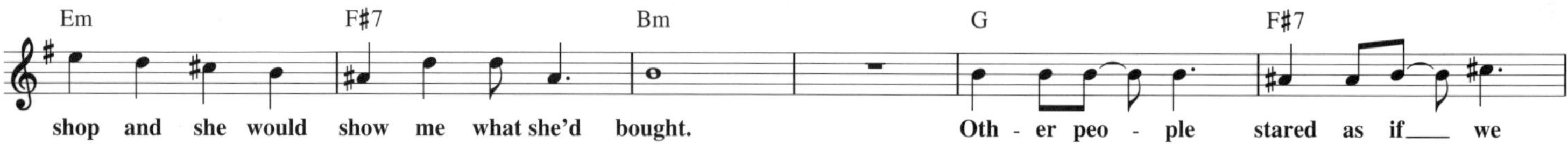
Em F♯7 Bm G F♯7
shop and she would show me what she'd bought. Oth - er peo - ple stared as if ___ we

Bm A G Em F♯7 Bm
were both quite in - sane. _ Some day my name and hers are go - ing to be the same.

Em
That's the way the whole _ thing start - ed sil - ly but it's true. Think - ing of a sweet _ ro - mance be -

G D Em C Bm
gin - ning in that queue. Came the sun the ice ___ was melt - ing no more shel - 'tring _ now. ______

Em
1 2
Nice to think that that _ um - brel - la led me to a vow. ___ ___

CALIFORNIA GIRLS

Copyright © 1965 IRVING MUSIC, INC.
Copyright Renewed

Words and Music by BRIAN WILSON
and MIKE LOVE

CALL ME THE BREEZE

Copyright © 1971 by Johnny Bienstock Music
Copyright Renewed

Words and Music by
JOHN CALE

- by; I got to keep mov - in' on.
D5 C♯5 C5 B5
Well, I got that green light, babe; I got to keep mov - in' on.
A5 E5
Well, I might go out to Cal - i - for -
D5 A5
- nia, might go down to Geor - gia, I don't know.
A5 Play 3 times
(Instrumental)
Well, I dig you Geor - gia peach - es, makes me feel right at home.
D5
Well now, I dig you Geor - gia peach-
C♯5 C5 B5 A5
- es; makes me feel right at home.
E5 D5
But I don't love me no one wom - an, so I can't
A5 D.C. al Coda
stay at Geor - gia's long. Well, now, they
CODA
A5 C♯5 D5 D♯5 Freely E5 N.C. B♭7 A7
Woo.
Spoken: Mister Breeze.

CAN'T YOU SEE

Copyright © 1973, 1975 Spirit One Music, A Division of Spirit Music Group, Inc.
Copyright Renewed

Words and Music by
TOY CALDWELL

Moderately fast

D C G D C G D C G D C G D7

Gon - na take a freight train down at the sta - tion, Lord, I don't care where it goes,
I'm gon - na find me a hole in the wall; gon - na crawl in side and die,
I'm gon - na buy a tick - et as far as I can; I ain't - a nev - er com - in' back.

Gon - na climb a moun - tain, the high - est moun - tain, Lord, and jump off, ain't no - bod - y gon - na know.
'cause my la - dy, now a mean old wom - an, Lord, nev - er told me good - bye.
I'm gon - na take me that south - bound, ride it all the way to Geor - gia, Lord, till the train, it run out of track.

Can't you see, oh, can't you see what that wom - an, what she been do - in' to me?

1, 2 | 3

(Instrumental)

CAUGHT UP IN YOU

Copyright © 1982 by Rude Music, Ensign Music Corporation, BMG Songs, Inc.,
Easy Action Music and WB Music Corp.
All Rights for Rude Music Controlled and Administered by Ensign Music Corporation
All Rights for Easy Action Music Administered by WB Music Corp.

Words and Music by FRANK SULLIVAN,
JIM PETERIK, JEFF CARLISI and DON BARNES

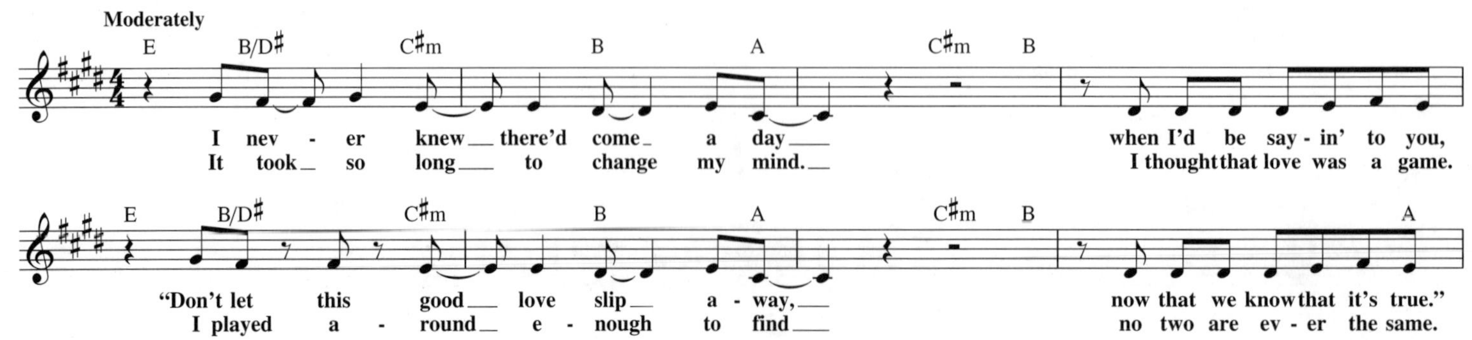

Moderately
E B/D♯ C♯m B A C♯m B
I nev - er knew there'd come a day when I'd be say - in' to you,
It took so long to change my mind. I thought that love was a game.
E B/D♯ C♯m B A C♯m B A
"Don't let this good love slip a - way, now that we know that it's true."
I played a - round e - nough to find no two are ev - er the same.

C♯m B A C♯m B

Don't, don't you know the kind of man I am? No? Said I'd nev-
You made me re - al - ize the love I'd missed. So hot; love

F♯m E/G♯ A F♯/A♯

- er fall in love a - gain. But it's real, and the feel - ing comes shin - ing through.
I could - n't quite re - sist. When it's right, the light just comes shin - ing through.

B A 𝄋 E/G♯ F♯m7

I'm so caught up in you, lit - tle girl, and I nev -
I'm so caught up in you, lit - tle girl, you're the one

C♯m E A E/G♯

- er did sus - pect a thing; } so caught up in you, lit - tle girl,
that's got me down on my knees; }

F♯m7 C♯m E A E/G♯

that I nev - er want to get my - self free. And, ba - by, it's true. You're the one

F♯m7 E/G♯ A F♯/A♯ B

who caught me, ba - by. You taught me how good it could be.

1 | 2 C♯m7 F♯m B

Fill your days and your nights, no need to ev - er ask me twice,

E B/D♯ C♯m7 F♯m9 B

oh, no, when - ev - er you want me. And if ev -

C♯m7 F♯m B E B/D♯

er comes a day when you should turn and walk a - way, oh

D.S. (lyric 2) and Fade

C♯m7 F♯m B A

no. I can't live with - out you. I'm so caught up in you.

CARRY ON WAYWARD SON

© 1976 EMI BLACKWOOD MUSIC INC. and DON KIRSHNER MUSIC
All Rights Controlled and Administered by EMI BLACKWOOD MUSIC INC.

Words and Music by
KERRY LIVGREN

COME TOGETHER

Copyright © 1969 Sony/ATV Songs LLC
Copyright Renewed
All Rights Administered by Sony/ATV Music Publishing, 8 Music Square West, Nashville, TN 37203

Words and Music by JOHN LENNON
and PAUL McCARTNEY

CENTERFOLD

© 1981 CENTER CITY MUSIC (ASCAP)/Administered by BUG MUSIC and PAL-PARK MUSIC
All Rights for PAL-PARK MUSIC Administered by ALMO MUSIC CORP.

Written by
SETH JUSTMAN

Slow and funky

(Instrumental) **Play 4 times**

Does she walk? Does she talk? Does she come com-plete? My home-room, home-room an-gel al-ways pulled me from my seat.
It's o-kay, I un-der-stand, this ain't no nev-er nev-er land. I hope that when this is-sue's gone, I'll see you when your clothes are on.

She was pure like snow-flakes; no one could ev-er stain the mem-o-ry of my an-gel, could nev-er cause me pain.
Take your car, yes, we will, we'll take your car and drive it. We'll take it to a mo-tel room and take 'em off in pri-vate.

The years go by, I'm look-in' through a girl-ie mag-a-zine, and there's my home-room an-gel on the pag-es in be-tween.
A part of me has just been ripped, the pag-es from my mind are stripped, Ah no! I can't de-ny it. Oh yeah, I guess I got-ta buy it.

My blood runs cold; my mem-o-ry has just been sold. My an-gel is the cen-ter-fold. An-gel is the cen-ter-fold.

My blood runs cold; my mem-o-ry has just been sold. *(Instrumental)* An-gel in the cen-ter-fold. **To Coda**

Slipped me notes un-der the desk, while I was think-in' a-bout her dress. I was shy, I turned a-way be-fore she caught my eye. I was shak-in' in my shoes, when-ev-er she flashed those ba-by blues. Some-thing had a hold on me when an-gel passed close by. Those soft fuz-zy sweat-ers, too mag-ic-al to touch! To see her in that neg-li-gee is real-ly just too much!

My blood runs cold; my mem-o-ry has just been sold. My an-gel is the cen-ter-fold. An-gel is the cen-ter-fold. My blood runs cold; my mem-o-ry has just been sold. *(Instrumental)* An-gel is the cen-ter-fold. **D.C. al Coda**

CODA **Repeat and Fade**

Na na na na na na na na na na na na na na na na. Na na na na na na na na na na na na na na na na.

COME SAIL AWAY
Copyright © 1977 ALMO MUSIC CORP. and STYGIAN SONGS
All Rights Controlled and Administered by ALMO MUSIC CORP.
Words and Music by
DENNIS DE YOUNG
Moderately slow
C Em/B Am Am/G F G
I'm sail - ing a - way. Set an o - pen course for the vir - gin sea. Cause
I've got to be free, free to face the life that's a-head of me.
Am G Am
On board I'm the cap - tain, so climb a - board. We'll search for to - mor - row
G C Em/B Am Am/G F G C F/C
on ev - 'ry shore, and I'll try, oh Lord, I'll try to car - ry on. A
C F/C C(add2) F/C C F/C
gath - er - ing of an - gels ap-peared a - bove my head. They sang to me this song of hope and
thought that they were an - gels but much to my sur - prise, we climbed a - board their star - ship and
C(add2) F/C To Coda C F/C C(add2) F/C
this is what they said. They said, "Come sail a-way, come sail a-way, come sail a - way with me, lads.
head - ed for the skies, sing - in', "Come sail a-way, come sail a-way, come sail a - way with me.
C F/C 1 C(add2) F/C 2 C(add2) F/C D.S. al Coda
Come sail a-way, come sail a-way, come sail a - way with me."
Come sail a-way, come sail a-way, come sail a-way with me." I
CODA
C F/C C(add2) F/C Repeat and Fade
"Come sail a - way, come sail a - way, come sail a - way with me."
COMIN' HOME
Copyright © 1970 by Eric Patrick Clapton and Embassy Music Corporation
Copyright Renewed
All Rights for Eric Patrick Clapton Administered by Unichappell Music Inc.
Words and Music by ERIC CLAPTON
and BONNIE BRAMLETT
Moderately
A
(Instrumental) Been out on the road 'bout six months too long.
Hitch - hi-kin' on the turn-pike all day long.
I want you so bad, I can hard - ly stand it I'm so tired
No-bod-y seemed to no - tice just pass me o - ver. To keep from go-in' cra-zy,
and I'm all a - lone. We'll soon be to - geth - er, and that's it,
I got - ta sing my song. Got a whole lot of lov - in' and ba - by that's
1 G D/F#
I'm com-in' home to your love. (Instrumental)
why I'm com-in' home
A G D/F# 2 A N.C.
to your love. (Instrumental)

CUTS LIKE A KNIFE

Copyright © 1983 IRVING MUSIC, ADAMS COMMUNICATIONS, INC., ALMO MUSIC CORP. and TESTATYME MUSIC
All Rights for ADAMS COMMUNICATIONS, INC. Controlled and Administered by IRVING MUSIC, INC.
All Rights for TESTATYME MUSIC Controlled and Administered by ALMO MUSIC CORP.

Words and Music by BRYAN ADAMS
and JIM VALLANCE

Moderate Rock

D
G
C(add2)
D
Driv - in' home_ this eve - nin' I could - a sworn_ we had it all worked out.___

G
C(add2)
D
G
C(add2)
You had this boy_ be - liev - in' way be - yond_ the shad - ow of a doubt._

D
G
C(add2)
D
Well, I heard it on___ the street,___ I
times I've been___ mis - tak - en, there's

G
C(add2)
D
G
C(add2)
heard you might___ have found___ some - bod - y new.____ Well,
times I thought_ I've been____ mis - un - der - stood.____ So

D
G
C(add2)
D
who__ is he, ba - by? Who is he__ and tell__ me what he means to you.
wait a min - ute dar - lin', can't you see__ we did______ the__ best we could?

A
Bm
I took it all__ for grant - ed, but how was I___ to know________ that
This would - n't be__ the first__ time that things have gone_ a - stray.________ Now you've

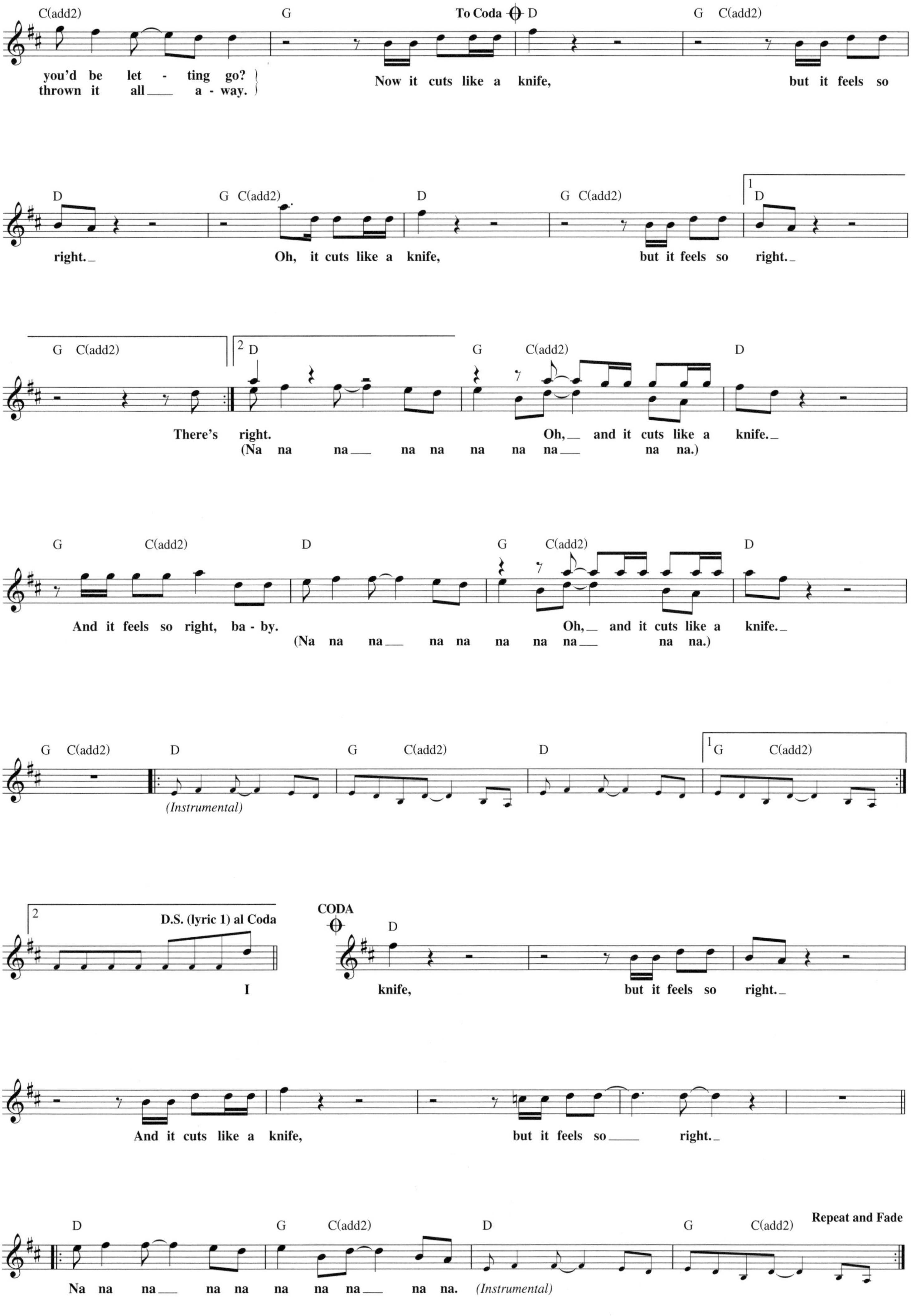

C(add2) G To Coda D G C(add2)
you'd be let - ting go?
thrown it all a - way.
Now it cuts like a knife, but it feels so
D G C(add2) D G C(add2) 1 D
right. Oh, it cuts like a knife, but it feels so right.
G C(add2) 2 D G C(add2) D
There's right. Oh, and it cuts like a knife.
(Na na na na na na na na na na.)
G C(add2) D G C(add2) D
And it feels so right, ba - by. Oh, and it cuts like a knife.
(Na na na na na na na na na na.)
G C(add2) D G C(add2) D 1 G C(add2)
(Instrumental)
2 D.S. (lyric 1) al Coda
I
CODA
D
knife, but it feels so right.
And it cuts like a knife, but it feels so right.
D G C(add2) D G C(add2) Repeat and Fade
Na na na na na na na na na na. (Instrumental)

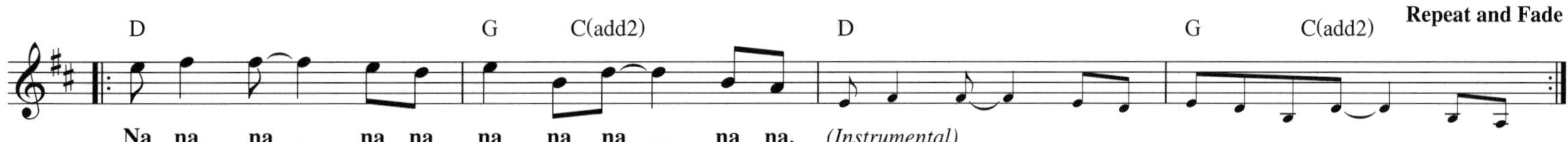

DARK HORSE

© 1974 GANGA PUBLISHING B.V.

By GEORGE HARRISON

DON'T DO ME LIKE THAT

Copyright © 1977 ALMO MUSIC CORP.

Words and Music by
TOM PETTY

DON'T BRING ME DOWN

© 1979 EMI BLACKWOOD MUSIC INC.

Words and Music by
JEFF LYNNE

Moderately

A

You got me run - ning, go - ing out of my mind.
You want to stay out with your fan - cy friends.

You got me think - ing that I'm wast - ing my time.
I'm tell - ing you it's got to be the end.

Don't bring me

D

down. No, no, no, no,

A

no. Oo, ee, hoo.

C

I'll tell you once more be - fore I

1 G D A

get off the floor. Don't bring me down.

2 G D

get off the floor. Don't bring me

A

down. Don't bring me down.

𝄋 F♯m

Grrooss.

A F♯m

Don't bring me down. Grrooss.

A

Don't bring me down.

F♯m A E

Grrooss. Don't bring me down.

To Coda

A

What hap - pened to the girl I used to know? You let your mind out some - where down the road.
You're al - ways talk - ing 'bout your cra - zy nights. One of these days your gon - na get it right.

Don't bring me

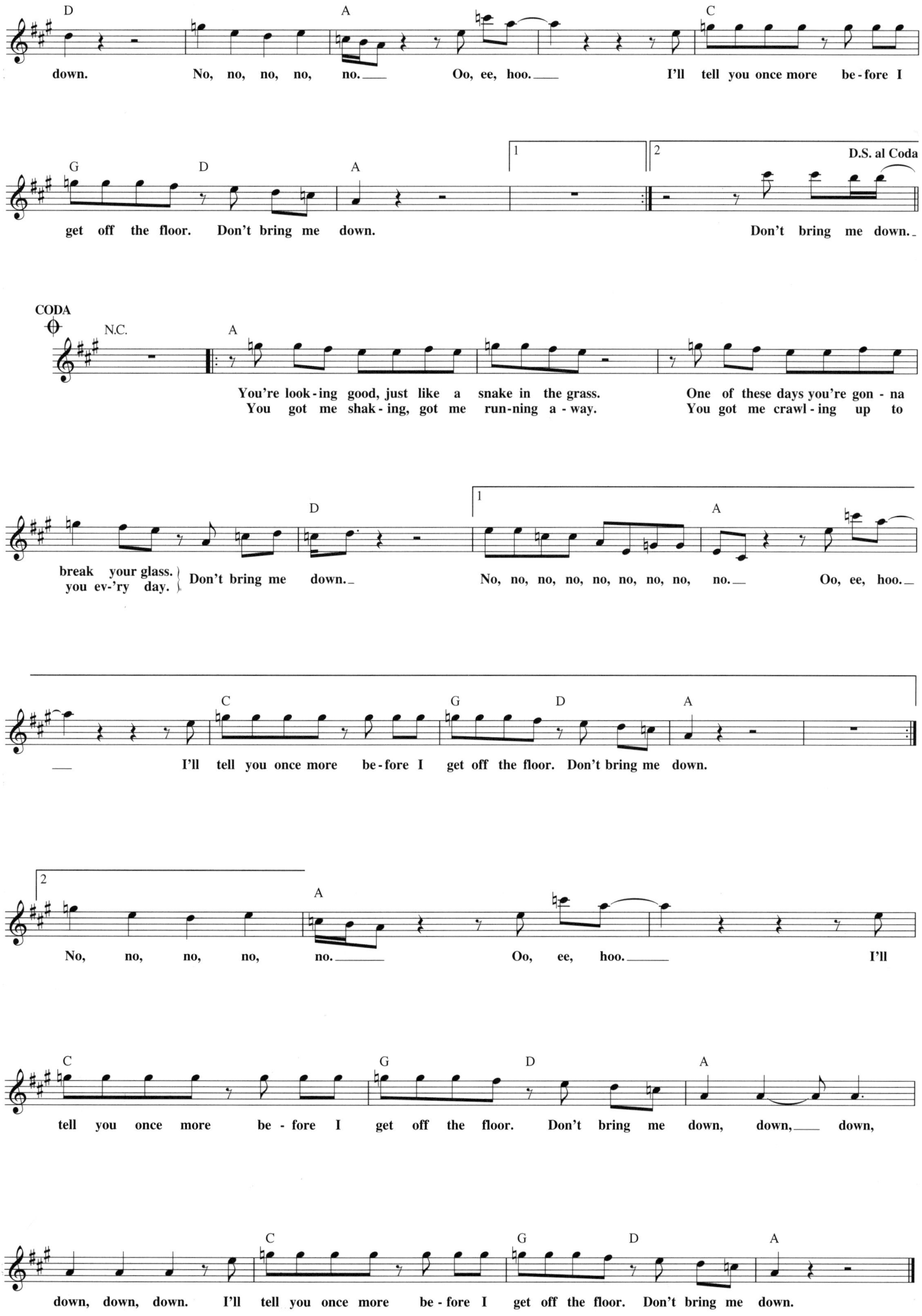

D A C

down. No, no, no, no, no. Oo, ee, hoo. I'll tell you once more be-fore I

G D A 1 2 D.S. al Coda

get off the floor. Don't bring me down. Don't bring me down.

CODA

N.C. A

You're look-ing good, just like a snake in the grass. One of these days you're gon-na

You got me shak-ing, got me run-ning a-way. You got me crawl-ing up to

D 1 A

break your glass.
you ev-'ry day. Don't bring me down. No, no, no, no, no, no, no, no, no. Oo, ee, hoo.

C G D A

I'll tell you once more be-fore I get off the floor. Don't bring me down.

2 A

No, no, no, no, no. Oo, ee, hoo. I'll

C G D A

tell you once more be-fore I get off the floor. Don't bring me down, down, down,

C G D A
down, down, down. I'll tell you once more be-fore I get off the floor. Don't bring me down.

DON'T FEAR THE REAPER

Copyright © 1976 Sony/ATV Tunes LLC
All Rights Administered by Sony/ATV Music Publishing, 8 Music Square West, Nashville, TN 37203

Words and Music by
DONALD ROESER

F5 G5 A5 G5 F6/9 G A5 G F6/9 G
oth - er for - ty thou-sand com-ing ev - 'ry day. Come on, bay - by. Ba - by, take my hand. _
A5 G F6/9 G A5 G F6/9 G A5 G F6/9 G
We'll be a - ble to fly. _ Ba - by, I'm your man.
A5 G F6/9 G A5 G F6/9 G A5 G F6/9 G
La, la, la, la, la. La, la, la, la, la. _
A5 G F6/9 G A5 G F6/9 G A5 G F6/9 G
Love of two is one.
A5 G F6/9 G A5 G F6/9 G F5 G5
Here but now they're _ gone. Came the last night of sad -
A5 G5 F5 G5 A5 G5 F5 G5 A5 G5
- ness, and it was clear she could-n't go on. And the door was o - pen and the wind _ a'peared. The
F5 G5 A5 G5 F5 G5 A5 G5 F G
can - dles blew _ and then dis - ap - peared. The cur - tains flew _ and then he ap-peared. Said don't be a - fraid. _ Come on ba -
Am G F G Am G F G Am G
- by. And she had no fear. _ And she ran _ to him. They looked back-ward and said _ good-bye.
F G Am G F G Am G F G Am
She had tak - en his hand. _ Come on, ba - by. Don't fear the reap - er.

DON'T LET THE SUN GO DOWN ON ME

Copyright © 1974 by Big Pig Music Ltd.
All Rights for the United States Administered by Intersong U.S.A., Inc.

Words and Music by ELTON JOHN
and BERNIE TAUPIN

I can't find oh the right ro - man-tic line.
(Instrumental)
But see me once and see the way I feel.
Don't dis-card me just be-cause you think I mean you harm.
D.S. al Coda
But these cuts I have, oh, they need love to help them heal.
CODA
me. (Instrumental)
DON'T STOP
Copyright © 1976 by Careers-BMG Music Publishing, Inc.
Words and Music by
CHRISTINE McVIE
Medium Rock beat (♫ = ♩♪)
If you wake up and don't want to smile; if it takes just a lit - tle while, o-pen your eyes and look at the day. You'll see things in a dif - f'rent way.
Why not think a-bout times to come, and not a-bout the things that you've done. If your life was bad to you, just think what to - mor-row will do.
All I want is to see you smile, if it takes just a lit - tle while. I know you don't be - lieve that it's true. I nev-er meant an - y harm to you.
Don't Stop think-ing a-bout to-mor-row. Don't Stop. It-'ll soon be here. It - 'll be bet-ter than be-fore. Yes-ter-day's gone. Yes - ter-day's gone.
1,2
3
- ter-day's gone.
Repeat and Fade
Ooh, don't you look back.

DON'T STAND SO CLOSE TO ME

© 1980 G.M. SUMNER
Published by MAGNETIC PUBLISHING LTD. and Administered by
EMI BLACKWOOD MUSIC INC. in the USA and Canada

Written and Composed by
STING

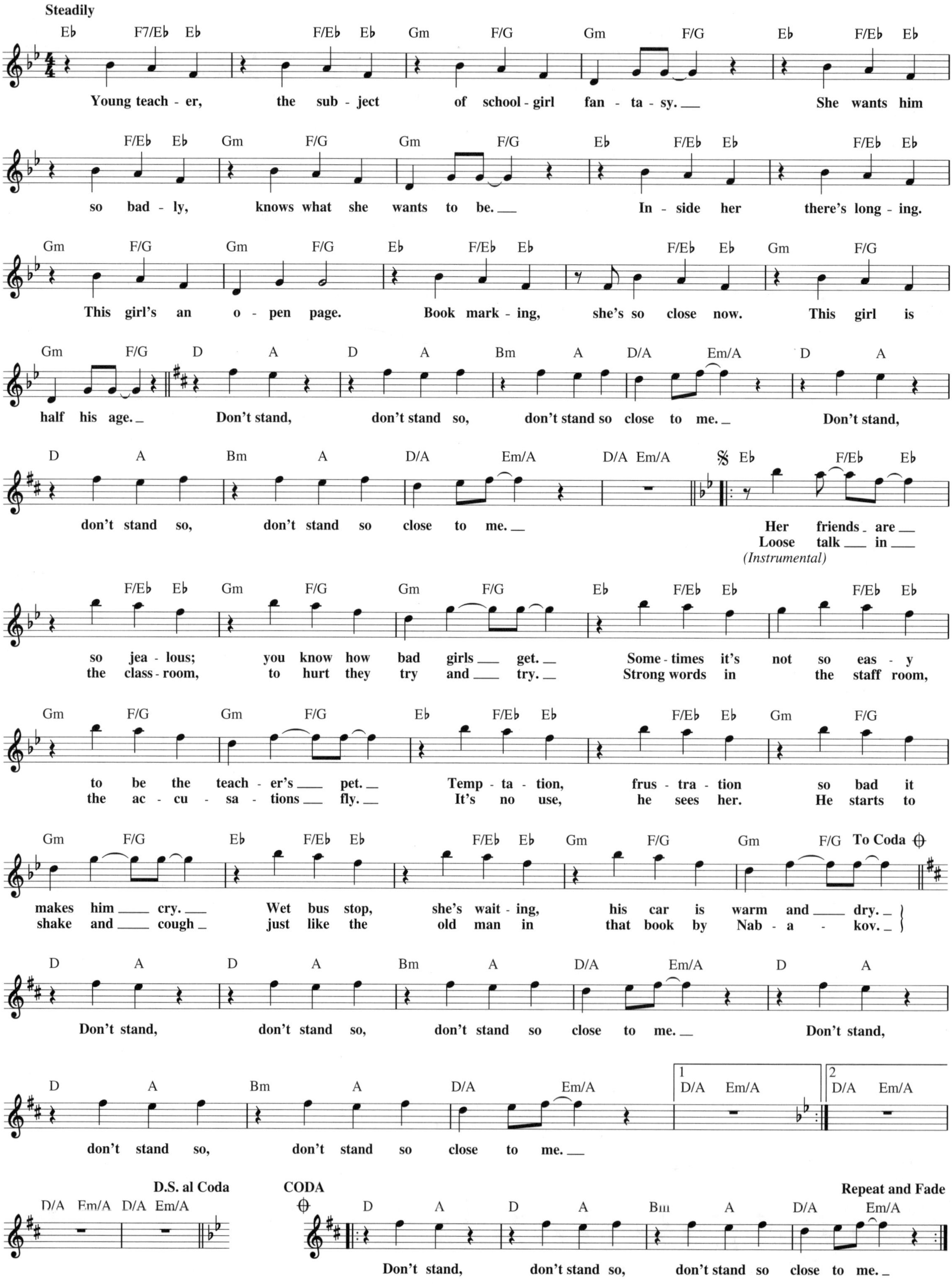
Steadily
Eb F7/Eb Eb F/Eb Eb Gm F/G Gm F/G Eb F/Eb Eb
Young teach - er, the sub - ject of school - girl fan - ta - sy. She wants him
F/Eb Eb Gm F/G Gm F/G Eb F/Eb Eb F/Eb Eb
so bad - ly, knows what she wants to be. In - side her there's long - ing.
Gm F/G Gm F/G Eb F/Eb Eb F/Eb Eb Gm F/G
This girl's an o - pen page. Book mark - ing, she's so close now. This girl is
Gm F/G D A D A Bm A D/A Em/A D A
half his age. Don't stand, don't stand so, don't stand so close to me. Don't stand,
D A Bm A D/A Em/A D/A Em/A Eb F/Eb Eb
don't stand so, don't stand so close to me. Her friends are
Loose talk in
(Instrumental)
F/Eb Eb Gm F/G Gm F/G Eb F/Eb Eb F/Eb Eb
so jea - lous; you know how bad girls get. Some - times it's not so eas - y
the class - room, to hurt they try and try. Strong words in the staff room,
Gm F/G Gm F/G Eb F/Eb Eb F/Eb Eb Gm F/G
to be the teach - er's pet. Temp - ta - tion, frus - tra - tion so bad it
the ac - cu - sa - tions fly. It's no use, he sees her. He starts to
Gm F/G Eb F/Eb Eb F/Eb Eb Gm F/G Gm F/G To Coda
makes him cry. Wet bus stop, she's wait - ing, his car is warm and dry.
shake and cough just like the old man in that book by Nab - a - kov.
D A D A Bm A D/A Em/A D A
Don't stand, don't stand so, don't stand so close to me. Don't stand,
D A Bm A D/A Em/A 1 D/A Em/A 2 D/A Em/A
don't stand so, don't stand so close to me.
D.S. al Coda
D/A Em/A D/A Em/A
CODA
D A D A Bm A D/A Em/A
Repeat and Fade
Don't stand, don't stand so, don't stand so close to me.

DOO DOO DOO DOO DOO
(Heartbreaker)

© 1973 (Renewed 2001) EMI MUSIC PUBLISHING LTD.
All Rights for the U.S. and Canada Controlled and Administered by COLGEMS-EMI MUSIC INC.

Words and Music by MICK JAGGER
and KEITH RICHARDS

DRAW THE LINE

Copyright © 1978 Daksel LLC
All Rights Administered by Sony/ATV Music Publishing, 8 Music Square West, Nashville, TN 37203

Words and Music by STEVEN TYLER
and JOE PERRY

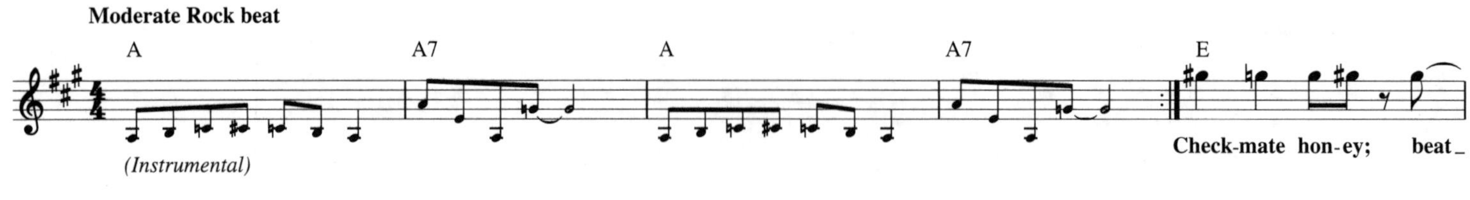
Moderate Rock beat
A
A7
A
A7
E
(Instrumental)
Check-mate hon-ey; beat

A
A7
E
you at your own damn game.
No dice, hon-ey; I'm liv-in' on the as - tral plane.

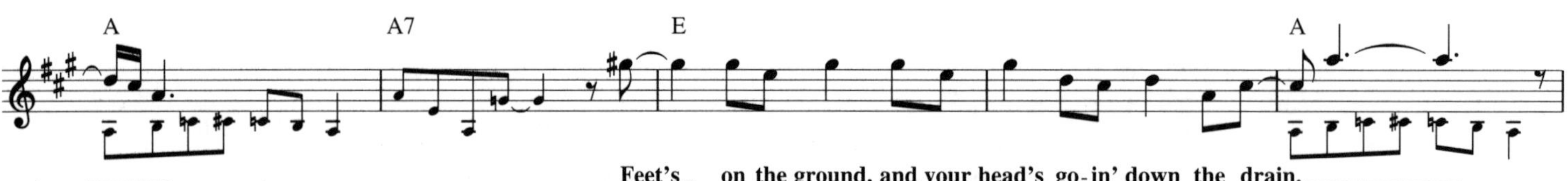
A
A7
E
A
Feet's on the ground, and your head's go-in' down the drain.

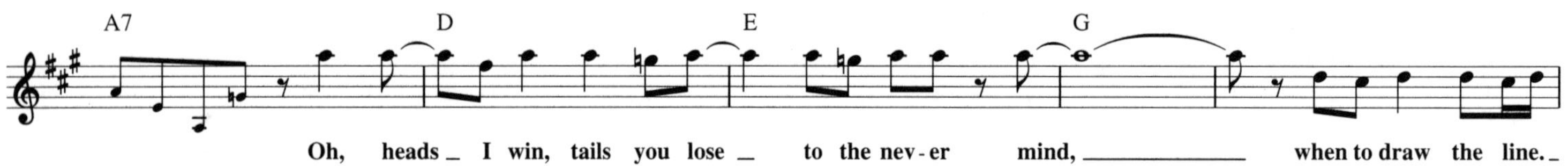
A7
D
E
G
Oh, heads I win, tails you lose to the nev-er mind, when to draw the line.

A
A7
A
A7
E
An In-di-an sum-mer, Ker-

A
E
- ry was all o-ver the floor.
She was a wet-nap win-ner and rare-ly ev-er left the store.

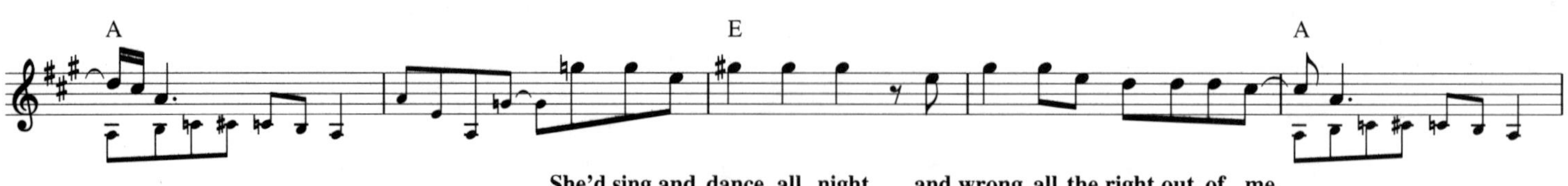
A
E
A
She'd sing and dance all night and wrong all the right out of me.

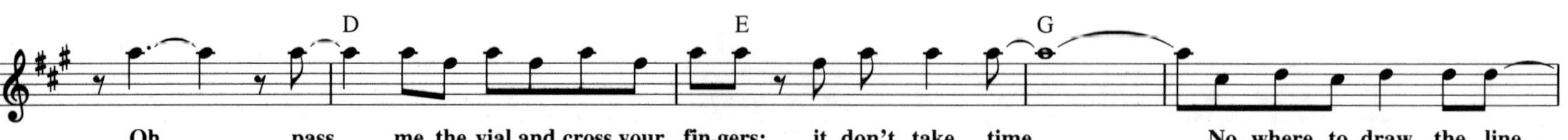
D
E
G
Oh, pass me the vial and cross your fin-gers; it don't take time. No-where to draw the line.

A
(Instrumental)

E
(End instrumental) Hi - ho, Sil-ver, we was - sing-in' all your cow-boy songs.

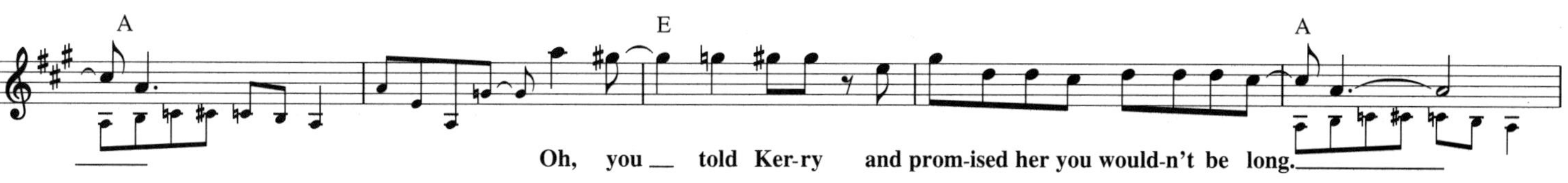
A
E
A
Oh, you told Ker-ry and prom-ised her you would-n't be long.

A7
D
E
G
Heads I win, tails you lose; Lord, it's such a crime.

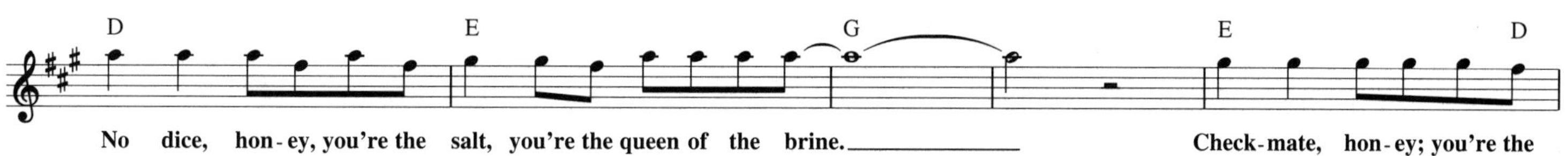
D
E
G
E
D
No dice, hon-ey, you're the salt, you're the queen of the brine. Check-mate, hon-ey; you're the

E
A
A7
on-ly one who's got to choose when I draw the line.
(Instrumental)

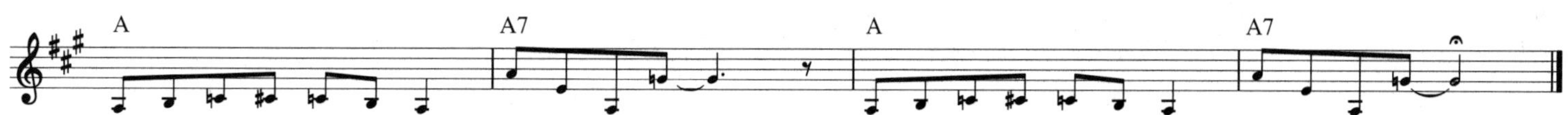
A
A7
A
A7

DREAM ON

Copyright © 1973 Daksel LLC
Copyright Renewed
All Rights Administered by Sony/ATV Music Publishing, 8 Music Square West, Nashville, TN 37203

Words and Music by
STEVEN TYLER

Db Eb Fm
dream on and dream un - til your dream comes true. (Instrumental)
Bb C Db Eb
Dream on, dream on, dream on, dream on.
F 8va G Ab Bb
Dream on, dream on, dream on, ah.
Bbm/C C Bbm/C C Bbm/C C Bbm/C C Bbm/C C Bbm/C C Bbm/C C Bbm/C C
Ah.
loco
Fm Eb Db Eb Fm Eb
Sing with me, sing for the years, sing for the laugh-ter 'n' sing for the tears. Sing with me if it's just for to-day,
1 Db Eb
may-be to-mor - row the good Lord will take you a-way.
2 Dm7b5 Db
may-be to-mor - row the good Lord will take you a -
Repeat and Fade
Bbm/C C Bbm/C C Bbm/C C Bbm/C C Bbm/C C Bbm/C C Bbm/C C Bbm/C C Bbm6/C C Bbm6/C C Bbm6/C C Bbm6/C C
way.

EIGHT MILES HIGH

Copyright © 1966 (Renewed) Sixteen Stars Music, Gene Clark Music/Administered by Bug Music and Songs Of DreamWorks
Rights for Songs Of DreamWorks Administered by Cherry River Music Co.

Words and Music by ROGER McGUINN, DAVID CROSBY and GENE CLARK

Moderately
Em G D C G
Eight miles high and when you touch down you'll find that
Signs in the street that say where you're go - ing are some - where
No - where is there warmth to be found a - mong those
D C 1,2 3 Em
it's strang - er than known.
just be - ing their own.
a - fraid of los - ing their ground. Rain gray
G D C G D
town, known for its sound in plac - es small fac - es un -
C Em G D C
bound. 'Round the squares, hud - dled in storms,
Side - walk scenes and black lim - ou - sines,
G D 1 C 2 C
some laugh - ing, some just shape - less forms.
some liv - ing, some stand - ing a - lone.

DREAMER

Copyright © 1974 RONDOR MUSIC (LONDON) LTD. and DELICATE MUSIC
All Rights Controlled and Administered by ALMO MUSIC CORP.

Words and Music by RICK DAVIES
and ROGER HODGSON

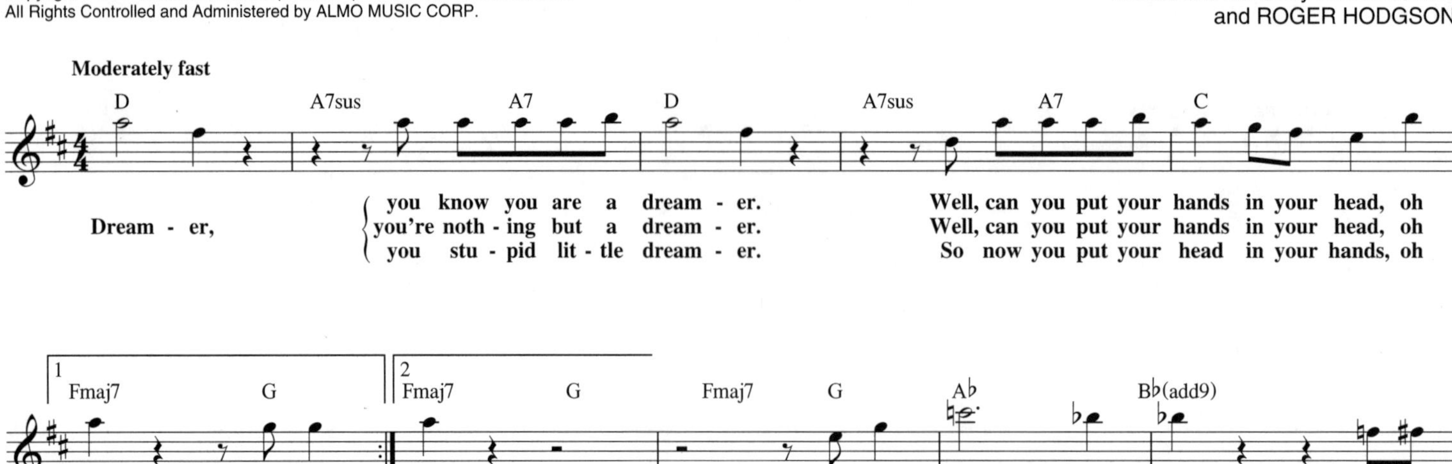

C
Gm7/C
Take a dream on a Sun - day.
(Instrumental)
I'll take a life, take a hol - i - day.
(Instrumental)
Take a lie, take a
Gm7/C
dream - er.
(Instrumental)
Dream, (dream,) dream, (dream,) dream, (dream,) dream, dream a - long...
C F/C C F/C
C F/C C F/C C Bbmaj7 C/Bb Bb C/Bb Bb C/Bb Bb C/Bb Bb
C
Dream - er. (Dream - er, dream a - long. Come on, you dream - er, dream a - long.) Roll it on.
Bbmaj7
(Come on, you dream - er, dream a - long.
D A7sus A7
Dream - er, you know you are a
D A7sus A7 C
dream - er. Can you put your hands in your head, oh
1 Fmaj7 G
no! I said,
2 Fmaj7 G Fmaj7 G N.C.
no! Oh no!
(Instrumental)
Fade out

DREAMS

Copyright © 1977, 1978 Welsh Witch Music
All Rights Administered by Sony/ATV Music Publishing, 8 Music Square West, Nashville, TN 37203

Words and Music by
STEVIE NICKS

DUST IN THE WIND

© 1977, 1978 EMI BLACKWOOD MUSIC INC. and DON KIRSHNER MUSIC
All Rights Controlled and Administered by EMI BLACKWOOD MUSIC INC.

Words and Music by
KERRY LIVGREN

EMOTIONAL RESCUE

© 1980 EMI MUSIC PUBLISHING LTD.
All Rights for the U.S. and Canada Controlled and Administered by COLGEMS-EMI MUSIC INC.

Words and Music by MICK JAGGER
and KEITH RICHARDS

EVERY BREATH YOU TAKE

© 1983 G.M. SUMNER
Published by MAGNETIC PUBLISHING LTD. and Administered by
EMI BLACKWOOD MUSIC INC. in the USA and Canada

Written and Composed by
STING

EVERY LITTLE THING SHE DOES IS MAGIC

© 1981 G.M. SUMNER
Published by MAGNETIC PUBLISHING LTD. and Administered by
EMI BLACKWOOD MUSIC INC. in the USA and Canada

Written and Composed by
STING

Additional Lyrics

2. Do I have to tell the story
Of a thousand rainy days since we first met.
It's a big enough umbrella
But it's always me that ends up getting wet.
Chorus: (Repeat)

EYE IN THE SKY

Copyright © 1982 by Careers-BMG Music Publishing, Inc. and Woolfsongs Ltd.
All Rights Administered by Careers-BMG Music Publishing, Inc.

Words and Music by ALAN PARSONS
and ERIC WOOLFSON

EVIL WOMAN

© 1975 UNART MUSIC CORPORATION and JET MUSIC INCORPORATED
All Rights Controlled and Administered by EMI BLACKWOOD MUSIC INC.

Words and Music by
JEFF LYNNE

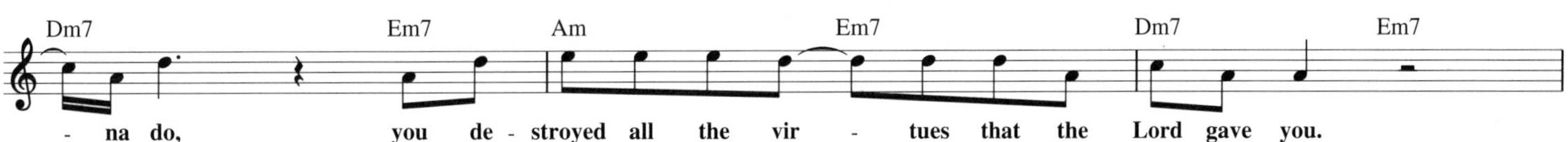
Dm7 Em7 Am Em7 Dm7 Em7
- na do, you de - stroyed all the vir - tues that the Lord gave you.

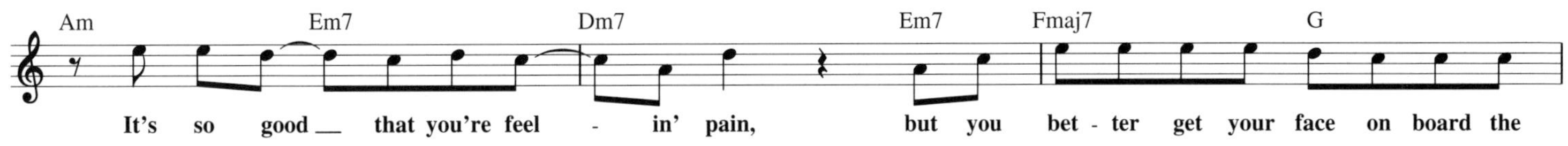
Am Em7 Dm7 Em7 Fmaj7 G
It's so good __ that you're feel - in' pain, but you bet - ter get your face on board the

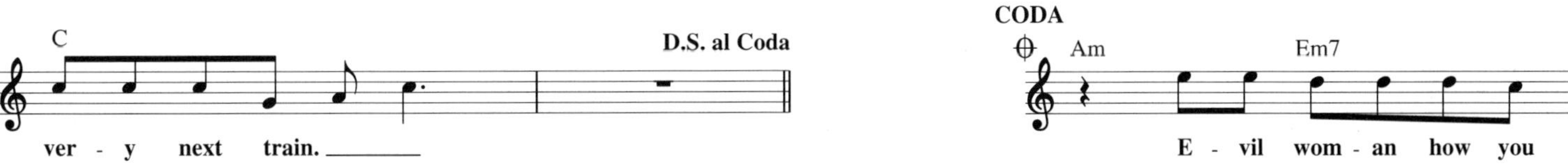
C
D.S. al Coda
CODA
Am Em7
ver - y next train. ____
E - vil wom - an how you

Dm7 Em7 Am Em7 Dm7 Em7
done me wrong, _ but now you're try - in' to wail a dif - f'rent song.

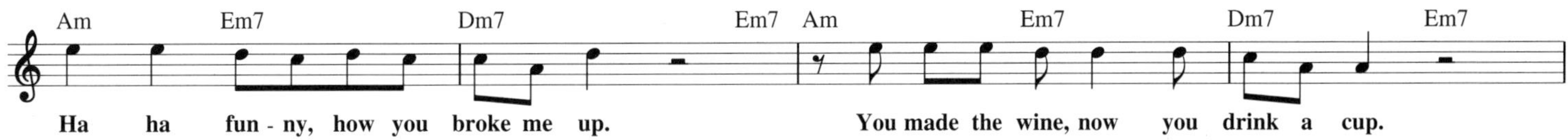
Am Em7 Dm7 Em7 Am Em7 Dm7 Em7
Ha ha fun - ny, how you broke me up. You made the wine, now you drink a cup.

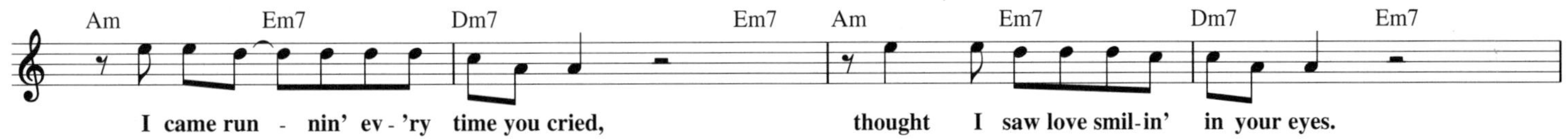
Am Em7 Dm7 Em7 Am Em7 Dm7 Em7
I came run - nin' ev - 'ry time you cried, thought I saw love smil - in' in your eyes.

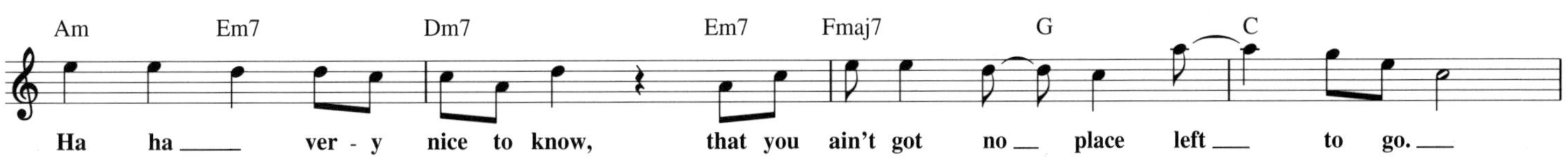
Am Em7 Dm7 Em7 Fmaj7 G C
Ha ha ____ ver - y nice to know, that you ain't got no __ place left ___ to go. ___

Am Em7 Dm7 Em7 Am Em7 Dm7 Em7
E - vil wom - an. E - vil wom - an.

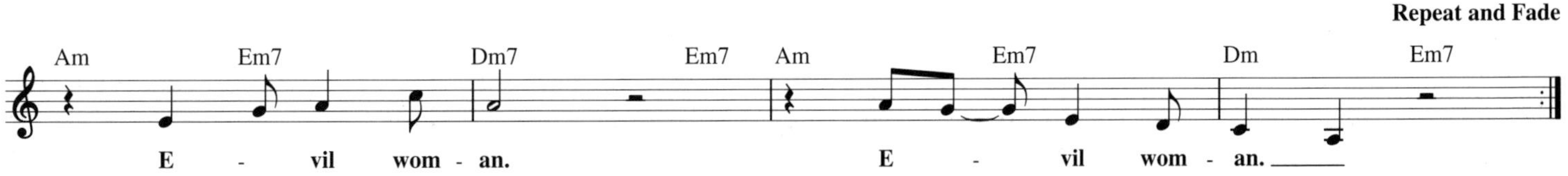
Repeat and Fade
Am Em7 Dm7 Em7 Am Em7 Dm Em7
E - vil wom - an. E - vil wom - an. ______

FAME

© 1975 EMI MUSIC PUBLISHING LTD., LENONO.MUSIC, JONES MUSIC AMERICA, 100 MPH MUSIC and CHRYSALIS MUSIC LTD.
All Rights for EMI MUSIC PUBLISHING LTD. Controlled and Administered by SCREEN GEMS-EMI MUSIC INC.
All Rights for LENONO.MUSIC Controlled and Administered by EMI BLACKWOOD MUSIC INC.
All Rights for JONES MUSIC AMERICA Administered by ARZO PUBLISHING

Words and Music by JOHN LENNON, DAVID BOWIE and CARLOS ALOMAR

FIELDS OF GOLD

© 1993 STEERPIKE LTD.
Administered by MAGNETIC PUBLISHING LTD. (PRS) and
EMI BLACKWOOD MUSIC INC. (BMI)

Written and Composed by
G.M. SUMNER

FIRE AND ICE

Copyright © 1981 Sony/ATV Tunes LLC, Big Tooth Music, Discott Music and Rare Blue Music, Inc.
All Rights on behalf of Sony/ATV Tunes LLC Administered by Sony/ATV Music Publishing,
8 Music Square West, Nashville, TN 37203
All Rights on behalf of Big Tooth Music and Discott Music Controlled by Rare Blue Music, Inc.

Words and Music by TOM KELLY,
SCOTT SHEETS and PAT BENATAR

CODA
Cm Abmaj7 Bb Bbsus Bb
You come on like a flame, then you turn a cold shoul - der.
Cm Abmaj7 Bb
Fire and ice, I wan - na give you my love, but you'll just
Bbsus Bb Cm Abmaj7 Repeat and Fade
take a lit - tle piece of my heart. You come
FOR YOUR LOVE
© 1965 (Renewed 1993) HERMUSIC LTD.
All Rights for the U.S.A. and Canada Controlled and Administered by
EMI BLACKWOOD MUSIC INC.
Words and Music by
GRAHAM GOULDMAN
Bright Rock
Em G A Am Am
(Instrumental)
For your love
Em G A Am
(Instrumental)
For your love.
Em G A Am
I'd give you ev - 'ry - thing and more and that's for sure.
I'd give the moon if it were mine to give.
(For your love.)
Em G A Am
I'd give you dia - mond rings and things right to your door.
I'd give that star and the sun 'fore I live.
(For your love.)
Em G A Am
To thrill you with de - light, I'd give you dia - monds bright.
Em G A Am To Coda
There'll be things that will ex - cite, to make you dream of me at night. For your
Em G A Am Am Em
love, For your
B A
For your love, for your love, I would give the stars a - bove.
E B A C#m B D.C. al Coda
For your love, for your love I would give you all I could.
CODA
Em G A Am Am Em
love. For your (Instrumental)

FOOLING YOURSELF
(The Angry Young Man)

Copyright © 1977 ALMO MUSIC CORP. and STYGIAN SONGS
All Rights Controlled and Administered by ALMO MUSIC CORP.

Words and Music by
TOMMY SHAW

Moderately
D5
D5
(Instrumental)

G A/G G
A/G G
A/G G
A/G G

A/G G
A/G G
A/G G
A/G G/A

D C/D G/D C/D D
C/D G/D C/D D

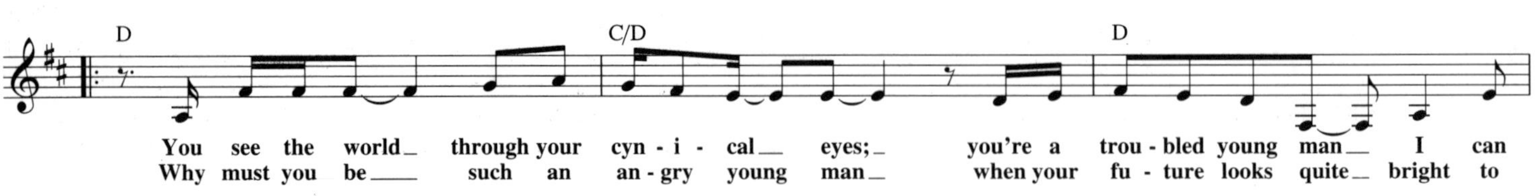
D C/D D
You see the world through your cyn - i - cal eyes; you're a trou - bled young man I can
Why must you be such an an - gry young man when your fu - ture looks quite bright to

C/D D C/D
tell. You've got it all in the palm of your hand, but your
me? And how can there be such a sin - is - ter plan that could

B♭ C/B♭ B♭ C/B♭ D/A
hand's wet with sweat, and your head needs a rest.
hide such a lamb, such a car - ing young man?
And you're fool - ing your - self if you don't be - lieve

G/A
D/A
G/A
it.
You're
kid - ding your - self if you don't be - lieve it.
kill - ing your - self if you don't be - lieve it.
Get

D
E♭/D D C/D D
C/D D E♭/D D C/D D
C
up! (Get up!) Get back on your feet. You're the one they can't beat and you know it. Come

D
E♭/D D C/D D
C/D D E♭/D D C/D D
C
on! (Come on!) Let's see what you've got. Just take your best shot and don't blow it. Oh.

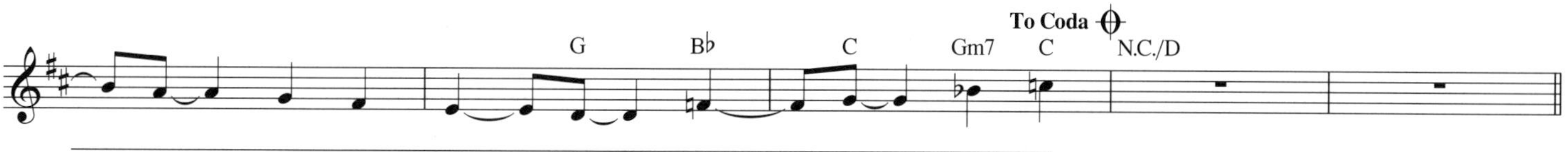
G
B♭
C
Gm7 C
To Coda
N.C./D

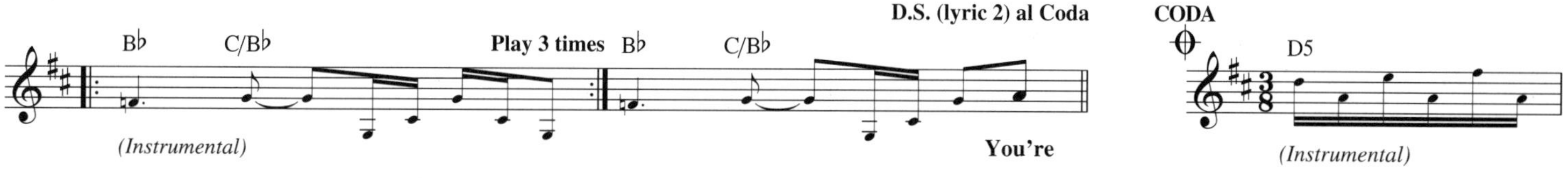
B♭
C/B♭
Play 3 times
B♭
C/B♭
D.S. (lyric 2) al Coda
(Instrumental)
You're
CODA
D5
(Instrumental)

C5

B♭5

Asus
D Em/D Dmaj7 G/D Dmaj7 Em/D D G A
Repeat and Fade

FOREVER YOUNG

© 1988 ROD STEWART, GRIFFON INVESTMENTS LTD., KEVIN SAVIGAR MUSIC and SPECIAL RIDER MUSIC
All Rights for ROD STEWART Controlled and Administered by EMI APRIL MUSIC INC.
All Rights for GRIFFON INVESTMENTS LTD. for the U.S.A. Administered by WB MUSIC CORP.
All Rights for KEVIN SAVIGAR MUSIC Administered by PSO LIMITED

Words and Music by ROD STEWART,
JIM CREGAN, KEVIN SAVIGAR, and BOB DYLAN

Driving beat

E A E 1 2
(Instrumental) **May the**

A E
good Lord be with you down ev - er - y road you roam. __ *(Instrumental)* **And may**

A E
sun - shine_ and hap - pi - ness _ sur - round you when you're far __ from home. __ *(Instrumental)* **And may you**

𝄋 A E
grow _ to be proud, _ dig - ni - fied __ and true. __ *(Instrumental)* **And**
for - tune be with you, may your guid - ing light __ be strong, _ **build a**
fi - n'lly fly a - way, I'll be hoping that I served _ you well. __ **For all the**

A E
do un - to oth - ers as you'd have done to you. __ *(Instrumental)* **Be cou -**
stair - way to heav - en with a prince or a vag - a - bond. _ **And may you**
wis - dom of a life - time, no one can ev - er tell. __ **But what -**

F♯m7 A C♯m7 A
ra - geous and __ be brave. _ And in my heart you'll al - ways stay ___
nev - er love __ in vain. __ And in my heart you will __ re - main ___ **for - ev - er**
ev - er road _ you choose, _ I'm right be - hind you win __ or lose, ___

E A/E E 1 2, 3
young, (for - ev - er young) for - ev - er young, (for - ev - er young.) _ May good young.) _

F♯m7 A E
For - ev - er young. ____ *(Instrumental)*

F♯m A E To Coda ⊕
For - ev - er ____ young. _ *(Instrumental)*

B A E B

A B E5

D.S. al Coda
(End instrumental) **And when you**

CODA ⊕
F♯m7 A
For For - ev - er

E F♯m7 A E
young. ____ *(Instrumental)* **For - ev - er young. _____**

FREEZE FRAME

© 1981 CENTER CITY MUSIC (ASCAP)/Administered by BUG MUSIC and PAL-PARK MUSIC
All Rights for PAL-PARK MUSIC Administered by ALMO MUSIC CORP.

Words and Music by SETH JUSTMAN
and PETER WOLF

FORTRESS AROUND YOUR HEART

© 1985 G.M. SUMNER
Administered by MAGNETIC PUBLISHING LTD. (PRS) and EMI BLACKWOOD MUSIC INC. (BMI)

Written and Composed by
G.M. SUMNER

F♯m9
— and years, you pro - bab - ly thought or e - ven wished that I was dead. While the ar - mies are
— the cit - y. We walked through its streets in the af - ter - noon, — as I re - turned a - cross the
all sleep - ing — be - neath the tat - tered flag — we'd made, —
lands I'd known, — I rec - og - nized — the fields where I once played. —
I had to stop in my tracks
B7
— for fear — of walk - ing on — the mines — I'd laid. — And if —
— I'd laid. — And if —
D.S. al Coda
CODA
Repeat and Fade
(Instrumental)
FREE RIDE
© 1972 (Renewed 2000), 1974 EMI BLACKWOOD MUSIC INC.
Words and Music by
DAN HARTMAN
With energy
The moun - tain is high, — the val - ley is low, — and you're con - fused — on
o - ver the coun - try I've seen it the same; — no - bod - y's win - ning at
(Instrumental)
which way to go. — So, I've come here — to give you a hand — and lead you in - to the
this kind of game. — We've got - ta do bet - ter, it's time to be - gin. — You know all the an - swers must
prom - ised land. — So, come on — and take a free ride, — (free ride. —) Come on — and sit here
come from with - in.
To Coda
N.C.
by my side. — Come on — and take a free ride.
(Instrumental)
(End instrumental)
All, Yeah, yeah, yeah, yeah.
D.S. al Coda
CODA
Repeat and Fade
Come on — and take a free ride. Yeah, yeah, yeah, yeah.

GET BACK

Copyright © 1969 Sony/ATV Songs LLC
Copyright Renewed
All Rights Administered by Sony/ATV Music Publishing, 8 Music Square West, Nashville, TN 37203

Words and Music by JOHN LENNON
and PAUL McCARTNEY

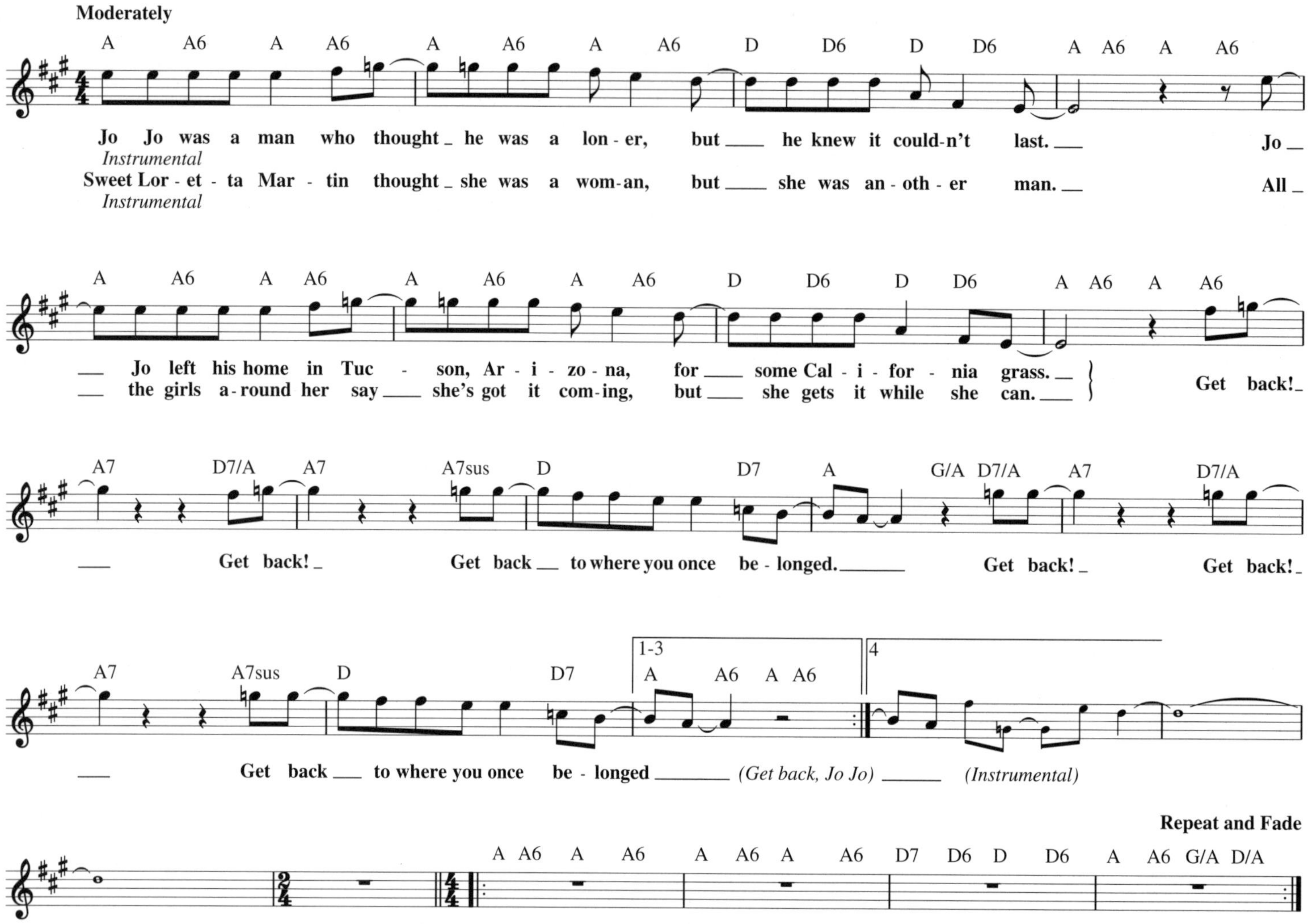

Moderately
A A6 A A6 A A6 A A6 D D6 D D6 A A6 A A6
Jo Jo was a man who thought he was a lon-er, but he knew it could-n't last. Jo
Instrumental
Sweet Lor-et-ta Mar-tin thought she was a wom-an, but she was an-oth-er man. All
Instrumental
A A6 A A6 A A6 A A6 D D6 D D6 A A6 A A6
Jo left his home in Tuc-son, Ar-i-zo-na, for some Cal-i-for-nia grass.
the girls a-round her say she's got it com-ing, but she gets it while she can.
Get back!
A7 D7/A A7 A7sus D D7 A G/A D7/A A7 D7/A
Get back! Get back to where you once be-longed. Get back! Get back!
A7 A7sus D D7
1-3
A A6 A A6
4
Get back to where you once be-longed (Get back, Jo Jo) (Instrumental)
Repeat and Fade
A A6 A A6 A A6 A A6 D7 D6 D D6 A A6 G/A D/A

Spoken: Get back, Loretta, your momma's waitin' for you
Wearin' her high heel shoes and a low-neck sweater.
Get back home, Loretta.

GIVE ME LOVE
(Give Me Peace on Earth)

© 1973 (Renewed) THE MATERIAL WORLD CHARITABLE FOUNDATION LTD.
Copyright Renewed 2001

By GEORGE HARRISON

Moderately slow
F Fmaj7 Gm7 C
Give me love, give me love, give me peace on earth. Give me light,
(D.S.) give me love give me love, give me
Bbm C Eb Bb
give me life, keep me free from birth. Give me
F Fmaj7 Gm7 C Bbm C
hope, help me cope with this heav-y load. Try-ing to touch and reach you with

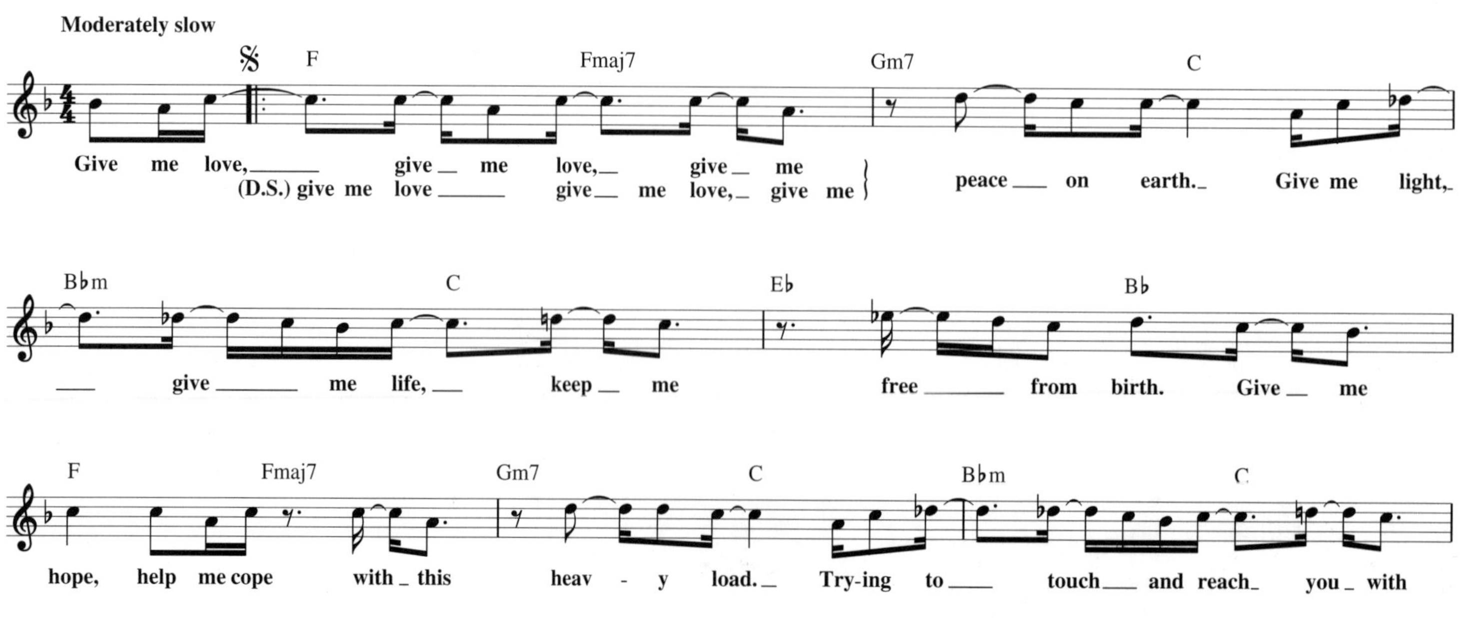

To Coda
Eb Bb F Fmaj7 F7
1
Bb7
heart and soul. Oh, my Lord.
F Fmaj7 F7 Bb
Please take hold of my hand that I
G7 C C7
might un - der - stand you. Won't you please. Oh, won't you
2
Bb7
Lord.
(Instrumental)
F Fmaj7
F7 Bb G7
(End instrumental)
C C7
D.S. al Coda
Won't you please. Oh, won't you
CODA
F Fmaj7
Give me love, give me love, give me
Gm7 C Bbm C Eb Bb
peace on earth. Give me light, give me life, keep me keep me free from birth. Now give
F Fmaj7 Gm7 C Bbm
me hope, help me cope with this heav - y load. Try-ing to touch and
C Eb Bb F
reach You with heart and soul. Oh,
Fmaj7 F7 Bb7 F
my Lord.
(Instrumental)
Fmaj7 F7 Bb7

GIVE A LITTLE BIT

Copyright © 1977 ALMO MUSIC CORP. and DELICATE MUSIC
All Rights Controlled and Administered by ALMO MUSIC CORP.

Words and Music by RICK DAVIES
and ROGER HODGSON

GLORIA

Copyright © 1965 by January Music Corp. and Hyde Park Music Company Ltd.
Copyright Renewed
Published in the U.S.A. and Canada by Unichappell Music Inc. and Bernice Music, Inc.
All Rights Administered by Unichappell Music Inc.

Words and Music by
VAN MORRISON

GODZILLA

Copyright © 1977 Sony/ATV Tunes LLC
All Rights Administered by Sony/ATV Music Publishing, 8 Music Square West, Nashville, TN 37203

Words and Music by
DONALD ROESER

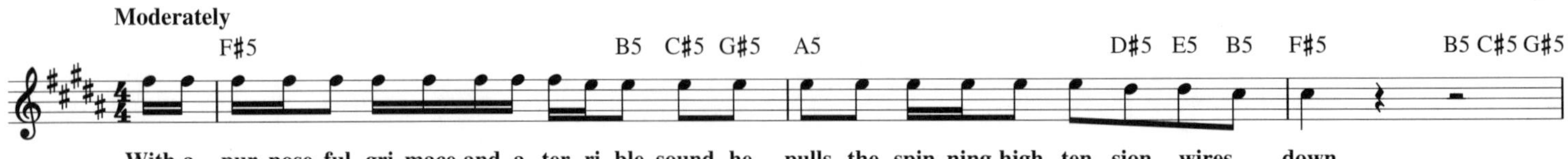
Moderately
F♯5 B5 C♯5 G♯5 A5 D♯5 E5 B5 F♯5 B5 C♯5 G♯5
With a pur-pose-ful gri-mace and a ter-ri-ble sound he pulls the spin-ning high ten-sion wires _ down.

A5 D♯5 E5 B5 F♯5 B5 C♯5 G♯5 A5 D♯5 E5 B5 F♯5 B5 C♯5 G♯5
Help-less peo-ple on sub-way trains scream bug-eyed _ as he looks in on them.

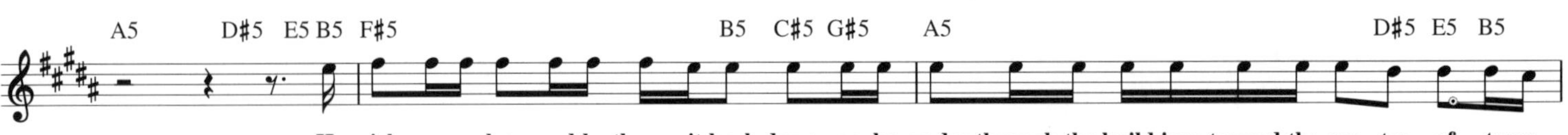
A5 D♯5 E5 B5 F♯5 B5 C♯5 G♯5 A5 D♯5 E5 B5
He picks up a bus and he throws it back down, as he wades through the build-ings toward the cen-ter of town. _

F♯5 B5 C♯5 G♯5 A5 D♯5 E5 B5 E5
Oh, no, they say he's got to go. Go, go God-

F♯5 E5
zil-la. Whoo. _ Oh, no

F♯5
there goes To-kyo. Go, go God-zil-la. Whoo. _

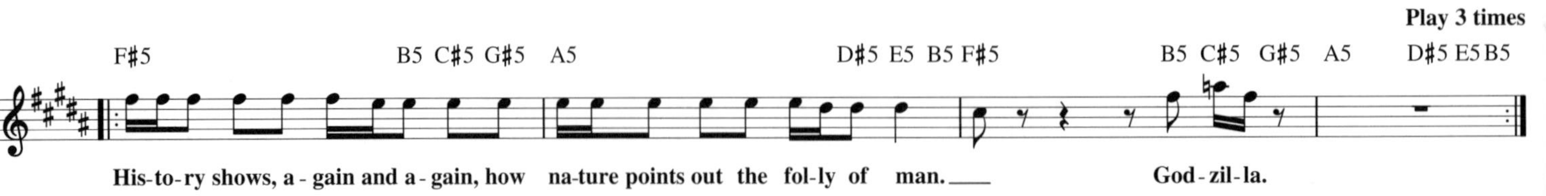
Play 3 times
F♯5 B5 C♯5 G♯5 A5 D♯5 E5 B5 F♯5 B5 C♯5 G♯5 A5 D♯5 E5 B5
His-to-ry shows, a-gain and a-gain, how na-ture points out the fol-ly of man. _ God-zil-la.

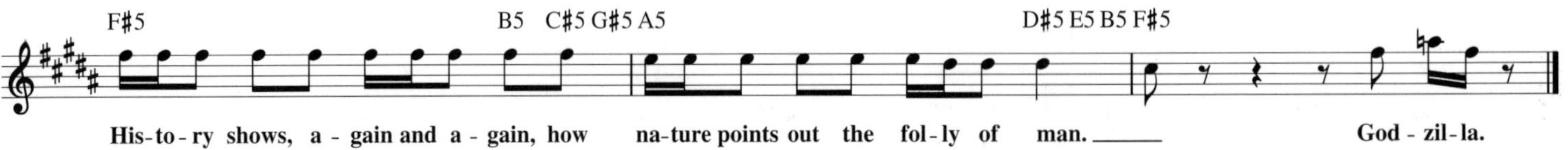
F♯5 B5 C♯5 G♯5 A5 D♯5 E5 B5 F♯5
His-to-ry shows, a-gain and a-gain, how na-ture points out the fol-ly of man. _ God-zil-la.

GO NOW

© 1963 (Renewed) TRIO MUSIC COMPANY, INC.

Words and Music by MILTON BENNETT
and LARRY BANKS

GOT MY MIND SET ON YOU

Copyright © 1978, 1987 by Carbert Music, Inc.

Words and Music by
RUDY CLARK

B♭
F
C
D.S. al Coda 1
to it, I know that I real - ly can do it. I Got My Mind
CODA 1
F
B♭
F
Dm
A7
Dm
do it, to do it right.
(Instrumental)
F
C7
F
Dm
A7
Dm
F
C7
F
Dm
A7
Dm
I Got My Mind Set On You.
F
C7
F
Dm
A7
Dm
I Got My Mind Set On You. I Got My Mind Set On You.
F
C7
F
I Got My Mind Set On You. And this time I know it's real,
B♭
F
B♭
F
the feel - ings that I feel. I know if I put my mind
B♭
F
C
D.S.S. al Coda 2
to it. I know that I real - ly can do it. But it's gon - na take mon -
CODA 2
F
B♭
F
do it, to do it right.
Dm
A7
Dm
F
C7
F
Repeat and Fade
Set on you. Set on you.

GOT TO GET YOU INTO MY LIFE

Copyright © 1966 Sony/ATV Songs LLC
Copyright Renewed
All Rights Administered by Sony/ATV Music Publishing, 8 Music Square West, Nashville, TN 37203

Words and Music by JOHN LENNON
and PAUL McCARTNEY

GREEN-EYED LADY

© 1970 (Renewed) CLARIDGE MUSIC COMPANY, A Division of MPL Communications, Inc.

Words and Music by JERRY CORBETTA,
J.C. PHILLIPS and DAVID RIORDAN

A HARD DAY'S NIGHT

Copyright © 1964 Sony/ATV Songs LLC
Copyright Renewed
All Rights Administered by Sony/ATV Music Publishing, 8 Music Square West, Nashville, TN 37203

Words and Music by JOHN LENNON
and PAUL McCARTNEY

HEART AND SOUL

Copyright © 1981 by BMG Songs, Inc.

Words and Music by MIKE CHAPMAN
and NICKY CHINN

HEARTACHE TONIGHT

© 1979 EMI BLACKWOOD MUSIC INC., WOODY CREEK MUSIC,
RED CLOUD MUSIC and GEAR PUBLISHING CO.

Words and Music by JOHN DAVID SOUTHER,
DON HENLEY, GLENN FREY and BOB SEGER

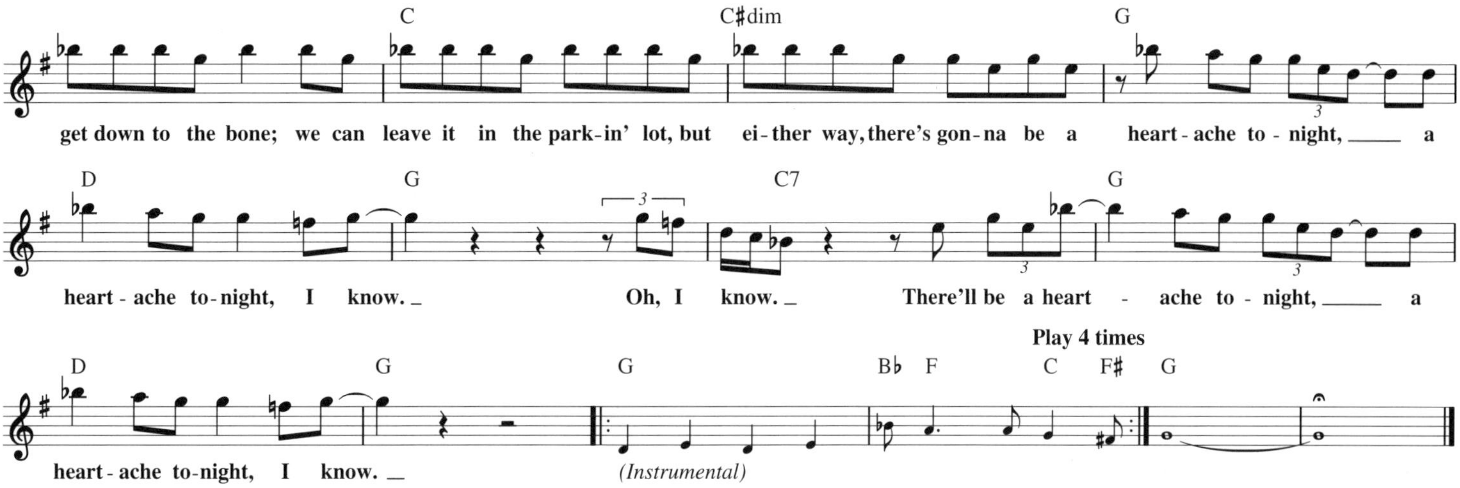

C C♯dim G

get down to the bone; we can leave it in the park-in' lot, but ei-ther way, there's gon-na be a heart-ache to-night, a

D G C7 G

heart-ache to-night, I know. Oh, I know. There'll be a heart - ache to-night, a

D G G B♭ F C F♯ G

Play 4 times

heart-ache to-night, I know. *(Instrumental)*

HAIR OF THE DOG

Copyright © 1975, 1978 by Mountain Music Ltd. and Carlin Music Corp.
All Rights for the United States and Canada Administered by
Bienstock Publishing Company

Words and Music by DAN McCAFFERTY, DARRELL SWEET,
PETE AGNEW and MANUEL CHARLTON

Rock

E

I'll break the soul-shak-er. I've been told a-bout you. She rode up, then I showed her,
Talkin' to her with poi-son i-vy, you ain't gon-na cling to me. Man tak-er, bone fin - ger,

A

what they've been sayin' must be true.
I ain't so blind I can't see.

Red hot ma-ma, love that charm-er;

E

just got to pay your dues. *(Instrumental)* *(End instrumental)*

E5 G5 A5 E5 D5 E5 G5

Now you're mess-in' with a, a son of a bitch.
Now you're mess-in' with a son of a bitch. Now you're mess-in' with a,

A5 E5 D5 E5

a son of a bitch.
Now you're mess-in' with a son of a bitch. *(Instrumental)*

E5 G5 A5 E Play 5 times

E5 G5 A5 E5

(End instrumental) Now you're mess-in' with a, a son of a bitch.
Now you're mess-in' with a

Repeat and Fade

D5 E5 G5 A5 E5 D5 E5

son of a bitch. Now you're mess-in' with a, a son of a bitch.
Now you're mess-in' with a son of a bitch.

HEAT OF THE MOMENT

Copyright © 1982 Palan Music Publishing Ltd., WB Music Corp. and Almond Legg Music Corp.
All Rights for Palan Music Publishing Ltd. in the United States and Canada Administered by
Palan Songs America
All Rights for Almond Legg Music Corp. Administered by WB Music Corp.

Words and Music by GEOFFREY DOWNES
and JOHN WETTON

HEAVEN

Copyright © 1983 IRVING MUSIC, INC., ADAMS COMMUNICATIONS, INC.,
ALMO MUSIC CORP. and TESTATYME MUSIC
All Rights for ADAMS COMMUNICATIONS, INC. Controlled and Administered by IRVING MUSIC, INC.
All Rights for TESTATYME MUSIC Controlled and Administered by ALMO MUSIC CORP.

Words and Music by BRYAN ADAMS
and JIM VALLANCE

HELLO, GOODBYE

Copyright © 1967 Sony/ATV Songs LLC
Copyright Renewed
All Rights Administered by Sony/ATV Music Publishing, 8 Music Square West, Nashville, TN 37203

Words and Music by JOHN LENNON
and PAUL McCARTNEY

HELLO, IT'S ME

© 1968 (Renewed 1996) SCREEN GEMS-EMI MUSIC INC.

Words and Music by
TODD RUNDGREN

Moderately slow

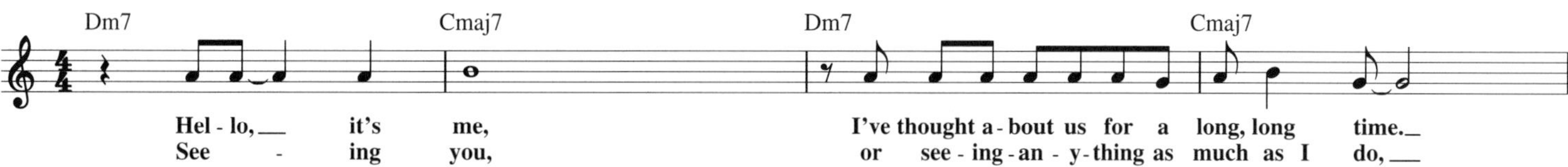
Dm7 Cmaj7 Dm7 Cmaj7
Hel - lo, it's me, I've thought a - bout us for a long, long time.
See - ing you, or see - ing - an - y - thing as much as I do,

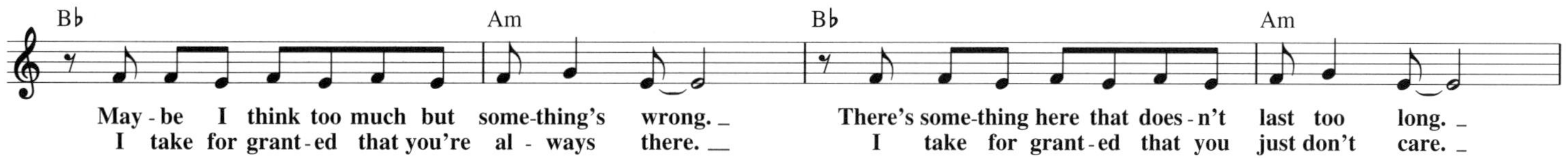
B♭ Am B♭ Am
May - be I think too much but some-thing's wrong. There's some-thing here that does - n't last too long.
I take for grant - ed that you're al - ways there. I take for grant - ed that you just don't care.

B♭ Fmaj7 B♭/F Fsus Fmaj7 B♭/F Fsus Fmaj7 𝄋 Dm7/F C/E C
May - be I should-n't think of you as mine.
Some-times I can't help see-ing all the way through.
(Instrumental)
(End instrumental)

Dm7 Cmaj7 B♭maj7 Fmaj7 B♭maj7 Fmaj7 Cmaj7 Gmaj7 Cmaj7 Gmaj7
It's im - por - tant to me that you know you are free, 'cause I

B♭ C B♭ Am Gsus/D G Dm7
nev - er want to make you change for me. (Instrumental) Think of

Cmaj7 Dm7 Cmaj7 B♭ Am
me. You know that I'd be with you if I could. I'll come a-round to see you once in a - while,

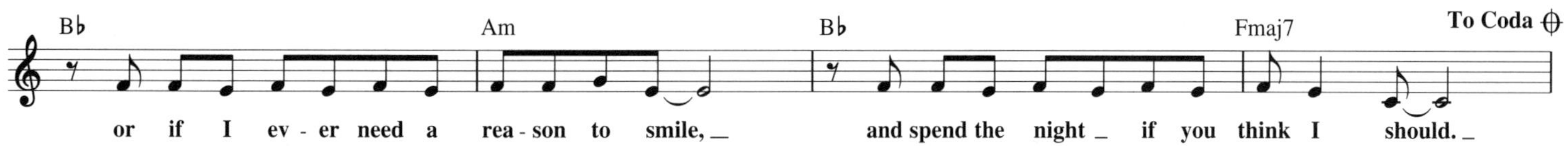
B♭ Am B♭ Fmaj7
To Coda 𝄌
or if I ev - er need a rea - son to smile, and spend the night if you think I should.

D.S. al Coda
B♭/F Fsus Fmaj7 B♭/F Fsus Fmaj7
(Instrumental)

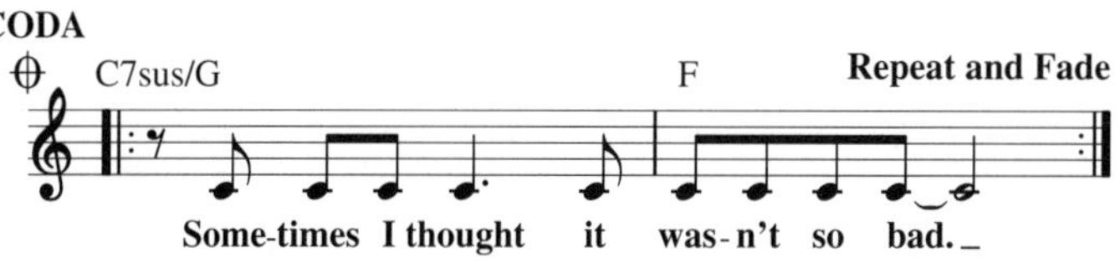
CODA
C7sus/G F
Repeat and Fade
Some-times I thought it was-n't so bad.

HELLO OLD FRIEND

Copyright © 1976 by Eric Patrick Clapton
All Rights for the U.S. Administered by Unichappell Music Inc.

Words and Music by
ERIC CLAPTON

you know I caught her mess-in' round with an - oth-er man. Huh! And that ain't too cool. Uh, hey, Joe,
I heard you shot your wom-an down, you shot her down now. Uh, hey, Joe,
I heard you shot your old la-dy down, you shot her down in the ground. Yeah. Yes, I did, I shot her.
You know I caught her mess-in' 'round mess-in' 'round town. Uh, yes I did, I shot her.
You know I caught my old la-dy mess-in' 'round town. And I gave her the gun. I shot her.
Al - right. Shoot her one more time a - gain, ba-by. Yeah.
Ah dig it. Ah! Ah! Al-right.
Hey, Joe, said now uh where you gon-na run to now? Where you gon-na run to? Yeah.
Hey, Joe, I said where you gon-na run to now? Where you, where you gon-na go? Well, dig it.
I'm go-in' way down south, way down to Mex-i-co way. Al - right. I'm go-in' way down south,
way down where I can be free. Ain't no one gon-na find me, babe. Ain't no hang-man gon-na.
Repeat ad lib. and Fade
He ain't gon-na put a rope a-round me. You bet-ter be-lieve it right now. I got-ta go now.

HELP!

Copyright © 1965 Sony/ATV Songs LLC
Copyright Renewed
All Rights Administered by Sony/ATV Music Publishing, 8 Music Square West, Nashville, TN 37203

Words and Music by JOHN LENNON
and PAUL McCARTNEY

Moderately, with a driving beat

Bm Bm/A G G/F# E7

Help! I need some-bod - y, Help! Not just an - y - bod - y, Help! You know I

A N.C. A

need some - one, Help!

1.,3. When I was young - er, so much
2. And now my life has changed in,

C#m F#m

young - er than to - day, I nev - er need - ed an - y - bod - y's
oh, so man - y ways, my in - de - pen-dence seems to

D G A C#m

Help in an - y way. But now these days are gone, I'm not so self - as - sured,
van - ish in the haze. But ev - 'ry now and then I feel so in - se - cure,

F#m D G A Bm

now I find I've changed my mind, I've o - pened up the doors.
I know that I just need you like I've nev - er done be - fore.
Help me if you

Bm/A G

can, I'm feel - ing down, and I do ap - pre - ci - ate you be-ing 'round,

G/F# E7 A N.C.

Help me get my feet back on the ground. Won't you please

1,2 | 3 F#m A A6

please, Help me? Help me, Help me! Oo.

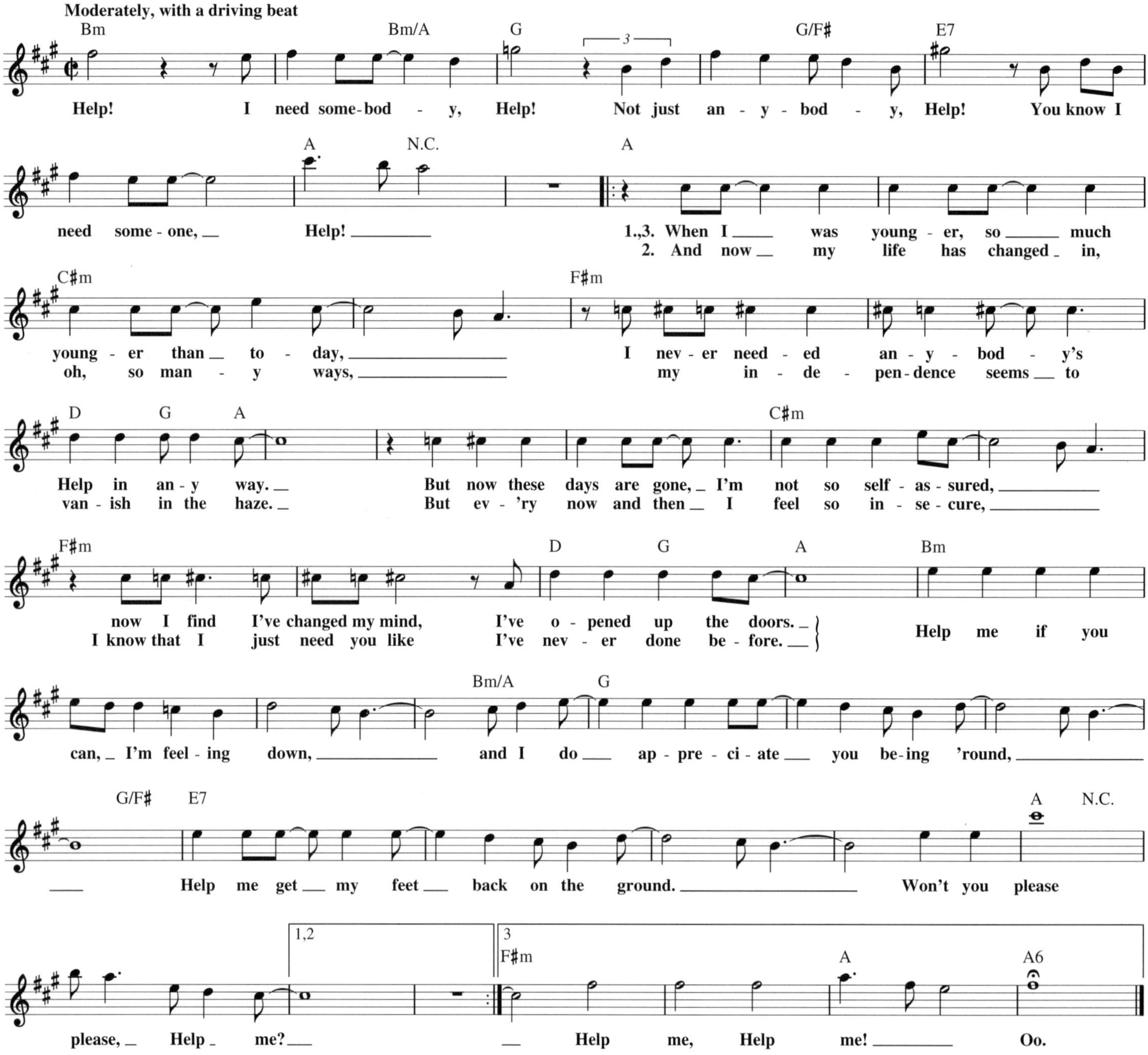

HELTER SKELTER

Copyright © 1968 Sony/ATV Songs LLC
Copyright Renewed
All Rights Administered by Sony/ATV Music Publishing, 8 Music Square West, Nashville, TN 37203

Words and Music by JOHN LENNON
and PAUL McCARTNEY

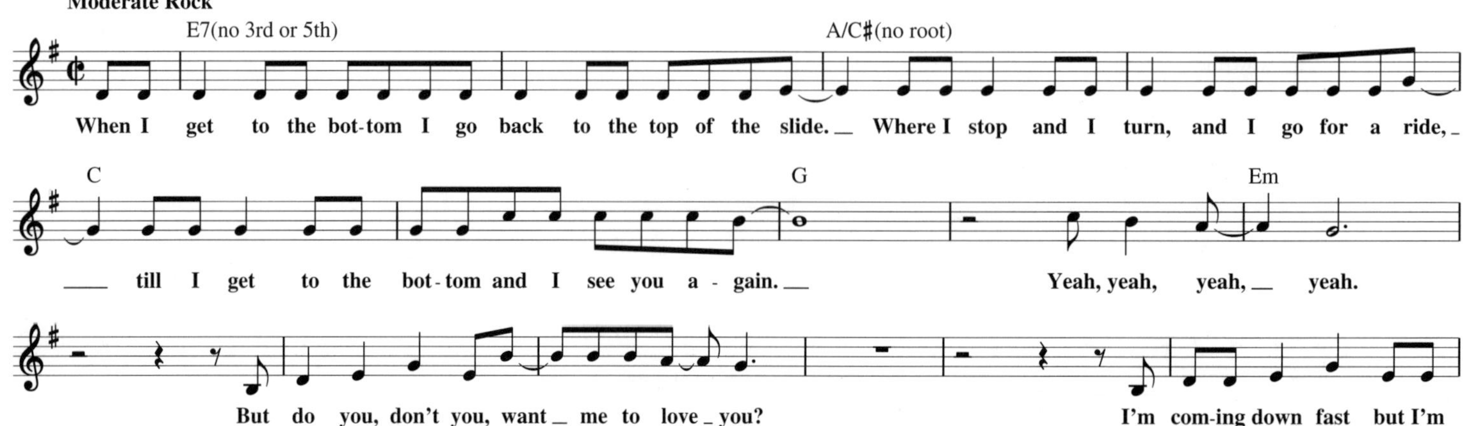

G
miles a - bove _ you. Tell me, tell me, tell ___ me, come on tell ___ me the an - swer. _
A Em A
___ Well you may be a lov - er but you ain't no _ danc - er. _ Now hel - ter, skel - ter,
Em A
(Instrumental) hel - ter, skel - ter, (Instrumental) hel - ter, skel - ter, (Instrumental)
Em %Em E
yeah, ___ Well will you, won't you want _ me to make _ you?
do you, don't you want _ me to make _ you? I'm
Em E G
com-ing down fast but don't let me break _ you. Tell me, tell me, tell ___ me _ the an - swer. You
A E A
may be a lov - er but you ain't no danc - er. Look out! _ Hel - ter, skel - ter,
Em A To Coda
(Instrumental) hel - ter, skel - ter, (Instrumental) hel - ter, skel - ter, (Instrumental)
Em
ooh. _ Look out! 'cause here she come! (Instrumental)
A E(#9) A Em
(End instrumental)
E7 A/E
When I get to the bot - tom, I go back to the top of the slide. _ And I stop and I turn, and I go for a ride _
C/E G E D.S. al Coda
___ and I get to the bot - tom and I see you a - gain. _ Yeah, yeah, yeah, _ yeah. Well
CODA
Em
Ad lib.
(Shout): Look out! Helter, skelter! She's coming down fast. Yes, she is. (etc.)

HIT ME WITH YOUR BEST SHOT

Copyright © 1978, 1980 Sony/ATV Songs LLC
All Rights Administered by Sony/ATV Music Publishing, 8 Music Square West, Nashville, TN 37203

Words and Music by
EDDIE SCHWARTZ

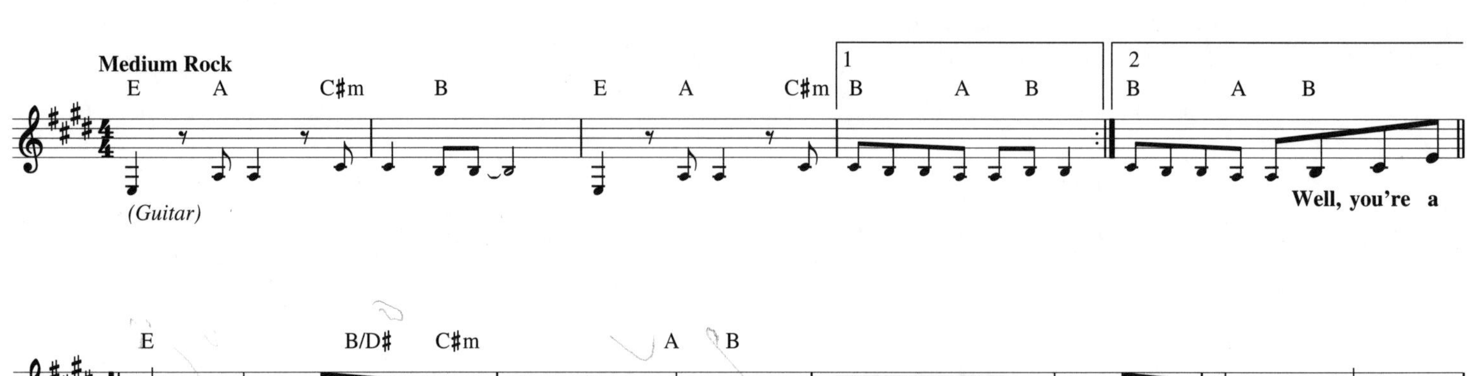

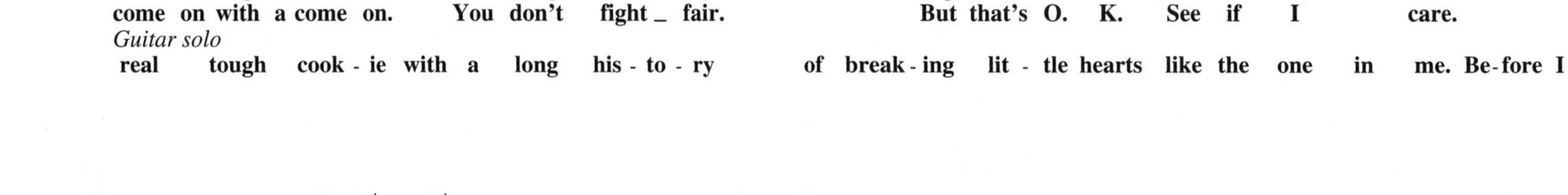

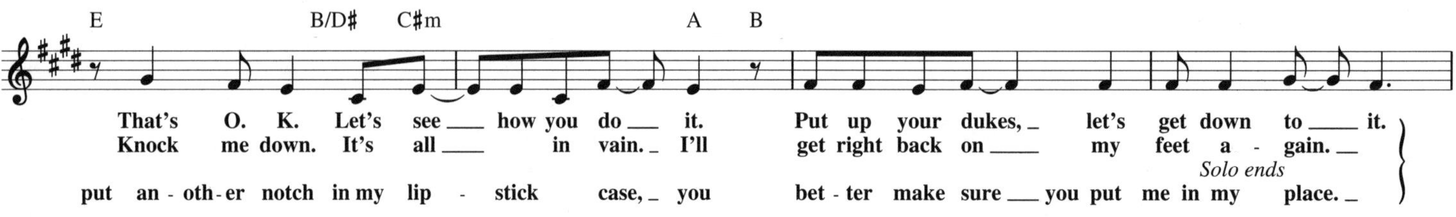

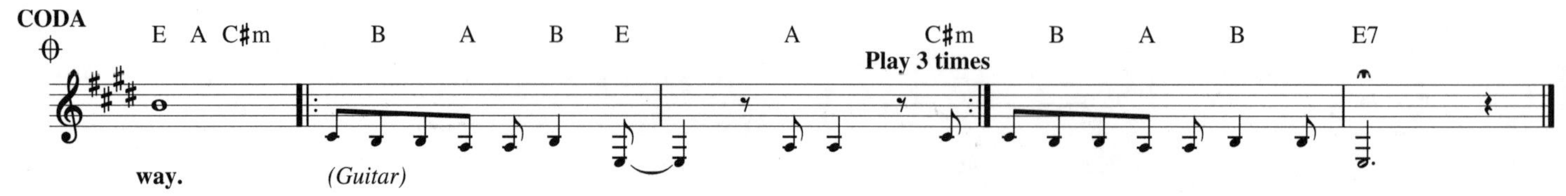

HONESTY

© 1978 IMPULSIVE MUSIC

Words and Music by
BILLY JOEL

HOT LEGS

© 1977 ROD STEWART
All Rights Controlled and Administered by EMI APRIL MUSIC INC.

Words and Music by
ROD STEWART

HURDY GURDY MAN

Words and Music by
DONOVAN LEITCH

Copyright © 1968 by Donovan (Music) Ltd.
Copyright Renewed
All Rights Administered by Peer International Corporation

Slowly

G Bm C D7 G Bm
Thrown like a star in my_ vast sleep I o-pen my eyes to take_ a peep_ to find that I was by_ the sea_
His-tor-ies_ of ag-es past_ un-en-light-ened shad-ows cast_ down through all_ e-ter-ni-ty,_ the

C D7 F C G
gaz-ing with tran-quil-i-ty._ 'Twas then when the hur-dy gur-dy man_ came sing-ing songs of love,
cry-ing of hu-man-i-ty._ 'Tis then when the hur-dy gur-dy man_ comes sing-ing songs of love,

F C G
then when the hur-dy gur-dy man_ came sing-ing songs_ of love._
then when the hur-dy gur-dy man_ comes sing-ing songs_ of love._

F C G F C
Hur-dy gur-dy hur-dy gur-dy hur-dy gur-dy, gur-dy he sang._ Hur-dy gur-dy hur-dy gur-dy hur-dy

G F C G
gur-dy, gur-dy he sang._ Hur-dy gur-dy hur-dy gur-dy hur-dy gur-dy, gur-dy he sang._

F C 1 G N.C. 2 G F C
(Instrumental)
Hur-dy gur-dy hur-dy gur-dy hur-dy

G F C
gur-dy, gur-dy he sang._ Here comes the ro-ly po-ly man_ and he's

G F C G
Repeat and Fade
sing-ing songs of love._ Ro-ly po-ly ro-ly po-ly po-ly ro-ly po-ly he sang._

HUSH

Copyright © 1970 Sony/ATV Songs LLC
Copyright Renewed
All Rights Administered by Sony/ATV Music Publishing, 8 Music Square West, Nashville, TN 37203

Words and Music by
JOE SOUTH

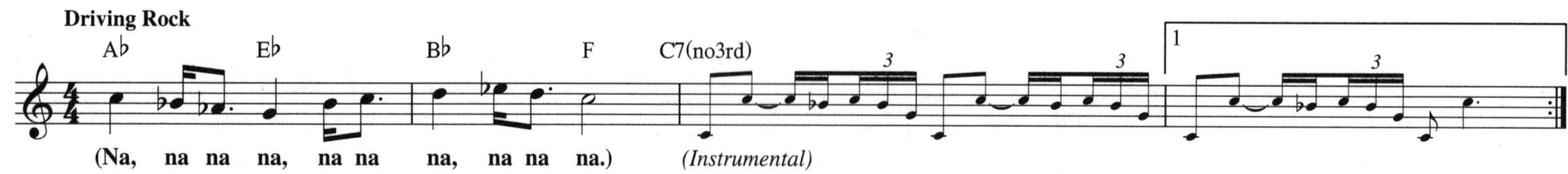
Driving Rock
A♭ E♭ B♭ F C7(no3rd)
1
(Na, na na na, na na na, na na na.)
(Instrumental)

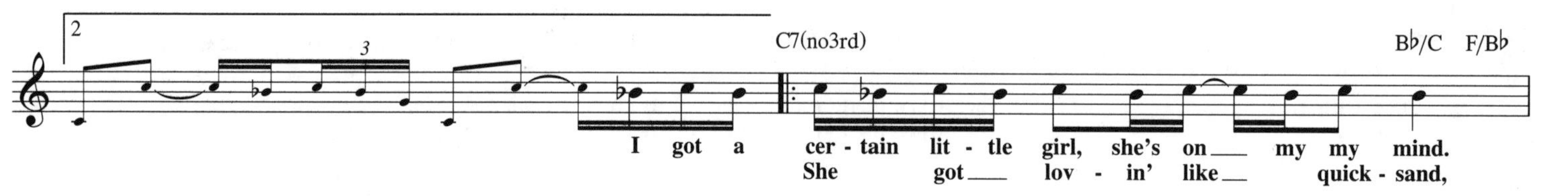
2
C7(no3rd) B♭/C F/B♭
I got a cer - tain lit - tle girl, she's on my my mind.
She got lov - in' like quick - sand,

C7(no3rd) B♭/C F/B♭ C7(no3rd) B♭/C F/B♭
No doubt a - bout it, she looks so fine. She's the best girl that I ev - er had.
On - ly took one touch of her hand to blow my mind, and I'm in so deep, that

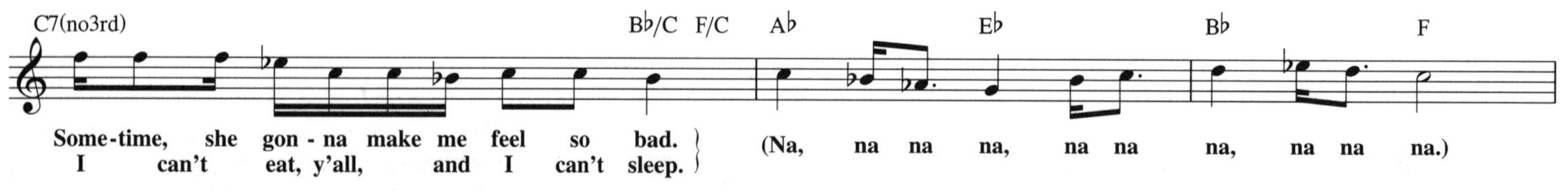
C7(no3rd) B♭/C F/C A♭ E♭ B♭ F
Some-time, she gon - na make me feel so bad.
I can't eat, y'all, and I can't sleep.
(Na, na na na, na na na, na na na.)

C7(no3rd) B♭/C F/B♭ C7(no3rd) B♭/C F/C A♭ E♭ B♭ F
(Instrumental)
(Na, na na na, na na na, na na na.)

C7(no3rd) C7
(Instrumental)
Hush, hush. I

F B♭ F C7 F B♭ F
thought I heard her call - in' my name now. Hush, hush. She broke my heart, but I love her just the same, now.

C7
F
B♭
F
C7
Hush, hush. I though I heard her call - in' my name, now. Hush, hush. I

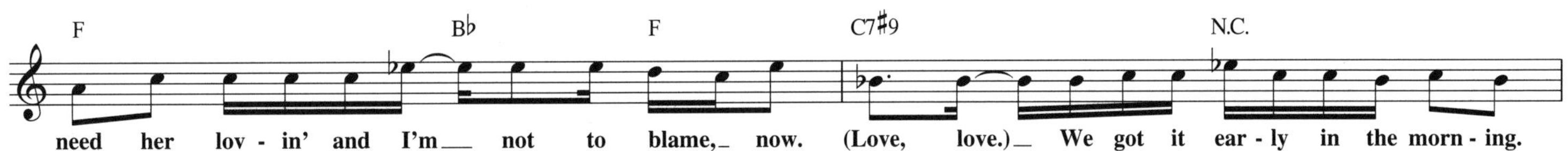
F
B♭
F
C7♯9
N.C.
need her lov - in' and I'm not to blame, now. (Love, love.) We got it ear - ly in the morn - ing.

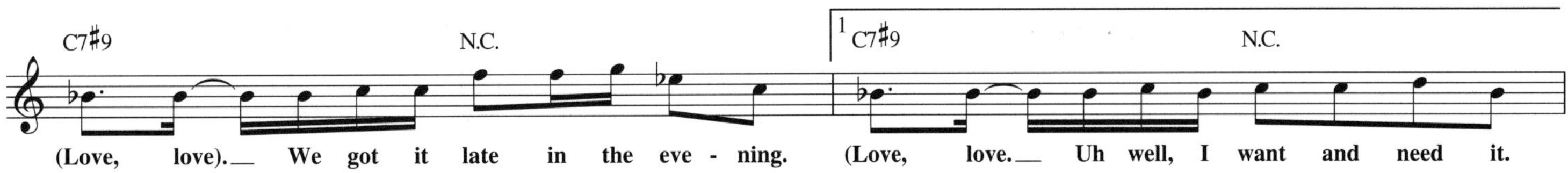
C7♯9
N.C.
1
C7♯9
N.C.
(Love, love). We got it late in the eve - ning. (Love, love. Uh well, I want and need it.

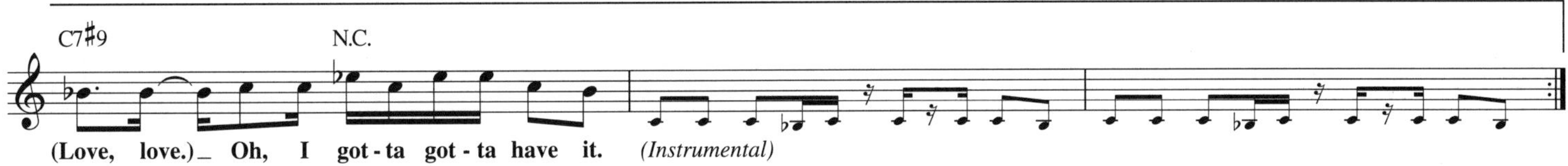
C7♯9
N.C.
(Love, love.) Oh, I got - ta got - ta have it. (Instrumental)

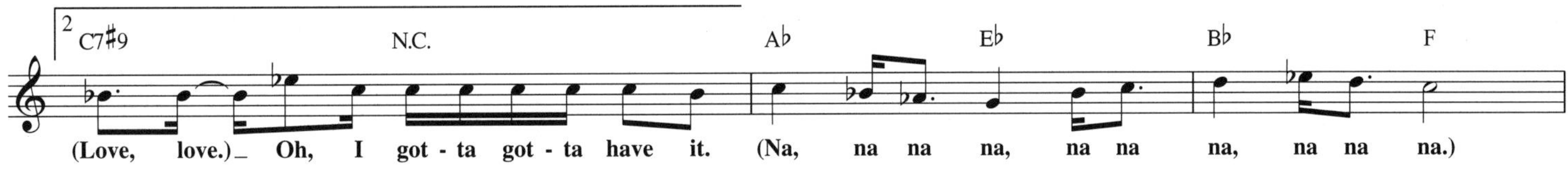
2
C7♯9
N.C.
A♭
E♭
B♭
F
(Love, love.) Oh, I got - ta got - ta have it. (Na, na na na, na na na, na na na.)

C7(no3rd)
A♭
E♭
(Instrumental)
(Na, na na na, na na

B♭
F
C7(no3rd)
na, na na na.)
(Instrumental)

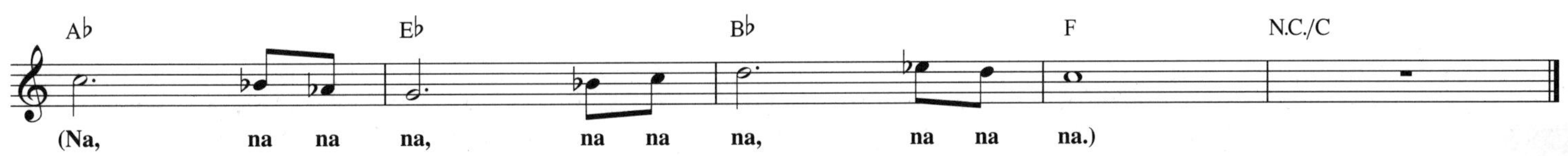
A♭
E♭
B♭
F
N.C./C
(Na, na na na, na na na, na na na.)

HURTS SO GOOD

© 1982 EMI FULL KEEL MUSIC

Words and Music by JOHN MELLENCAMP
and GEORGE GREEN

I CAN SEE FOR MILES

© Copyright 1967 (Renewed) Fabulous Music Ltd., London, England
TRO - Essex Music, Inc., New York, controls all publication rights for the U.S.A. and Canada

Words and Music by
PETER TOWNSHEND

I CAN'T STAND IT
Copyright © 1981 by Eric Patrick Clapton
All Rights for the U.S. Administered by Unichappell Music Inc.
Words and Music by
ERIC CLAPTON
Slowly
You've been told, so may-be it's time you learned. You've been sold; may-be it's time that you earned. I can't stand it. Your fool-ing a-round, I can't stand it. Your run-ning a-round, I won't stand it. You're fool-ing a-round with my heart.
I feel like I'm be-in' used. Make it plain, so you don't get con-fused. I can't stand it. Your fool-ing a-round, I won't stand it. Your run-ning a-round, I can't stand it. You're fool-ing a-round with my heart.
time for me to let you know. Ain't no crime, no crime to let your feel-ings show. I can't stand it. Your run-ning a-round, I can't stand it. Your play-ing a-round, I can't stand it. Your fool-ing a-round, I can't stand
To Coda
I'll ex-plain,
(Instrumental)
(End instrumental)
I can't stand it. Your fool-ing a-round, I won't stand it. Your run-ning a-round, I can't stand it. You're fool-ing a-round with my heart.
D.S. al Coda
It was time,
CODA
it. Your run-ning a-round, I won't stand it, Your
fool-ing a-round, I won't stand it, Your
play-ing a-round, I won't stand it, Your run-ning a-round, I won't stand it. You're
run-ning a-round with my heart. Your
Play 3 times
Repeat and Fade
I FOUGHT THE LAW
Copyright © 1961 (Renewed 1990) by Acuff-Rose Music, Inc.
Words and Music by
SONNY CURTIS
Driving Rock
A break-in' rocks in the hot sun.
need-ed mon-ey 'cause I had none.
rob-bin' peo-ple with a six gun.
miss my ba-by and the good fun.
I fought the law and the law won. I fought the law and the law won.
I
I left my ba-by and I feel so bad. I guess my race is run. Well, she's the best girl

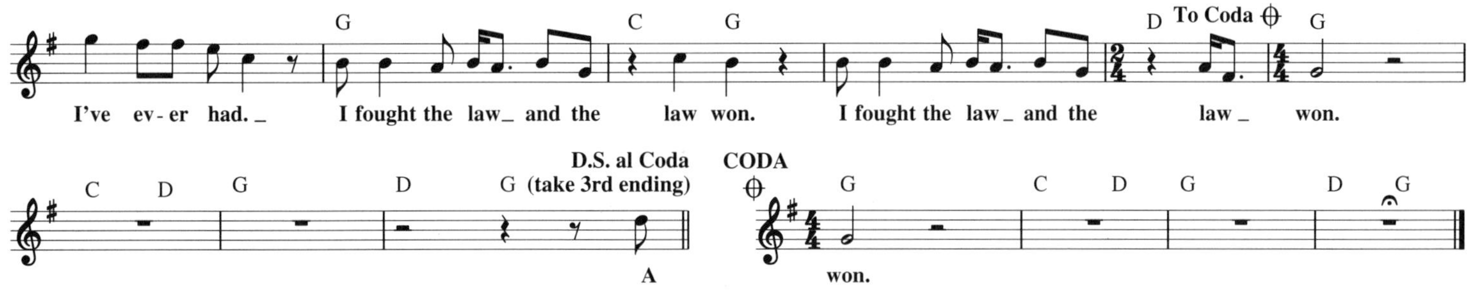

I LOVE ROCK 'N ROLL

Copyright © 1975, 1982 Rak Publishing Ltd. for the World
All Rights for the U.S.A. and Canada Controlled by Finchley Music Corp.
Administered by Music & Media International, Inc.

Words and Music by ALAN MERRILL
and JAKE HOOKER

Moderately

E5 N.C. E5
I saw him danc - ing there _ by the re - cord ma - chine. I knew he must have been _
smiled, so I got up ___ and asked _ for his name. "That don't mat - ter," he

B5 N.C. A5 B5 E5
_ a - bout sev - en - teen. The beat was go - ing strong, _ play - ing my fa - v'rite
said, "cause it's all the same." I said, "Can I take you home ___ where we can be a -

A5 N.C.
song, and I could tell it would - n't be long ___ till he was with me, yeah,
lone?" And next, we were mov - ing on, and he was with me, yeah,

B5 E5
me. And I could tell it would - n't be long _ till he was with me, yeah, me, sing - in', I Love
me. And next, we were mov - ing on, and he was with me, yeah, me, sing - in',

A5 B5 E5
Rock 'N' Roll. _ So put an - oth - er dime in the juke - box ba - by. I Love Rock 'N' Roll. _ So

A5 B5 E5 1 N.C. 2 N.C.
come and take your time and dance with me. He I

A5 B5 E5 A5
said, "Can I take you home _ where we can be a - lone?" Next we were mov - in' on, _

N.C.
___ and he was with me, yeah, me. And we'll be mov - in' on ___ and sing - in' that same old

E5 A5
song, yeah, with me, ___ sing - in', I Love Rock 'N' Roll. _ So put an - oth - er dime in the

B5 E5 A5 B5 E5
juke - box, ba - by. I Love Rock 'N' Roll. _ So come and take your time and dance with me.

I WANT YOU TO WANT ME

© 1977, 1978 SCREEN GEMS-EMI MUSIC INC. and ADULT MUSIC
All Rights Controlled and Administered by SCREEN GEMS-EMI MUSIC INC.

Words and Music by
RICK NIELSEN

A A/G♯ F♯m7 B7 G
shirt. I'll get home early from work if you say that you love
F♯m A E
me. (Instrumental) Did-n't I, did-n't I, did-n't I see you cry-in' (cry-in',
F♯m D7 C
cry-in'). Oh, did-n't I, did-n't I, did-n't I see you cry-in' (cry-in', cry-in'). (Instrumental)
A E F♯m
Feel-in' all a-lone with-out a friend you know you feel like dy-in' (dy-in', dy-in'). Oh, did-n't I, did-n't I,
D7 A E
did-n't I see you cry-in' (cry-in', cry-in'). (Guitar solo)
F♯m D7 C 1 A
(End solo) I Feel-in' all a-lone with-out a friend you know you feel like
E F♯m
dy-in'. Oh, did-n't I, did-n't I, did-n't I see you
D7 2 A A(add2) A
cry-in' (cry-in', cry-in'). want you to want me.
A/G♯ F♯m A/E D
I need you to need me. I'd love
D(add2) D A/C♯ A Asus A
you to love me. I'm beg-gin' you.

IF YOU LEAVE ME NOW

Copyright © 1976 by BMG Songs, Inc. and Big Elk Music

Words and Music by
PETER CETERA

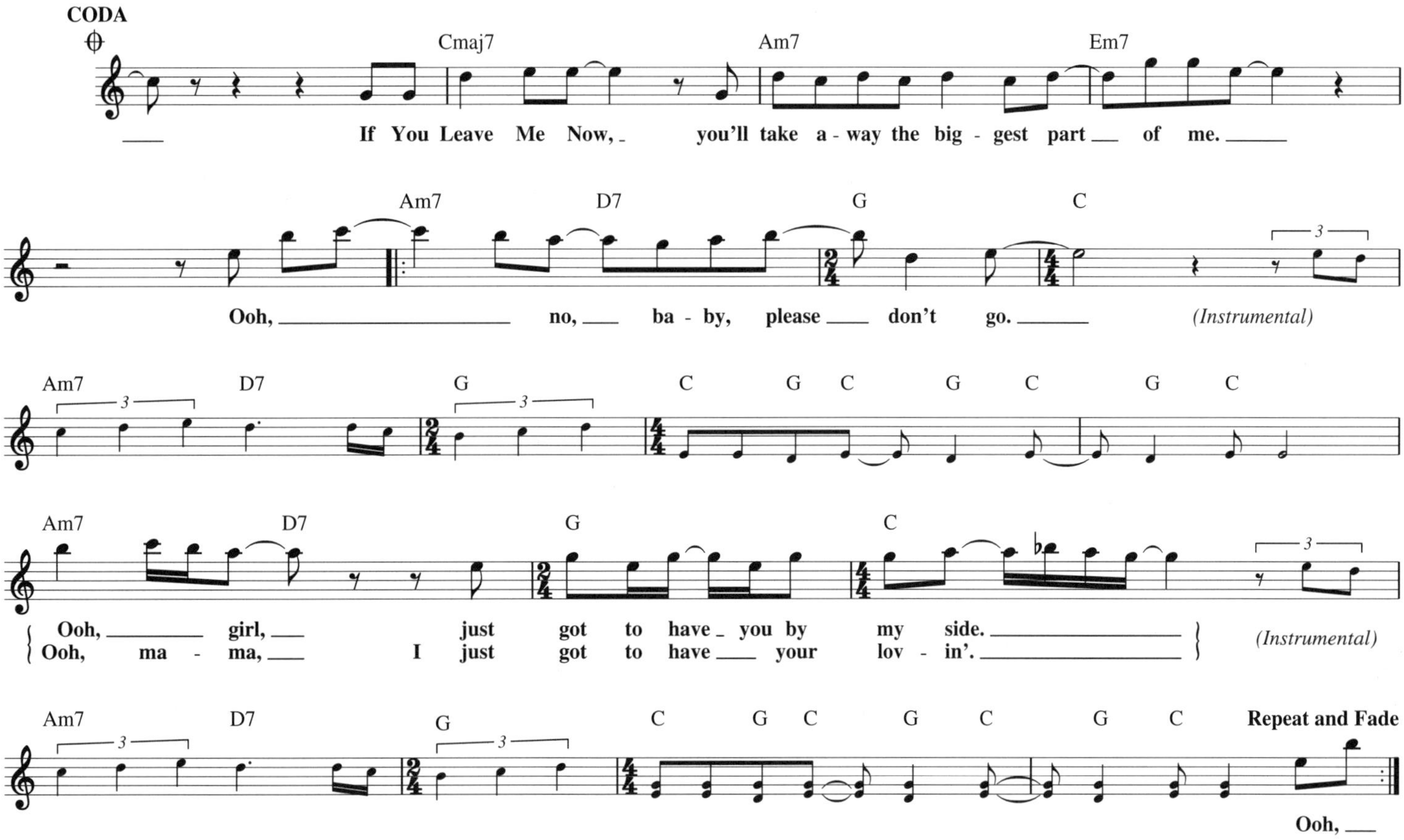

CODA
Cmaj7 Am7 Em7
If You Leave Me Now, you'll take a-way the big-gest part of me.
Am7 D7 G C
Ooh, no, ba-by, please don't go.
(Instrumental)
Am7 D7 G C G C G C G C
Am7 D7 G C
Ooh, girl, just got to have you by my side.
Ooh, ma-ma, I just got to have your lov-in'.
(Instrumental)
Am7 D7 G C G C G C G C
Repeat and Fade
Ooh,

I SHOT THE SHERIFF

Copyright © 1974 Fifty-Six Hope Road Music, Ltd., Odnil Music, Ltd. and Blue Mountain Music, Ltd.
All Rights for North and South America Controlled and Administered by Rykomusic, Inc.
All Rights for the rest of the world Controlled and Administered by Rykomusic, Inc.

Words and Music by
BOB MARLEY

Moderately slow, with a beat
Gm7 Cm7 Gm Gm7 Cm7
1. I shot the sher-iff, but I did not shoot the dep-u-ty. I shot the sher-iff, but I did-n't shoot the
2. - 4. (See additional lyrics)
Gm Ebmaj7 Dm7 Gm Ebmaj7 Dm7 Gm
dep-u-ty. All a-round in my home town, they're try-ing to track me down. They
Ebmaj7 Dm7 Gm Ebmaj7 Dm7 Gm Ebmaj7 Dm7
say they want to bring me in guilt-y for the kill-ing of a dep-u-ty, for the life of a dep-u-
Gm N.C. 1-3 4
ty. But I say: (Instrumental)
D.C. and Fade

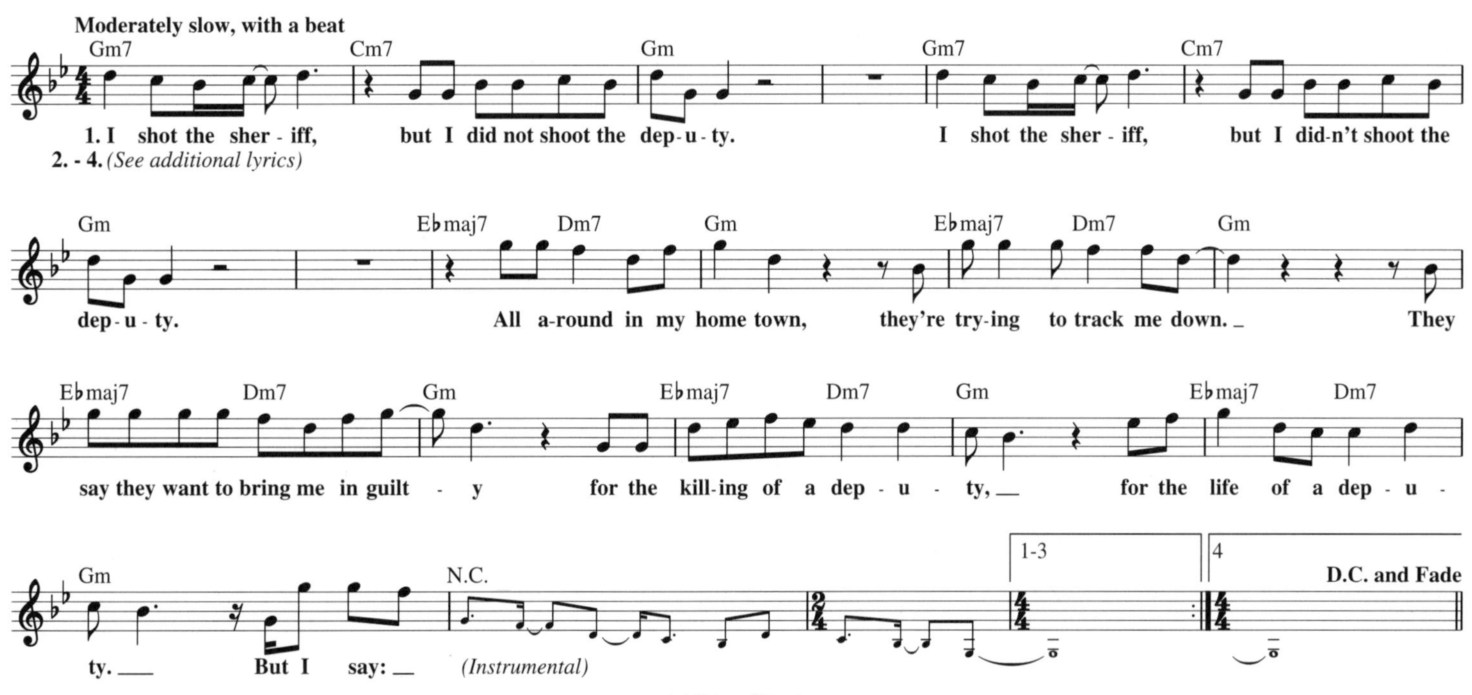

Additional Lyrics

2. I shot the sheriff, but I swear it was in self-defense.
I shot the sheriff, and they say it is a capital offense.
Sheriff John Brown always hated me; for what, I don't know.
Every time that I plant a seed, he said, "Kill it before it grows."
He said, "Kill it before it grows." But I say:

3. I shot the sheriff, but I swear it was in self-defense.
I shot the sheriff, but I swear it was in self-defense.
Freedom came my way one day, and I started out of town.
All of a sudden, I see Sheriff John Brown aiming to shoot me down.
So I shot, I shot him down. But I say:

4. I shot the sheriff, but I did not shoot the deputy.
I shot the sheriff, but I didn't shoot the deputy.
Reflexes got the better of me, and what is to be must be.
Every day, the bucket goes to the well, but one day the bottom will drop out.
Yes, one day the bottom will drop out. But I say:

IF YOU LOVE SOMEBODY SET THEM FREE

© 1985 G.M. SUMNER
Administered by MAGNETIC PUBLISHING LTD. (PRS) and EMI BLACKWOOD MUSIC INC. (BMI)

Written and Composed by
G.M. SUMNER

C Gm7 F C/E
With so man - y rich - es, so many souls, with ev - 'ry-thing we see that we
C Dm7 G
D.S. al Coda
want to pos-sess. If you need some-bod - y,
Repeat and Fade with vocal ad lib.
CODA
Dm9 G Am7 G
free. (Free, free, set them free.) Set them
IMAGINE
© 1971 (Renewed 1999) LENONO.MUSIC
All Rights Controlled and Administered by EMI BLACKWOOD MUSIC INC.
Words and Music by
JOHN LENNON
Slowly
C Cmaj7 F C Cmaj7 F
I-mag-ine there's no hea-ven. It's eas - y if you try.
C Cmaj7 F C Cmaj7 F Am/E
No hell be-low us, a-bove us on - ly sky. I-mag-ine all the peo -
Dm7 F/C G C/G G7 C Cmaj7
ple liv - ing for to - day. Ah. I-mag-ine there's no coun -
F C Cmaj7 F C Cmaj7 F
tries. It is-n't hard to do. Noth-ing to kill or die for
sions. I won-der if you can. No need for greed or hun - ger,
C Cmaj7 F Am/E Dm7 F/C
and no re - li - gion, too. I-mag - ine all the peo - ple
a broth - er - hood of man. I-mag - ine all the peo - ple
G C/G G7 F G C E7 F G
liv - ing life in peace. You you may say I'm a dream - er. But I'm not the on - ly one.
shar - ing all the world.
C E7 F G C E7 1 F G
I hope some day you'll join us and the world will
C Cmaj7 2 F G C
be as one. I-mag-ine no pos - ses - and the world will live as one.

IN MY LIFE

Copyright © 1965 Sony/ATV Songs LLC
Copyright Renewed
All Rights Administered by Sony/ATV Music Publishing, 8 Music Square West, Nashville, TN 37203

Words and Music by JOHN LENNON
and PAUL McCARTNEY

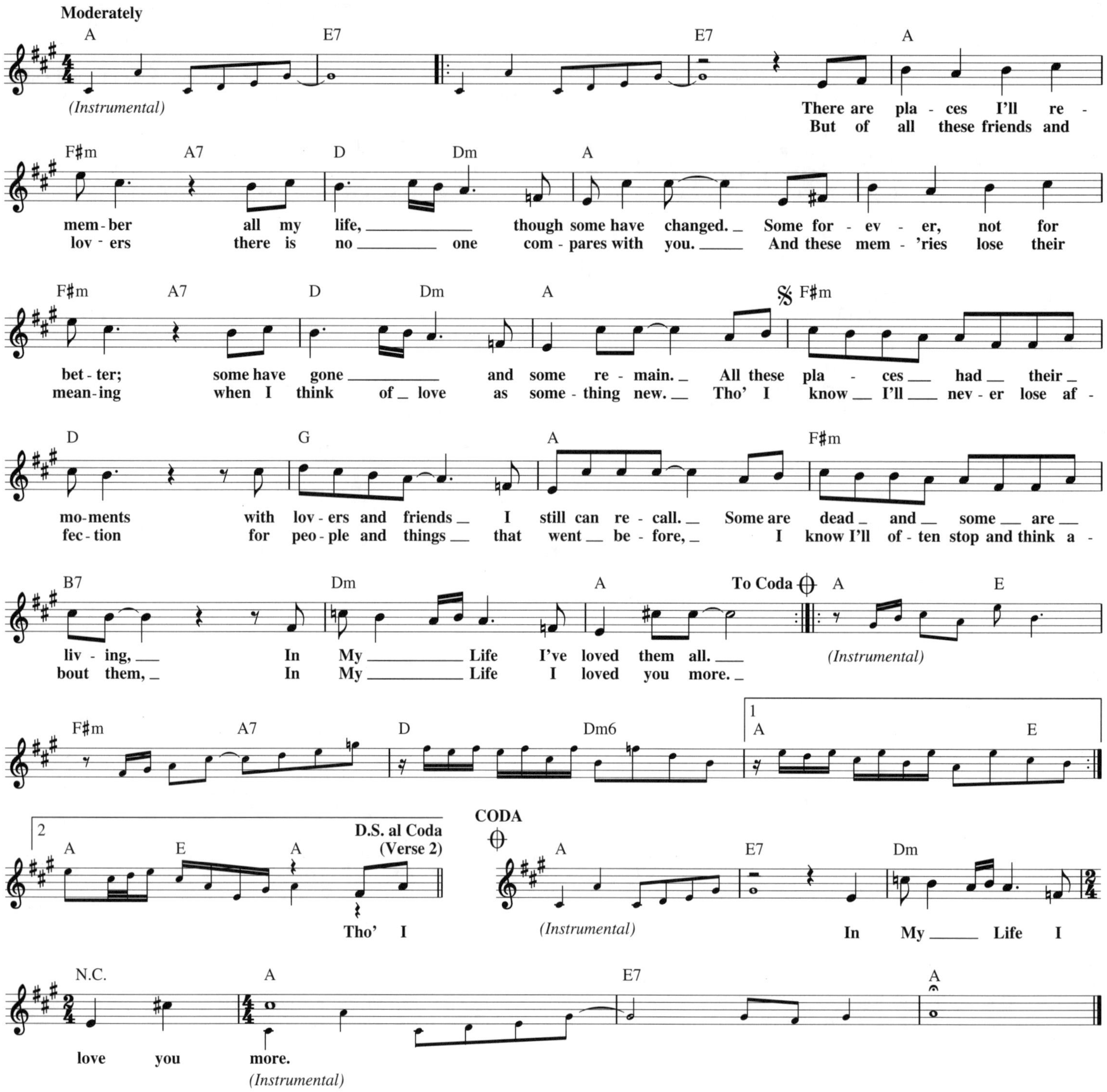

Moderately

A E7 E7 A
(Instrumental)
There are pla - ces I'll re -
But of all these friends and

F#m A7 D Dm A
mem - ber all my life, ___ though some have changed. ___ Some for - ev - er, not for
lov - ers there is no ___ one com - pares with you. ___ And these mem - 'ries lose their

F#m A7 D Dm A 𝄋 F#m
bet - ter; some have gone ___ and some re - main. ___ All these pla - ces ___ had ___ their ___
mean - ing when I think of ___ love as some - thing new. ___ Tho' I know ___ I'll ___ nev - er lose af -

D G A F#m
mo - ments with lov - ers and friends ___ I still can re - call. ___ Some are dead ___ and ___ some ___ are ___
fec - tion for peo - ple and things ___ that went ___ be - fore, ___ I know I'll of - ten stop and think a -

B7 Dm A **To Coda** 𝄌 A E
liv - ing, ___ In My ___ Life I've loved them all. ___ (Instrumental)
bout them, ___ In My ___ Life I loved you more. ___

F#m A7 D Dm6 1 A E

2 A E A **D.S. al Coda (Verse 2)**
Tho' I

CODA 𝄌
A E7 Dm
(Instrumental) In My ___ Life I

N.C. A E7 A
love you more.
(Instrumental)

INSTANT KARMA

© 1970 (Renewed 1998) LENONO.MUSIC
All Rights Controlled and Administered by EMI BLACKWOOD MUSIC INC.

Words and Music by
JOHN LENNON

F G A D D/C#
Pret - ty soon you're gon - na be dead. What in the world you think - ing
Join the hu - man race. How in the world you gon - na
ev - 'ry - one you meet. Why in the world are we
To Coda
Bm D D/C# Bm
of? Laugh - ing in the face of love,
see? Laugh - in' at fools like me,
here?
C C/B Am7 D 1 E9
what on earth you try'n to do? It's up to you, yeah, you.
who on earth d'you think you are, a su - per - star? Well, al -
2 E9 G Bm Em G Bm
right, you are. Well, we all shine on like the moon and the stars and the
Em G Bm Em D E9 D.C. al Coda
sun. Well, we all shine on. Ev - 'ry - one, come on.
CODA
D D/C# Bm C C/B Am
Sure - ly not to live in pain and fear. Why on earth are you there when you're
D Em7 G Bm Em
ev - 'ry - where? Come and get your share. Well, we all shine on like the
G Bm Em G Bm Em
moon and the stars and the sun. Well, we all shine on.
D 1 E7 A A/G# F#m
Come on and on and on, on, yeah yeah, al -
On and on and on and
A A/G# F#m A A/G# F#m C G A
- right, ah ha, ah. Well, we
2 E9 G Bm Em G Bm Em
Repeat and Fade
on and on. Well, we all shine on like the moon and the stars and the sun. Well, we

INVISIBLE TOUCH

© 1986 ANTHONY BANKS LTD., PHILIP COLLINS LTD., MICHAEL RUTHERFORD LTD. and HIT & RUN MUSIC (PUBLISHING) LTD.
All Rights Controlled and Administered by EMI APRIL MUSIC INC.

Words and Music by TONY BANKS, PHIL COLLINS and MIKE RUTHERFORD

IRON MAN

© Copyright 1970 (Renewed) and 1974 (Renewed) Westminster Music Ltd., London, England
TRO - Essex Music International, Inc., New York, controls all publication rights for the U.S.A. and Canada

Words and Music by FRANK IOMMI, JOHN OSBOURNE,
WILLIAM WARD and TERENCE BUTLER

ISLAND GIRL

Copyright © 1975 by Big Pig Music Ltd.
All Rights for the United States Administered by Intersong U.S.A., Inc.

Words and Music by ELTON JOHN
and BERNIE TAUPIN

IT'S ONLY LOVE

Copyright © 1984 IRVING MUSIC, ADAMS COMMUNICATIONS, INC., ALMO MUSIC CORP. and TESTATYME MUSIC
All Rights for ADAMS COMMUNICATIONS, INC. Controlled and Administered by IRVING MUSIC, INC.
All Rights for TESTATYME MUSIC Controlled and Administered by ALMO MUSIC CORP.

Words and Music by BRYAN ADAMS
and JIM VALLANCE

IT'S ONLY ROCK 'N' ROLL
(But I Like It)

© 1974 EMI MUSIC PUBLISHING LTD.
All Rights for the U.S. and Canada Controlled and Administered by COLGEMS-EMI MUSIC INC.

Words and Music by MICK JAGGER
and KEITH RICHARDS

IT'S STILL ROCK AND ROLL TO ME

© 1980 IMPULSIVE MUSIC

Words and Music by
BILLY JOEL

Moderately fast Rock/Shuffle
C Em B♭ F
What's the mat - ter with the clothes I'm wear - ing? "Can't you tell that your tie's too wide?"
What's the mat - ter with the car I'm driv - ing? "Can't you tell that it's out of style?"
How a - bout a pair of pink side - wing - ers and a bright or - ange pair of pants?
What's the mat - ter with the crowd I'm see - ing? "Don't you know that they're out of touch?"
C Em B♭
May - be I should buy some old tab col - lars? "Wel - come back to the age of jive.
Should I get a set of white wall - tires? "Are you gon - na cruise the mir - a - cle mile?
Well you could real - ly be a Beau Brum - mel, ba - by, if you just give it half a chance.
Should I try to be a straight 'A' stu - dent? "If you are, then you think too much."
F Em Am
Where have you been hid - in' out late - ly hon - ey? You
Now - a - days you can't be too sen - ti - men - tal. Your
Don't waste your mon - ey on a new set of speak - ers. You
"Don't you know a - bout the new fash - ion, hon - ey?
Em G C Em
can't dress trash - y till you spend a lot of mon - ey."
best bet's a true ba - by blue con - ti - nen - tal."
get more mile - age from a cheap pair of sneak - ers."
All you need are looks and a whole lot of mon - ey." It's the next phase, new wave
Ev - 'ry - bod - y's talk - in' 'bout the
Hot funk, cool punk,
Next phase, new wave
B♭ F Am G
4th time To Coda C
1
new sound. Fun - ny, but
e - ven if it's old junk,
dance craze, an - y - ways,
dance craze, an - y - ways,
It's Still Rock And Roll To Me.
2,3
G F E7
Oh, it does - n't mat - ter what they say in the pa - pers 'cause it's al - ways been the same old scene.
Instrumental
Am G F
There's a new band in town but you can't get the sound from a
E7 A♭ E♭ F G
2nd time D.C. al Coda
sto - ry in a mag - a - zine, aimed at your av - er - age teen. Oooh!
(2nd time only)
CODA
C Em
Ev - 'ry - bod - y's talk - in' 'bout the
B♭ F G C C9
new sound. Fun - ny, but It's Still Rock And Roll To Me.

JACK AND DIANE

© 1982 EMI FULL KEEL MUSIC

Words and Music by
JOHN MELLENCAMP

D E A E
thrill of liv - ing is gone. Say - in', oh yeah,
To Coda
D E A E D E A
life goes on, long af - ter the thrill of liv - ing is gone.
1
E/A A E/A D N.C.
Now, walk on. (Instrumental)
A E/A A E/A D N.C.
2
N.C. A/E D/F# N.C.
Oh, let it rock,
D/F# E/G# N.C. A/E D/F# G/B D/A
let it roll. Let the Bi - ble belt come and save my soul.
A5 A/E D/F# G D/F#
Hold - in' on to six - teen as long as you can.
D.S. al Coda
A5 N.C. A/E D/F# E A N.C.
Change is com - in' 'round real soon, make us wom - en and men.
CODA
E D E
A lit - tle dit - ty a - bout Jack and Di - ane,
A E D E A
two A - mer - i - can kids do - in' the best that they can.
Repeat and Fade
A E/A A E/A A E/A D N.C.
(Instrumental)

JESUS IS JUST ALRIGHT

Copyright © 1969 by Artists Music, Inc. and Music Sales Corporation
Copyright Renewed
All Rights for Artists Music, Inc. Administered by BMG Songs, Inc.

Words and Music by
ARTHUR REYNOLDS

took me by the hand, lead me far from this land. Je - sus,
he's my friend.
(End solo)
Bright Rock
N.C.
(Instrumental)
D.S. al Coda
(End instrumental)
CODA
oh yeah.
JOY TO THE WORLD
Copyright © 1970 IRVING MUSIC, INC.
Copyright Renewed
Words and Music by
HOYT AXTON
Moderate Gospel Rock
Jer - e - mi - ah was a bull - frog, was a good friend of mine.
If I were the king of the world, tell you what I'd do.
know I love the la - dies, love to have my fun.
Nev - er un - der - stood a sin - gle word he said, but I
Throw a - way the cars and the bars and the wars, and
I'm a high night fly - er and a rain - bow rid - er, a
helped him a - drink - in' his wine. Yes he al - ways had some might - y fine wine.
make sweet love to you. Yes I'd make sweet love to you.
straight shoot - in' son - of - a - gun. Yes a straight shoot - in' son - of - a - gun.
Sing - ing
joy to the world, all the boys and girls now. Joy to the fish - es in the
To Coda
deep blue sea. Joy to you and me.
(Instrumental)
D.C. al Coda
You
CODA
Joy to the world, all the boys and girls. Joy to
the world, joy to you and me. Joy to the world, all the boys and
Repeat and Fade
girls. Joy to the fish - es in the deep blue sea. Joy to you and me.

KILLER QUEEN

© 1974 B. FELDMAN & CO., LTD., Trading As TRIDENT MUSIC
All Rights Controlled and Administered by GLENWOOD MUSIC CORP.

Words and Music by
FREDDIE MERCURY

mo - men - tar - i - ly out of ac - tion, tem - po - rar - i - ly out of gas, to ab - so - lute - ly drive you
D.S. al Coda
(take 1st ending)
CODA
wild, wild. She's a
what a drag.
(Instrumental)
Repeat and Fade
LADY MADONNA
Copyright © 1968 Sony/ATV Songs LLC
Copyright Renewed
All Rights Administered by Sony/ATV Music Publishing, 8 Music Square West, Nashville, TN 37203
Words and Music by JOHN LENNON
and PAUL McCARTNEY
Brightly, with a beat
(Instrumental)
La - dy Ma - don - na, chil - dren at your feet, won - der how you man - age to make
La - dy Ma - don - na, ba - by at your breast, won - ders how you man - age to feed
La - dy Ma - don - na, ly - ing on the bed, lis - ten to the mu - sic play - ing
La - dy Ma - don - na, chil - dren at your feet, won - der how you man - age to make
4th time To Coda
ends meet. Who finds the mon - ey when you pay the rent, did you think that
the rest. (Instrumental)
in your head. (Instrumental)
ends meet.
mon - ey was heav - en sent? Fri - day night ar - rives with - out a suit - case,
3. Tues - day af - ter - noon is nev - er end - ing,
Sun - day morn - ing creep - ing like a nun, Mon - day's child has learned to tie his
Wednes - day morn - ing pa - pers did - n't come, Thurs - day night your stock - ings need - ed
1,2
3 D.S. al Coda
boot - lace. See how they run!
mend - ing.
CODA
(Instrumental)

KISS YOU ALL OVER

Copyright © 1979 by BMG Songs, Inc.

Words and Music by NICKY CHINN
and MIKE CHAPMAN

LAST CHILD

Copyright © 1976 Daksel LLC
All Rights Administered by Sony/ATV Music Publishing, 8 Music Square West, Nashville, TN 37203

Words and Music by STEVEN TYLER
and BRAD WHITFORD

LAND OF CONFUSION

© 1986 ANTHONY BANKS LTD., PHILIP COLLINS LTD., MICHAEL RUTHERFORD LTD.
and HIT & RUN MUSIC (PUBLISHING) LTD.
All Rights Controlled and Administered by EMI APRIL MUSIC INC.

Words and Music by TONY BANKS,
PHIL COLLINS and MIKE RUTHERFORD

To Coda II
D.C.
(take 3rd ending)
D♭ B♭m A♭ A♭m D♭
place worth liv - ing in.
lives are go - ing to.
(Instrumental)
Cm A♭maj7/C
E♭ Gm/D Cm F Cm
I re-mem - ber long a - go,
F/C A♭maj7/C
ooh, when the sun was shin - ing.
Yes, and the stars were bright
E♭ Gm/D Cm F
all through the night, and the sound of your laugh - ter as I held you
A♭ C♭
tight so long a - go. (Instrumental)
D.C. al Coda I
(take 4th ending)
D♭ C♭ D♭ E♭m D♭
CODA I
D.S. al Coda II
D♭ B♭m
place worth fight - ing
CODA II
A♭m D♭ E♭m

LAY DOWN SALLY

Copyright © 1977 by Eric Patrick Clapton and Throat Music Ltd.
All Rights for the U.S. Administered by Unichappell Music Inc.

Words and Music by ERIC CLAPTON, MARCY LEVY and GEORGE TERRY

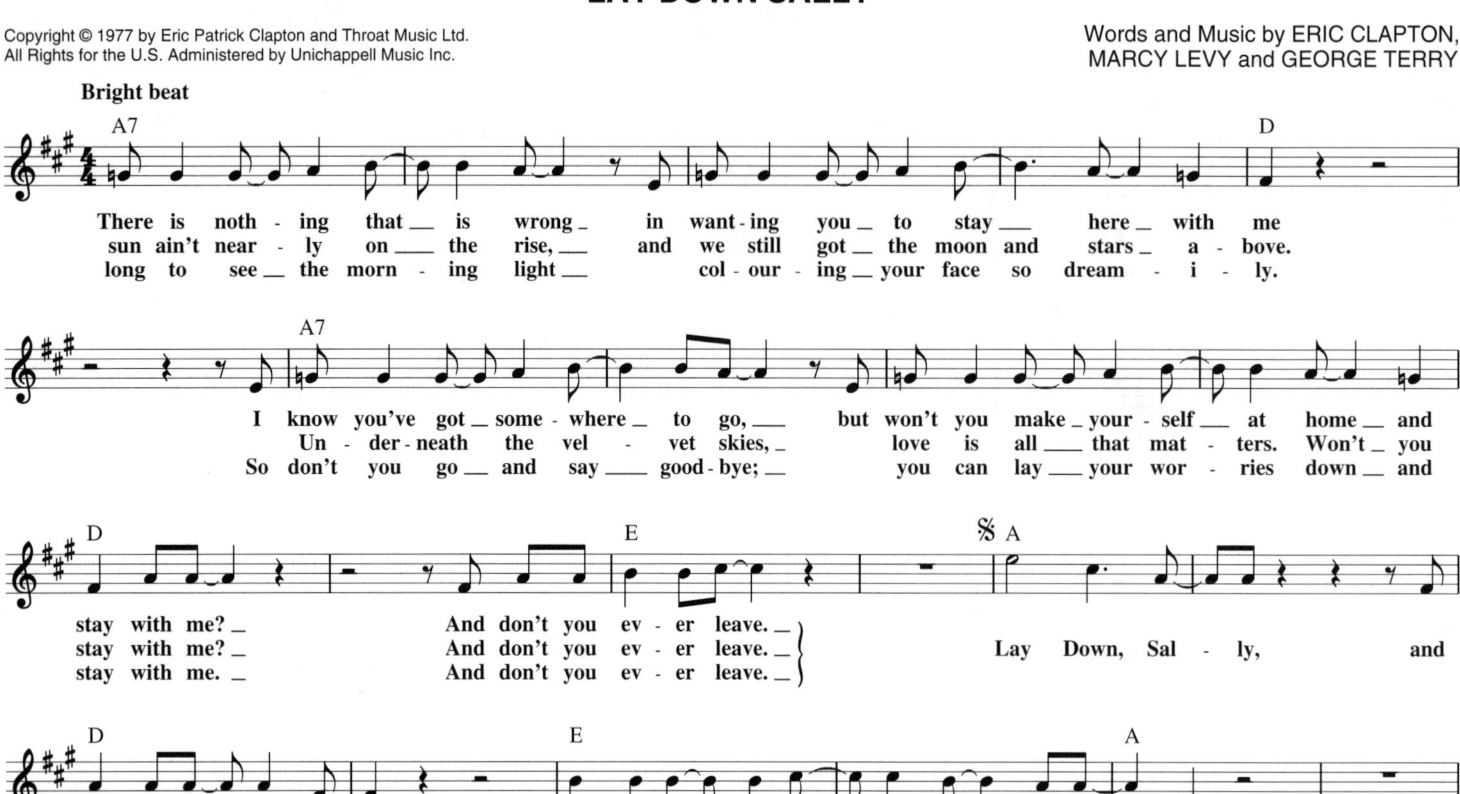
Bright beat
A7
D
There is noth - ing that is wrong in want - ing you to stay here with me
sun ain't near - ly on the rise, and we still got the moon and stars a - bove.
long to see the morn - ing light col - our - ing your face so dream - i - ly.
A7
I know you've got some - where to go, but won't you make your - self at home and
Un - der - neath the vel - vet skies, love is all that mat - ters. Won't you
So don't you go and say good - bye; you can lay your wor - ries down and
D
E
A
stay with me? And don't you ev - er leave.
stay with me? And don't you ev - er leave.
stay with me. And don't you ev - er leave.
Lay Down, Sal - ly, and
D
E
A
rest you in my arms. Don't you think you want some - one to talk to?

D
E
To Coda
Lay Down, Sal - ly; no need to leave so soon. I've been try - ing all night long just to

1,2
A
3
A
D.S. al Coda
CODA
A
talk to you.
The
I
talk to you.
talk to you.

LEATHER AND LACE

Copyright © 1981 Welsh Witch Music
All Rights Administered by Sony/ATV Music Publishing, 8 Music Square West, Nashville, TN 37203

Words and Music by STEVIE NICKS

Moderately slow, in 2
Eb
Eb/Db
Ab/C
Eb/Bb
Ab
(Female) Is love so frag - ile? And the hearts so hol - low shat - ter with
Eb/G
Bb7sus4
Eb
Eb/Db
words im - pos - si - ble to fol - low. You're say - in' I'm frag - ile.
Ab/C
Eb/Bb
Ab
Eb/G
Bb7sus
I try not to be. I search on - ly for some - thin' I can't see.
Eb
Eb/Db
Ab/C
Eb/Bb
I have my own life, and I am strong - er than you

Ab Eb/G Bb7sus Eb
know. But I car - ry this
Eb/Db Ab/C Eb/Bb Ab Eb/G
feel - in' when you walked in - to my house that you won't be walk-in' out the door.
Bb7sus Eb Eb/Db Ab/C
Still I car - ry this feel - in' when you walked in -
Eb/Bb Ab Eb/G Bb7sus
to my house that you won't be walk - in' out the door.
Ab Bb Ab Bb Ab
Lov - ers for - ev - er, face to face, my cit - y or
Bb Ab Bb Ab Bb
moun - tains. Stay with me, stay. I need you to love me. I
Ab Bb Ab Bb Ab To Coda
need you to - day. Give to me your leath - er. Take from me my
Bb7sus Eb Eb/Db
lace. (Male) You in the moon - light
Ab/C Eb/Bb Ab Eb/G Bb7sus
with your sleep - y eyes, could you ev - er love a man like me?
Eb Eb/Db Ab/C Eb/Bb
And you were right: when I walked in - to your house,
Ab Eb/G Bb7sus Eb
I knew I'd nev - er want to leave. Some - times I'm a
Eb/Db Ab/C Eb/Bb Ab Eb/G
strong man, some-times cold and scared, and some - times I cry.
Bb7sus Eb Eb/Db Ab/C
But that time I saw you, I knew with you to light
Eb/Bb Ab Eb/G Bb7sus D.S. (Male and Female Sing) al Coda
my nights, some-how I'd get by.
CODA
Bb7sus Ab Eb/G Bb7sus Repeat and Fade
lace. Take from me my lace. Take

LAYLA

Copyright © 1970 by Eric Patrick Clapton and Throat Music Ltd.
Copyright Renewed
All Rights for the U.S. Administered by Unichappell Music Inc.

Words and Music by ERIC CLAPTON
and JIM GORDON

Moderately
(Instrumental)
D5 C5 B♭5 C5 D5 N.C. D5 C5 B♭5 C5 D5 N.C.
C♯m G♯m C♯m7 C7 D7 E7
Ah, what-'ll you do when you get lone-ly, and no-bod-y's wait - in' by your side?
I tried to give you con-so-la-tion, when your old man he let you down.
So make the best of the sit-u-a-tion, be-fore I fi - n'lly go in - sane.
F♯m(add9) B E A F♯m B5
You been run - nin' and hid-in' much too long, you know it's just your fool - ish
Like a fool, I fell in love with you, you turned my whole world up - side
Please don't say we'll nev-er find a way, and tell me all my love's in
E N.C. D5 C5 B♭5 C5 D5 N.C. D5 C5 B♭5 C5
pride.
down.
vain.
Lay - la. You got me on my knees. Lay - la. I
D5 N.C. D5 C5 B♭5 C5 D5 N.C.
To Coda
D5 C5 B♭5
beg you dar - lin' please. Lay - la. Dar - lin', won't you ease my wor-ried mind.
1, 2
C5
3
D.S. al Coda
Lay -
CODA
D5 C5 B♭5 C5
mind.
C C/E F C C/E
Instrumental with guitar solo ad lib.
F B♭7 C 1, 2 3 G/B
Am Dm G C G/B Am
D G C C/E
F C C/E F
B♭7 C
Repeat and Fade

LIDO SHUFFLE

Copyright © 1976 by BMG Songs, Inc. and Hudmar Publishing

Words and Music by BOZ SCAGGS
and DAVID PAICH

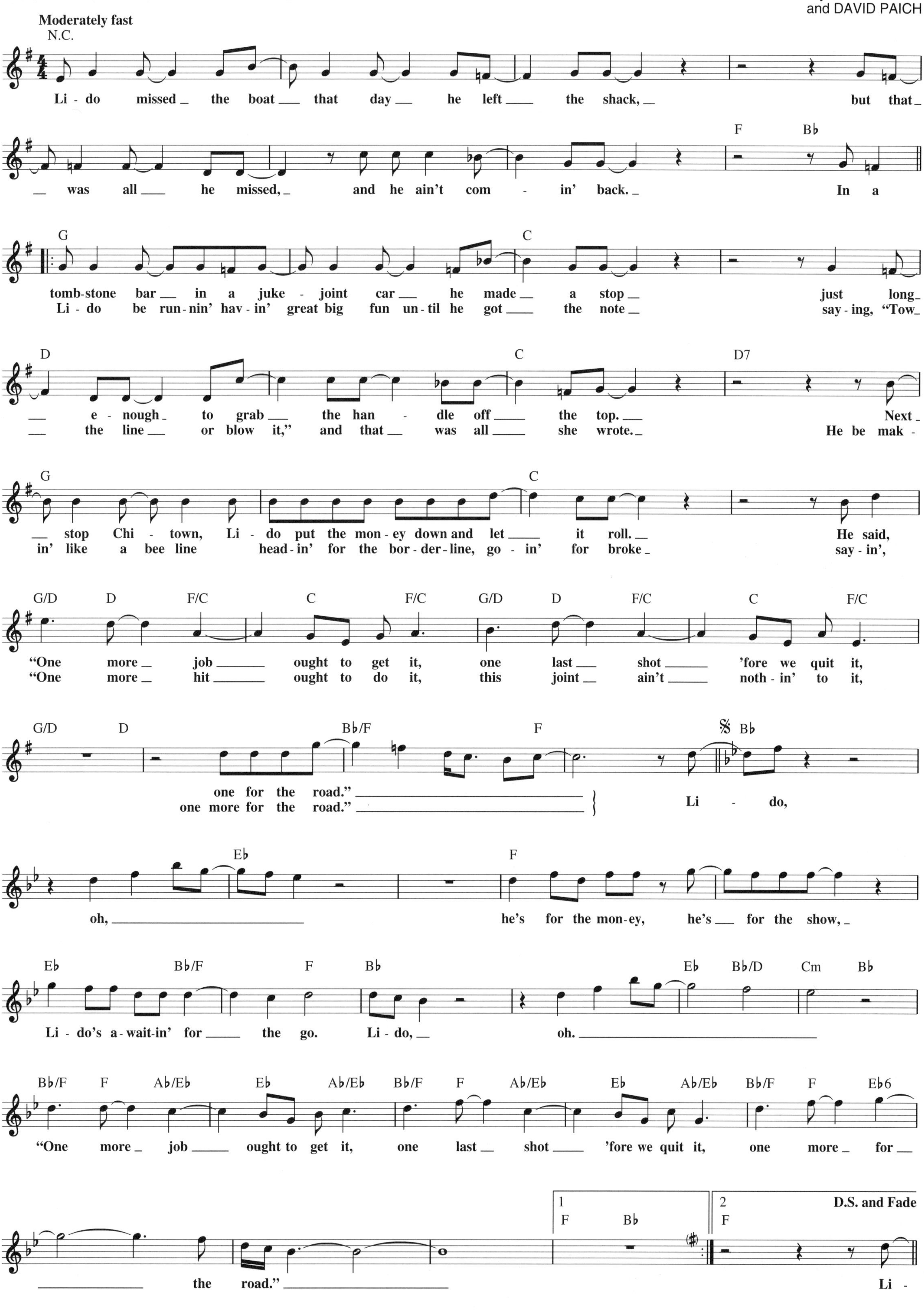
Moderately fast
N.C.
Li - do missed _ the boat ___ that day ___ he left ___ the shack, _ but that _
F Bb
_ was all ___ he missed, _ and he ain't com - in' back. _ In a
G C
tomb-stone bar ___ in a juke - joint car ___ he made ___ a stop ___ just long _
Li - do be run-nin' hav-in' great big fun un-til he got ___ the note _ say - ing, "Tow _
D C D7
___ e - nough _ to grab ___ the han - dle off ___ the top. ___ Next _
___ the line ___ or blow it," and that ___ was all ___ she wrote. _ He be mak -
G C
___ stop Chi - town, Li - do put the mon - ey down and let ___ it roll. ___ He said,
in' like a bee line head - in' for the bor - der - line, go - in' for broke _ say - in',
G/D D F/C C F/C G/D D F/C C F/C
"One more _ job ___ ought to get it, one last ___ shot ___ 'fore we quit it,
"One more _ hit ___ ought to do it, this joint ___ ain't ___ noth - in' to it,
G/D D Bb/F F Bb
one for the road." ___
one more for the road." ___
Li - do,
Eb F
oh, ___ he's for the mon-ey, he's ___ for the show, _
Eb Bb/F F Bb Eb Bb/D Cm Bb
Li - do's a-wait-in' for ___ the go. Li - do, ___ oh. ___
Bb/F F Ab/Eb Eb Ab/Eb Bb/F F Ab/Eb Eb Ab/Eb Bb/F F Eb6
"One more _ job ___ ought to get it, one last ___ shot ___ 'fore we quit it, one more _ for ___
1 F Bb 2 F D.S. and Fade
___ the road." ___ Li -

LET IT RAIN

Copyright © 1970 by Eric Patrick Clapton, Cotillion Music, Inc. and Delbon Publishing Co.
Copyright Renewed
All Rights for Eric Patrick Clapton in the U.S. Administered by Unichappell Music Inc.
All Rights for Cotillion Music, Inc. and Delbon Publishing Co. in the U.S. and Canada
Administered by Warner-Tamerlane Publishing Corp.

Words and Music by ERIC CLAPTON
and BONNIE BRAMLETT

LET IT RIDE

Copyright © 1973 Sony/ATV Songs LLC
Copyright Renewed
All Rights Administered by Sony/ATV Music Publishing, 8 Music Square West, Nashville, TN 37203

Words and Music by RANDY BACHMAN
and CHARLES TURNER

F♯m
While you've been out run - nin' I've been wait - in' half the night.
Ba - by you want the for-giv - in' kind and that's just not my style.
I've been do - in' things worth - while and you've been book - in' time.
Ride, ride, ride, let it ride.
E
D
A
E
F♯m
And would you cry if I told you that I lied, and would you
Bm7
F♯m7
D
A
say good - bye or would you let it ride?
And would you cry if I
To Coda
E
F♯m
Bm7
1
F♯m
told you that I lied, and would you say good - bye or would you let it ride?
(Instrumental)
2
F♯m
(Instrumental)
D.S. al Coda
(End instrumental)
CODA
F♯m
Would you let it ride?
Would you let it ride?
Would you let it ride?
N.C.
F♯m
Would you let it ride?
(Drum break)
Ride, ride, ride, let it ride.
Ride, ride, ride, let it ride.
Ride, ride, ride, let it ride.
Would you let it ride?
D
A
Would you let it ride?
(Instrumental)
E
F♯m
Bm9
F♯m7
Repeat and Fade

LITTLE BIT O' SOUL

Copyright © 1965 by Carter-Lewis Music Pub. Co. Ltd.
Copyright Renewed
All Rights Administered by Peer International Corporation

Words and Music by JOHN SHAKESPEARE
and KENNETH LEWIS

LIVIN' ON A PRAYER

Words and Music by DESMOND CHILD,
JON BON JOVI and RICHIE SAMBORA

© 1986 EMI APRIL MUSIC INC., DESMOBILE MUSIC CO., INC.,
UNIVERSAL - POLYGRAM INTERNATIONAL PUBLISHING, INC., BON JOVI PUBLISHING and
NEW JERSEY UNDERGROUND MUSIC INC.
All Rights for DESMOBILE MUSIC CO., INC. Controlled and Administered by EMI APRIL MUSIC INC.

Moderate Rock
Em Em(add2)
Spoken: Once upon a time, not so long ago...
Tom - my used to work on the docks,
Tom - my's got his six - string in hock, now
Em C D
un - ion's been on strike. He's down on his luck, it's tough, so tough.
he's hold - ing in what he used to make it talk. So tough, it's tough.
Em Em(add2) Em
Gi - na works the din - er all day work - ing for her man. She
Gi - na dreams of run - ning a - way; when she cries in the night, Tom - my
C D Em
brings home her pay, for love, for love. She says we've got to
whis - pers: ba - by, it's O. K. some - day. We've got to
C D Em C D Em
hold on to what we've got. It does - n't make a dif - f'rence if we make it or not. We've
C D Em C D
got each oth - er and that's a lot for love. We'll give it a shot.
Em C D G D7sus Em C
Whoa, we're half - way there. Whoa, liv - in' on a prayer. Take my hand, we'll
D G C D7sus 1 Em7
make it, I swear. Whoa, liv - in' on a prayer.
2 C Em C D G C D
Liv - in' on a prayer. (Instrumental)
Em C D G C Em
(End instrumental) Oh, we've got to
C D Em D C D
hold on, read - y or not, you live for the fight when it's all that you've got.
Gm Eb Fsus F Bb Eb F7sus
Whoa, we're half - way there. Whoa, liv - in' on a prayer.
Gm Eb F Bb Eb F7sus
Repeat and Fade
Take my hand and we'll make it, I swear. Whoa, liv - in' on a prayer.

LONG COOL WOMAN (IN A BLACK DRESS)

Copyright © 1972 by Timtobe Music Ltd. and Dick James Music Ltd.
Copyright Renewed
All Rights for Timtobe Music Ltd. for the United States and Canada Assigned to Bienstock Publishing Company
All Rights for Dick James Music Ltd. for the United States and Canada Administered by
Universal - Polygram International Publishing, Inc.

Words and Music by ALLAN CLARKE,
ROGER COOK and ROGER GREENAWAY

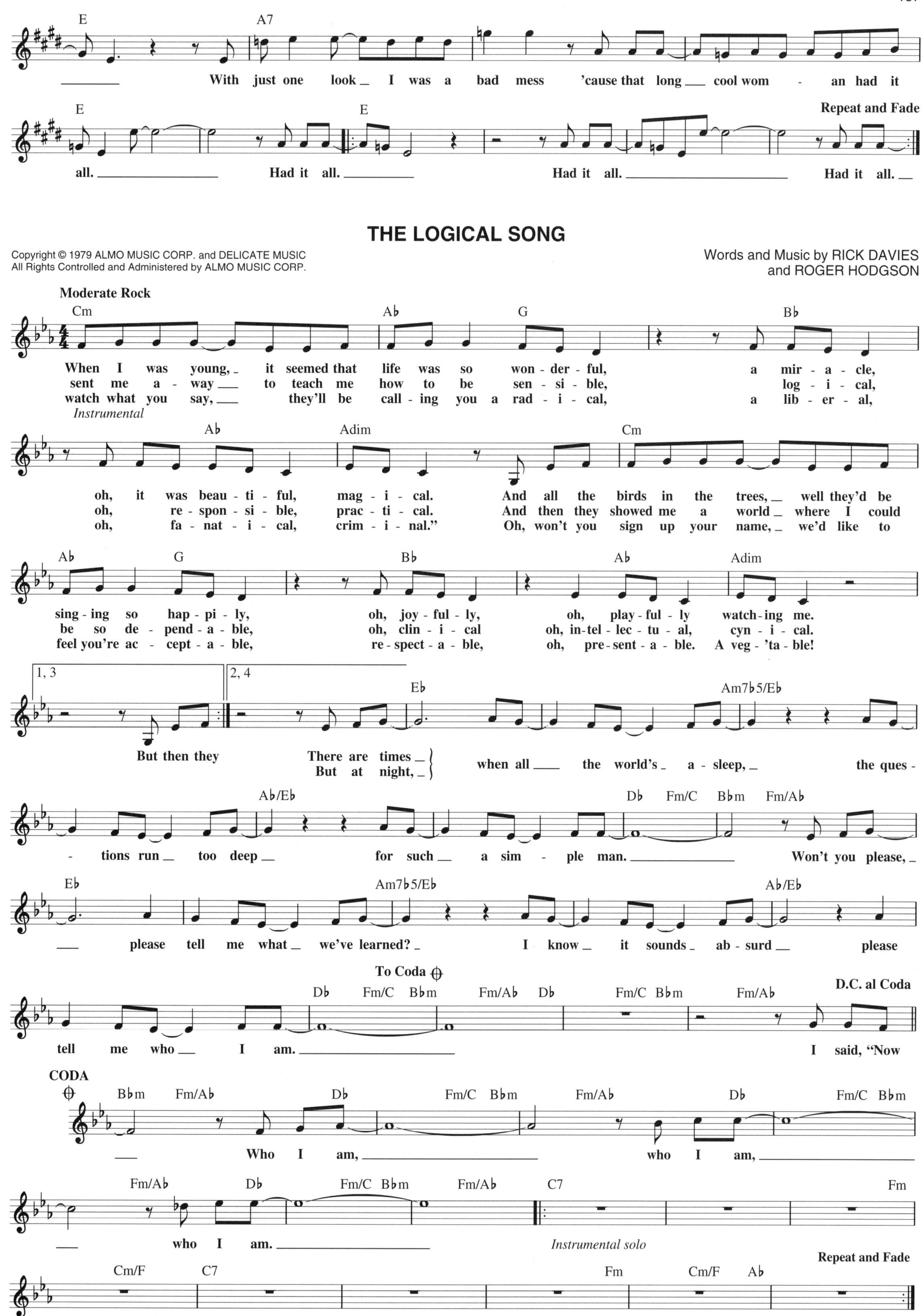
E A7
With just one look I was a bad mess 'cause that long cool wom - an had it
E E
Repeat and Fade
all. Had it all. Had it all. Had it all.
THE LOGICAL SONG
Copyright © 1979 ALMO MUSIC CORP. and DELICATE MUSIC
All Rights Controlled and Administered by ALMO MUSIC CORP.
Words and Music by RICK DAVIES
and ROGER HODGSON
Moderate Rock
Cm Ab G Bb
When I was young, it seemed that life was so won - der - ful, a mir - a - cle,
sent me a - way to teach me how to be sen - si - ble, log - i - cal,
watch what you say, they'll be call - ing you a rad - i - cal, a lib - er - al,
Instrumental
Ab Adim Cm
oh, it was beau - ti - ful, mag - i - cal. And all the birds in the trees, well they'd be
oh, re - spon - si - ble, prac - ti - cal. And then they showed me a world where I could
oh, fa - nat - i - cal, crim - i - nal." Oh, won't you sign up your name, we'd like to
Ab G Bb Ab Adim
sing - ing so hap - pi - ly, oh, joy - ful - ly, oh, play - ful - ly watch - ing me.
be so de - pend - a - ble, oh, clin - i - cal oh, in - tel - lec - tu - al, cyn - i - cal.
feel you're ac - cept - a - ble, re - spect - a - ble, oh, pre - sent - a - ble. A veg - 'ta - ble!
1, 3 2, 4 Eb Am7b5/Eb
But then they There are times But at night, when all the world's a - sleep, the ques -
Ab/Eb Db Fm/C Bbm Fm/Ab
- tions run too deep for such a sim - ple man. Won't you please,
Eb Am7b5/Eb Ab/Eb
please tell me what we've learned? I know it sounds ab - surd please
To Coda
Db Fm/C Bbm Fm/Ab Db Fm/C Bbm Fm/Ab
D.C. al Coda
tell me who I am. I said, "Now
CODA
Bbm Fm/Ab Db Fm/C Bbm Fm/Ab Db Fm/C Bbm
Who I am, who I am,
Fm/Ab Db Fm/C Bbm Fm/Ab C7 Fm
who I am.
Instrumental solo
Cm/F C7 Fm Cm/F Ab
Repeat and Fade

LOVE IS A BATTLEFIELD

Copyrght © 1983 by BMG Songs, Inc. and Mike Chapman Enterprises, Inc.

Words and Music by MIKE CHAPMAN
and HOLLY KNIGHT

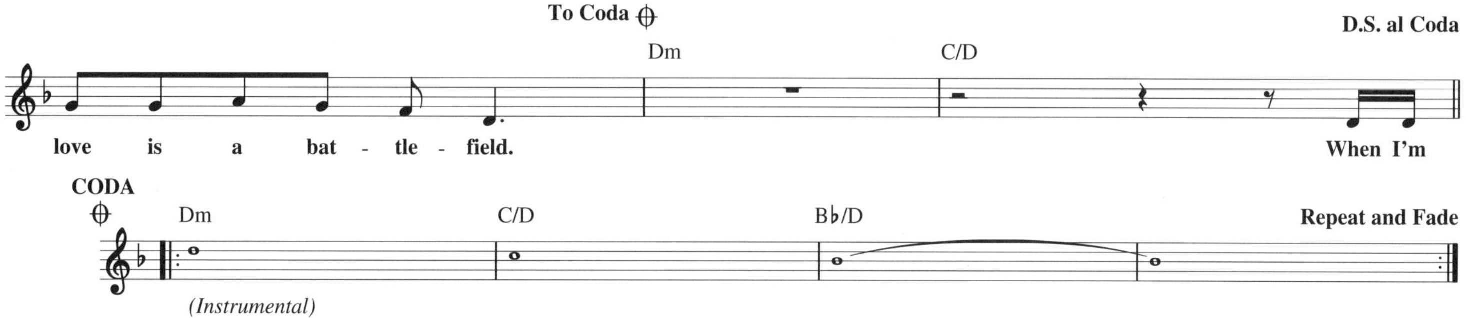

LUCY IN THE SKY WITH DIAMONDS

Copyright © 1967 Sony/ATV Songs LLC
Copyright Renewed
All Rights Administered by Sony/ATV Music Publishing, 8 Music Square West, 37203

Words and Music by JOHN LENNON
and PAUL McCARTNEY

Moderately

N.C. (*Instrumental*)

A A/G F♯m7 F+ A A/G F♯m7 F

Pic - ture your - self in a boat on a riv - er with tan - ger - ine trees and mar - ma - lade skies.
Fol - low her down to a bridge by a foun - tain where rock - ing horse peo - ple eat marsh - mal - low pies.
Pic - ture your - self on a train in a sta - tion with plas - ti - cine por - ters with look - ing glass ties.

A/E A/G F♯m7 F+ A/E A/G **To Coda**

Some - bod - y calls you, you an - swer quite slow - ly, a girl with ka - lei - do - scope
Ev - 'ry - one smiles as you drift past the flow - ers that grow so in - cred - i - bly
Sud - den - ly some - one is there at the turn - stile, the girl with ka - lei - do - scope

F♯m Dm Dm/C B♭ C9

eyes. Cel - lo - phane flow - ers of yel - low and green
high. News - pa - per tax - is ap - pear on the shore

F6 B♭ C6 G

tow - er - ing o - ver your head. Look for the girl with the sun in her
wait - ing to take you a - way. Climb in the back with your head in the

D7 Em (♩. = 𝅗𝅥) D G C D7 G C

eyes and she's gone.
clouds and you're gone.
Lu - cy In The Sky With Dia - monds, Lu - cy In The Sky With

D7 G C D7 1. D 2. D **D.S. al Coda**

Dia - monds, Lu - cy In The Sky With Dia - monds, ah. ah.

CODA

F♯m G C D7

eyes. Lu - cy In The Sky With Dia - monds,

G C D7 G C D7 D A **Repeat and Fade**

Lu - cy In The Sky With Dia - monds, Lu - cy In The Sky With Dia - monds, ah.

THE MAGIC BUS

Words and Music by
PETER TOWNSHEND

© Copyright 1967 (Renewed) and 1969 (Renewed) Fabulous Music Ltd., London, England
TRO - Essex Music, Inc., New York, controls all publication rights for the U.S.A. and Canada

N.C.
want it, I want __ it, I want it, you can't have it. (I
A5
want it, I want it. I want.) Thrup-pence and six - pence ev - e - ry - day. __
N.C. Asus N.C. Asus N.C. N.C. A5
(Instrumental) Just to drive _ to my ba - by. __ (Instrumental)
N.C. A5 N.C. N.C. A D/A A7 D/A
Thrup-pence and six - pence each day. __ (Instrumental) 'Cause I
N.C. A D/A N.C. A7 D/A N.C. A D/A Dsus D/A
drive my ba - by ev - e - ry way. ______
A G/D D D/A A 1 - 9 G/D D D/A 10 G/D D
(Mag-ic bus. _) Mag - ic bus. _ (Mag-ic bus. _) (I said)
A G/D D A G/D D A
now I get my mag - ic bus. _ (Too much, ____ the mag - ic bus. _) Said now I got my
G/D D A G/D D A G/D D
mag - ic bus. _ I drive my ba - by ev - e - ry way.
A G/D D A G/D D A G/D D
Each time I go a dif - f'rent way. _ I want _
A G/D D A G/D D A
___ it, I want it, I want it, I want it, I want it, I
G/D D A G/D D A G/D D
want it, I want it, I want _ it. Ev - 'ry - day __ you'll see the dust. _
Repeat and Fade
A G/D D A G/D D A G/D D
I drive my ba - by in my mag - ic bus. _

MAYBE I'M AMAZED

Copyright © 1970 Sony/ATV Songs LLC
Copyright Renewed
All Rights Administered by Sony/ATV Music Publishing, 8 Music Square West, Nashville, TN 37203

Words and Music by
PAUL McCARTNEY

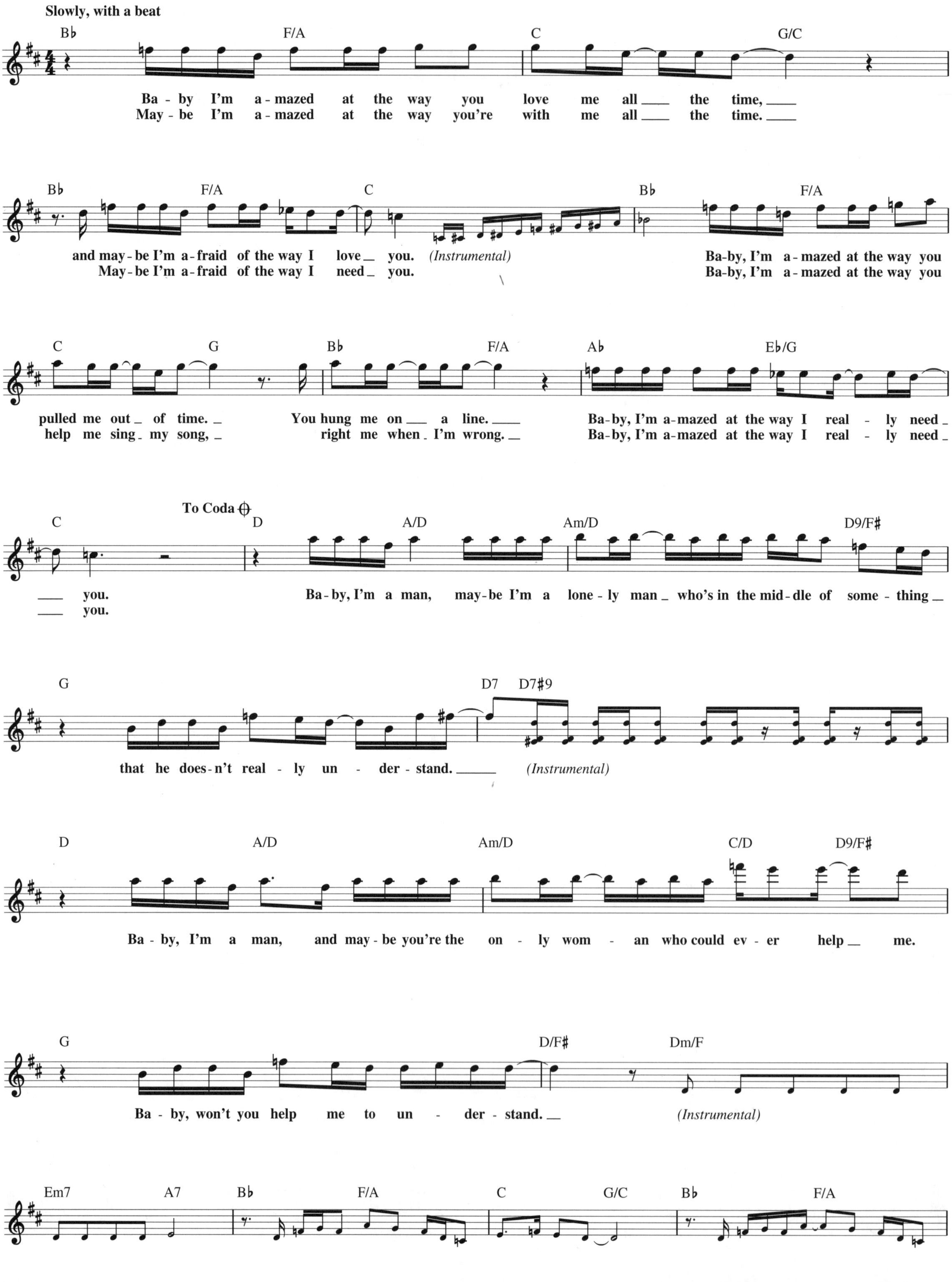

Slowly, with a beat
Bb F/A C G/C
Ba - by I'm a - mazed at the way you love me all the time,
May - be I'm a - mazed at the way you're with me all the time.
Bb F/A C Bb F/A
and may - be I'm a - fraid of the way I love you. (Instrumental) Ba - by, I'm a - mazed at the way you
May - be I'm a - fraid of the way I need you. Ba - by, I'm a - mazed at the way you
C G Bb F/A Ab Eb/G
pulled me out of time. You hung me on a line. Ba - by, I'm a - mazed at the way I real - ly need
help me sing my song, right me when I'm wrong. Ba - by, I'm a - mazed at the way I real - ly need
To Coda
C D A/D Am/D D9/F#
you. Ba - by, I'm a man, may - be I'm a lone - ly man who's in the mid - dle of some - thing
you.
G D7 D7#9
that he does - n't real - ly un - der - stand. (Instrumental)
D A/D Am/D C/D D9/F#
Ba - by, I'm a man, and may - be you're the on - ly wom - an who could ev - er help me.
G D/F# Dm/F
Ba - by, won't you help me to un - der - stand. (Instrumental)
Em7 A7 Bb F/A C G/C Bb F/A

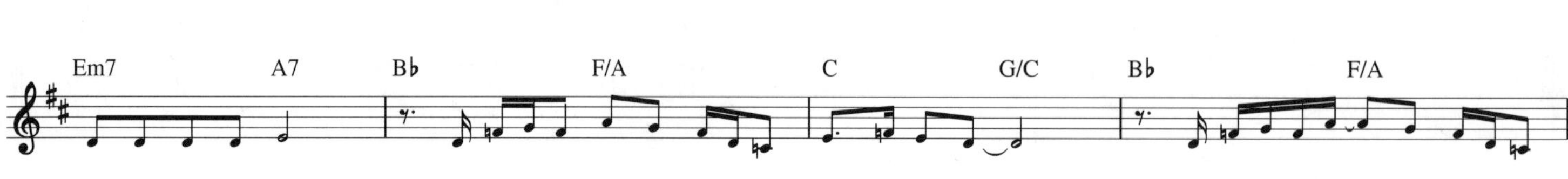

C
Bb
F/A
C
G
Bb
F/A
Ab
Eb/G
C
D
A/D
Ba-by, I'm a man, and may-be I'm a
Am/D
D9/F#
G
D7
D7#9
lone-ly man _ who's in the mid-dle of some-thing _ that he does-n't real-ly un - der-stand. ___
(Instrumental)
D
A/D
Am/D
C/D
D9/F#
Ba - by, I'm a man, and may-be you're the on - ly wom - an who could ev - er help _ me.
D.C. al Coda
G
D/F#
Dm/F
Em7
A7
Ba - by, won't you help me to un - der - stand. _
(Instrumental)
CODA
D
A/D
Am/D
C/D
D9/F#
G
D7#9
D
A/D
(Instrumental)
Am/D
C/D
D9/F#
G
D/F#
Dm/F
Em7
A7
Bb
F/A
C
G
Bb
F/A
C
Bb
F/A
C
G
Bb
F/A
Ab
Eb/G
C
Repeat and Fade

ME AND BOBBY McGEE

© 1969 (Renewed 1997) TEMI COMBINE INC.
All Rights Controlled by COMBINE MUSIC CORP. and Administered by EMI BLACKWOOD MUSIC INC.

Words and Music by KRIS KRISTOFFERSON
and FRED FOSTER

E D/E D A
hold - in' Bob - by's bod - y next to mine. Free - dom's just an - oth - er word for noth - in' left to lose.
E A D
Noth - in', and that's all that Bob - by left me, yeah. But if feel - in' good was eas - y, Lord,
A E
when he sang the blues, hey, feel - in' good was good e - nough for me, mm hmm,
E7 A
good e - nough for me and my Bob - by Mc - Gee. La da da da, la da da da, la da
Instrumental
E
da da da da da, la da da da la da la da Bob - by Mc - Gee, yeah.
A
La da la la la la, la da da da da, la la la la la Bob - by Mc - Gee. La da
da la da da la da da la da da, la da lo la da da la da la,
E7
hey now, Bob - by, lo now, Bob - by Mc - Gee, yeah. Lo na lo na na lo - na, na, lo na na na
na na na na na na na na na na na, hey now, Bob - by, lo now, Bob - by Mc - Gee,
A
yeah. And then when I called him my lov - er, called him my man; I said I
To Coda
called him my lov - er, did the best I can. Come on, hey now, Bob - by, now, hey now, Bob - by Mc - Gee,
E7
yeah. Lo la lo la lo la lo la lo la lo la lo la lo lo,
A
D.S. al Coda
CODA
E7
ley, hey, hey, Bob - by Mc - Gee, Lord.
Instrumental ends La la la
A
la la la la la la la la la la la la, hey, hey, hey, Bob - by Mc - Gee, ah.

MAGGIE MAY

Copyright © 1971 by Unichappell Music Inc., Rod Stewart and EMI Full Keel Music
Copyright Renewed 1999
All Rights for Rod Stewart Controlled and Administered by EMI Blackwood Music Inc.

Words and Music by ROD STEWART
and MARTIN QUITTENTON

Additional Lyrics

3. All I needed was a friend
To lend a guiding hand.
But you turned into a lover, and, mother, what a lover!
You wore me out.
All you did was wreck my bed,
And, in the morning, kick me in the head.
Oh, Maggie, I couldn't have tried any more.
You led me away from home
'Cause you didn't want to be alone.
You stole my heart. I couldn't leave you if I tried.

4. I suppose I could collect my books
And get on back to school.
Or steal my daddy's cue
And make a living out of playing pool.
Or find myself a rock 'n' roll band
That needs a helping hand.
Oh, Maggie, I wish I'd never seen your face.
You made a first-class fool out of me.
But I'm as blind as a fool can be.
You stole my heart, but I love you anyway.

MELISSA

Copyrght © 1968 by Unichappell Music Inc., EMI Longitude Music and Elijah Blue Music
Copyright Renewed
All Rights for Elijah Blue Music Administered by Songs Of Windswept Pacific

Words and Music by GREGG ALLMAN
and STEVE ALAIMO

MESSAGE IN A BOTTLE

© 1979 G.M. SUMNER
Published by MAGNETIC PUBLISHING LTD. and Administered by
EMI BLACKWOOD MUSIC INC. in the USA and Canada

Written and Composed by
STING

Brightly

C♯m9 Amaj7 B7 F♯m C♯m9 Amaj7 B7

Just a cast - a - way, __ an is - land lost __ at sea -
A year __ has passed _ since I wrote my note, __
Walked out this morn - ing, I don't be - lieve __ what I

F♯m C♯m9 Amaj7 B7 F♯m

- o. __ A - nuz - zer lone - ly day __
but I should have known this right from the
saw. A hun - dred bil - lion bot - tles __

C♯m9 Amaj7 B7 F♯m C♯m9 Amaj7

no one here __ but me - o. __ More
start. Only hope
washed up on __ the shore. Seems like I'm

B7 F♯m C♯m9 Amaj7 B7 F♯m

lone - li - ness __ than an - y man __ could bear. __
can keep me __ to - geth - er.
not a - lone in being a - lone. A

C♯m9 Amaj7 B7 F♯m C♯m9 Amaj7 B7

Res - cue me __ be - fore __ I fall __ in - to __ de - spair -
Love __ can mend __ your life __ but love __ can break _ your heart. _
hun - dred bil - lion cast - a - ways __ look - ing for __ a home. _

F♯m A D E

- o. __ I'll send __ an S. __ O. __ S. __ to the world. _

A D E F♯m

__ I'll send __ an S. __ O. __ S. __ to the world. _ I hope __ that some -

D F♯m D

- one gets __ my, I hope __ that some - one gets __ my,

F♯m D C♯m

I hope __ that some - one gets __ my __ mes - sage in __ a bot -

To Coda ⊕

A C♯m A C♯m

- tle __ yeah, mes - sage in __ a bot -

A 1. F♯m

- tle __ yeah.

2
F♯m
D.C. al Coda
CODA
C♯m A C♯m A
mes - sage in a bot - tle,
C♯m A F♯m
mes - sage in a bot - tle, oh yeah.
C♯m9 Amaj7 B7 F♯m C♯m9 Amaj7 B7
(Instrumental)
F♯m C♯m9 Amaj7 B7 F♯m
Repeat and Fade
(End instrumental) I'm send - ing out an S. O. S. I'm
MONEY
TRO - © Copyright 1973 (Renewed) Hampshire House Publishing Corp., New York, NY
Words and Music by
ROGER WATERS
Moderately
N.C.
Play 4 times
Bm7
Play 4 times
(Instrumental)
(End instrumental)
Bm7
Mon - ey, ya get a - way. Ya get a good job with more pay, and you're O. K.
Mon - ey, you get back. I'm all right, Jack. Keep your hands off my stack.
Mon - ey, it's a crime. Share it fair - ly, but don't take a slice of my pie.
Mon - ey, it's a gas. Grab that cash with both hands and make a stash.
Mon - ey, it's a hit. But don't give me that do - good - y good bull - shit. I'm in the
Mon - ey so they say, is the root of all e - vil to - day. But if
F♯m
1,2
Em
New car, cav - i - ar, four - star day - dream. Think I'll buy me a foot - ball team.
high fi - del - i - ty, first - class trav - 'ling set, and I think I need a Lear jet.
you ask for a rise, it's no sur -
Bm7
3
Em Bm7
Repeat and Fade
Bm7 E7/D
prise that they're giv - ing none a - way.
(Instrumental)

MELLOW YELLOW

Copyright © 1966 by Donovan (Music) Ltd.
Copyright Renewed
All Rights Administered by Peer International Corporation

Words and Music by
DONOVAN LEITCH

Moderately slow

Eb Ab Eb

I'm just mad a - bout Saf - fron, _ Saf - fron's mad a - bout me. _
I'm just mad a - bout Four - teen, _ Four - teen's mad a - bout me. _
Born high for - ev - er to ___ fly, _ wind ve - loc - i - ty: nill. _
(Instrumental)

Bb7 A Ab Ab7

I'm - a just mad a - bout Saf - fron, ___
I'm - a just mad a - bout Four - teen, ___
Born ___ high for - ev - er to ___ fly, ___

Bb7 Eb

she's just mad a - bout me. ___
she's just mad a - bout me. ___
if you want your cup I will fill. ___
They call me Mel - low Yel - low. ___ *Spoken: Quite rightly.*
(4.) *(Instrumental continues)*

Ab Bb7 Eb Ab Bb7

They call me Mel - low Yel - low. ___ *Quite rightly.* They call me Mel - low

1, 2, 4

Eb Ab Bb

To Coda (last time)

Yel - low. ___
(4.) *(End instrumental)*

3

Bb

D.C. al Coda

He's so mel - low, he's so mel - low,

CODA

Eb

E - lec - tri - cal ba - na -
I'm just ___ mad a-bout Saf -

Ab Eb Bb7 A

- na, _ is gon - na be a sud - den craze. ___
- fron, _ I'm ___ just ___ mad a - bout her. ___

Ab Ab7 Bb7

E - lec - tri - cal ___ ba - na - na ___ is bound to be the ve - ry next phase. _
I'm ___ just mad a - bout ___ Saf - fron, ___ a - she's ___ just ___ mad a-bout me. ___

Eb Ab Bb7

They call me Mel - low Yel - low. ___ *Spoken: Quite rightly.* They call me Mel - low

1

Eb Ab Bb7 Eb Ab

Yel - low. ___ *Quite rightly.* They call me Mel - low Yel - low. ___

Bb

2

Eb Ab Bb7

Repeat and Fade

Yel - low. ___ They call me Mel - low

MISSISSIPPI QUEEN

Copyright © 1970 by BMG Songs, Inc.
Copyright Renewed

Words and Music by LESLIE WEST,
FELIX PAPPALARDI, CORKY LAING and DAVID REA

Moderately
F
Mis - sis - sip - pi Queen, if you know what I mean
Mis - sis - sip - pi Queen, she taught me ev - 'ry-thing.
B♭
Way down a-round Bicks - burg,
a-round Lou - i - si - an - a way,
F
lives a Ca - jun la - dy called the
Mis - sis - sip - pi Queen.
C7
You know she was a danc - er,
B♭7
she moved bet - ter on wine. While the
F
rest of them dudes was get - tin' their kicks,
bud - dy, beg your par - don, I was get - tin' mine.
To Coda
Mis - sis - sip - pi Queen, if you know what I mean
Mis - sis - sip - pi Queen, she taught me ev - 'ry-thing.
B♭
This la - dy, she asked me,
if I would be her man.
F
You know that I told her
I'd do what I can
C7
to keep her look - in' pret - ty,
B♭7
buy her dress - es that shine. While the
F
rest of them dudes was mak - in' their bread,
bud - dy, beg your par - don, I was los - in' mine.
C7
D.S. al Coda
You know
CODA
F
Hey, Mis - sis - sip - pi Queen.

MISS YOU

© 1978 EMI MUSIC PUBLISHING LTD.
All Rights for the U.S. and Canada Controlled and Administered by COLGEMS-EMI MUSIC INC.

Words and Music by MICK JAGGER
and KEITH RICHARDS

Steady beat
Am
Dm
(Instrumental)
Am
Dm
1
2
(End instrumental)
Am
I've been hold - ing out so long, I've been sleep - ing all a - lone, Lord I
hang - ing on the phone, I've been sleep - ing all a - lone, I want to
Dm
1
2
miss you. I've been Hoo hoo
kiss you.
Am
Dm
hoo hoo hoo hoo hoo hoo hoo hoo hoo hoo
1
2
Am
Hoo hoo Well, I've been haunt - ed in my sleep, you've been
Dm
star - ring in my dreams, Lord I miss you, child. I've been
Am
Dm
wait - ing in the hall, been wait - ing on your call when the phone rings, Spoken: It's just some
Am
friends of mine that say, "Hey, what's the matter man? We're gonna come around at twelve o'clock
Dm
Am
with some Puerto Rican girls that are just dyin' to meet you. We're gonna bring a case of wine,
Dm
hey, let's go mess and fool around, you know we used to." Sung: Ha ha
Am
Dm
1
ha ha ha ha ha ha ha ha ha ha ha ha ha ha Ha ha

2
F
Em
Am
Oh! Ev - 'ry - bod - y waits so long,
F
Em
Dm
Oh! Ba - by, why you wait so long? Won't you
E
Am
come on? Come on! (Instrumental)
Dm
Am
Spoken: I've been walk - ing Cen - tral Park,
Dm
sing - ing af - ter dark, peo - ple think I'm cra - zy. I've been
Am
stum - bling on my feet, shuf - fling thro' the street ask - ing
Dm
Am
peo - ple, "What's the mat - ter with you Jim boy?" Some - times
Dm
what I want to say to my - self, some-times I say Sung: hoo hoo
3
Am
Dm
(1., 2.) hoo hoo hoo hoo hoo hoo hoo hoo hoo hoo hoo hoo hoo hoo.
(3., 4.) (Instrumental)
1 - 3
4
Am
(1.) Hoo hoo
(2., 3.) (Instrumental)
I guess I'm ly - ing to my - self, it's just
Dm
you and no-one else, Lord I won't miss you child. You've just been
Am
Dm
blot-ting out my mind, fool - ing on my time, no I won't miss you ba - by.
Am
Dm
D.S. and Fade
Lord I miss your touch. Oh ooh. Ha ha

MR. SPACEMAN

Copyright © 1966; Renewed 1994 Songs Of DreamWorks (BMI) and Sixteen Stars Music (BMI)
Worldwide Rights for Songs Of DreamWorks Administered by Cherry River Music Co.

Written by
ROGER McGUINN

CODA
C
G
Hey, Mis - ter
F
Freely
Space - man, won't you please take me a -
N.C.
C
long for a ride?
MONY, MONY
© 1968 (Renewed 1996) EMI LONGITUDE MUSIC
Words and Music by BOBBY BLOOM, TOMMY JAMES, RITCHIE CORDELL and BO GENTRY
Moderately
C
F C
Here she comes now, say, Mo - ny Mo - ny. Shoot 'em down, turn a - round,
Wake me, shake me, Mo - ny Mo - ny. Shot - gun get it done,
come on, Mo - ny. Hey, she give me lov - in', I feel all right now.
come on, Mo - ny. Don't stop look - in', it feels so good, yeah.
You've got me toss - in', turn - in' the mid - dle of the night, and I feel
Don't stop now. Come on, Mo - ny.
G
all right. I say Yeah! (Yeah!) Yeah! (Yeah!) Yeah! (Yeah!) Yeah! (Yeah!) Yeah!
Come on, Mo - ny, Yeah!
Bb
(Yeah!) Yeah! You make me feel (Mo - ny Mo - ny) so (Mo - ny Mo - ny) good. (Mo - ny Mo - ny)
Eb
Yeah! (Mo - ny Mo - ny) Yeah! (Mo - ny Mo - ny) Yeah! (Mo - ny Mo - ny) Yeah! (Mo - ny Mo - ny)
Yeah! (Mo - ny Mo - ny) Yeah! (Yeah!) Yeah! (Yeah!) Yeah! (Yeah!) Yeah! (Yeah) Yeah!
(Yeah!) Yeah! (Yeah!)
1
N.C.
2
Repeat and Fade

MOTHER

Copyright © 1971 Sony/ATV Songs LLC
Copyright Renewed
All Rights Administered by Sony/ATV Music Publishing, 8 Music Square West, Nashville, TN 37203

Words and Music by
JOHN LENNON

F Bb Bb/D C C/Bb
- ey?
- ders. And it seems such a waste of time, if
A7 A7/C# Dm Dm/C Bb Bb/D Em7
that's what it's all a - bout. Ma - ma, if that's mov - in' up then I'm
A7 N.C. Dm Gm7 C7 C7/E
mov - in' out. Mm I'm mov - in' out. Mm
Fmaj7 Dm Gm7 C7 C7/E Fmaj7
Oo Oo Uh huh Mm Hm
Dm G9 Gm7
You should nev - er ar - gue with a cra - zy mi mi mi mi mi mind. You ought - a know by now.
C Dm G7
You can pay Un - cle Sam with the o - ver - time. Is
C7 C7/E F Bb Bb/D
that all you get for your mon - ey? And if that's what you have in mind,
C C/Bb A7 A7/C# Dm Dm/C
then that's what you're all a - bout. Good
Bb Bb/D Em7 A7 N.C. Dm
luck mov - in' up 'cause I'm mov - in' out. Mm
Gm7 C7 C7/E Fmaj7 Dm
I'm mov - in' out. Mm Oo
Gm7 C7 C7/E Fmaj7
Oo Uh huh Mm Hm
Repeat and Fade
D G/D D Gsus G A G/A A G/D D
(1., 2.) (Instrumental)
(3.) out.
(2.) I'm mov - in'

MY GENERATION

© Copyright 1965 (Renewed) Fabulous Music Ltd., London, England
TRO - Devon Music, Inc., New York, controls all publication rights for the U.S.A. and Canada

Words and Music by
PETER TOWNSHEND

MY LIFE

© 1978 IMPULSIVE MUSIC

Words and Music by
BILLY JOEL

NEW KID IN TOWN

© 1976 EMI BLACKWOOD MUSIC INC.

Words and Music by JOHN DAVID SOUTHER,
DON HENLEY and GLENN FREY

Am7 D Am7 D C D
mind you that is does-n't real-ly mat-ter which side
G
you're on. You're walk-ing a-way and they're talk-ing be-
Am7 D Am7 D C
hind you. They will nev-er for-get you till
D G B7
some-bod-y new comes a-long.
Em7 A Em7 A
Where you been late-ly? There's a new kid in town.
Em7 A Am7
Ev-'ry-bod-y loves him, don't they? Now he's hold-ing
B E G♯m7 A
her, and you're still a-round. Oh, my, my.
B E G♯m7 A B
There's a new kid in town, just an-oth-er new kid in
E G♯m7 A Am E
town. Ooh, hoo. Ev-'ry-bod-y's talk-ing 'bout the
Ooh, hoo. Ev-'ry-bod-y's walk-ing like the
C♯m 1 2 E
new kid in town. There's a new kid in town.
new kid in town.
C♯m
I don't want to hear it. There's a new kid in town. I don't want to hear it. There's a
Repeat and Fade
E C♯m
new kid in town. There's a new kid in town. There's a

NIGHTS IN WHITE SATIN

Words and Music by
JUSTIN HAYWARD

© Copyright 1967 (Renewed), 1968 (Renewed) and 1970 (Renewed) Tyler Music Ltd. London, England
TRO - Essex Music, Inc., New York, controls all publication rights for the U.S.A. and Canada

Moderately
Em
D
Em
D
C
Nights in white sat - in,
nev - er reach - ing the end.
Let - ters I've

G
F
Em
writ - ten,
nev - er mean - ing to send.
Beau - ty I'd
Some try to

D
Em
D
C
G
al - ways missed with these eyes be - fore, just what the truth is
tell me thoughts they can - not de - fend. Just what you want to be

F
Em
A
I can't say an - y - more, 'cause I love you,
you'll be in the end, and I love you,
yes, I

To Coda
C
Em
D(add2)
D
Em
love you. Oh, how I love you.

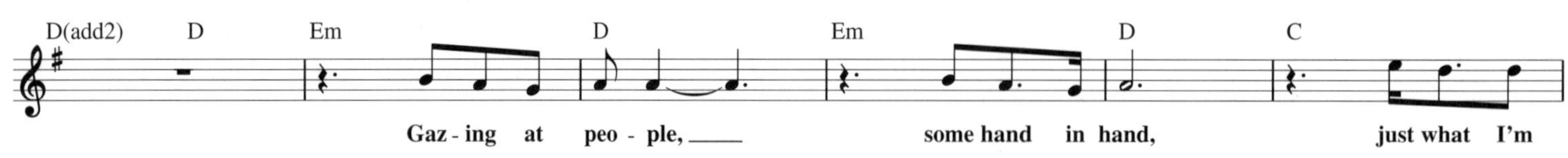
D(add2)
D
Em
D
Em
D
C
Gaz - ing at peo - ple, some hand in hand, just what I'm

D.S. al Coda
CODA
G
F
Em
Em
go - ing thru they can't un - der - stand.

OVER MY HEAD

Copyright © 1975 by Careers-BMG Music Publishing, Inc.

Words and Music by
CHRISTINE McVIE

ONLY THE GOOD DIE YOUNG

© 1977, 1978 IMPULSIVE MUSIC

Words and Music by
BILLY JOEL

Fast Shuffle

Come out Vir - gin - ia, don't let me wait. __ You Cath - o - lic girls __ start
showed you a sta - tue, told you to pray. __ They built you a tem - ple and

much too late, __ ah but soon - er or la - ter it comes down to fate. __ I
locked you a - way, __ ah but they nev - er told __ you the price that you pay, __ the

might as well be the one. __ Well they
things that you might have done, _ __ for on - ly the good __ die

young, ____ that's what I said. On - ly the good __ die young, _

__ on - ly the good die young. __ You might have heard I run __ with a
say there's a heav-en for

dan - ger - ous crowd. _ We ain't too pret - ty we ain't too proud. _ We
those who will wait. __ Some say it's bet - ter but I say it ain't. I'd rath - er

might be laugh - ing a bit too loud, __ but that nev - er hurt no one. __
laugh with the sin - ners than cry with the saints; __ the sin-ners are much more fun. __

To Coda

__ So come on Vir-gin - ia, show me a sign, __ send up a sig - nal, I'll

throw you a line. __ That stained glass cur-tain you're hid - ing be - hind __ nev - er lets in the sun. __

__ Dar - lin', on - ly the good __ die young, ____ whoa, ____

on - ly the good __ die young. __ On - ly the good die young. __

C G F C
You got a nice white dress and a par - ty on your con - fir - ma - tion.
D F
You've got a brand new soul and a cross of gold.
G F C
It's a pi - ty they did - n't give you quite e - nough in - for - ma - tion.
D F
You did - n't count on me when you were count - ing on your ro - sa - ry.
C/E Dm C G
D.S. al Coda
Oh, oh, oh. And they
CODA
G N.C.
You know that on - ly the good die
C F G C
young, that's what I say. On - ly the good
F G C
die young, on - ly the good die young.
G F C
(Instrumental)
D F
G F
(End instrumental) Said your moth - er told you all I could give you was a rep - u - ta -
C D
- tion. She nev - er cared for me,
F C/E Dm C G
D.C. and Fade
but did she ev - er say a pray'r for me? Come out

OWNER OF A LONELY HEART

Copyright © 1983 by Carlin Music Corp., Unforgettable Songs and Affirmative Music
All Rights for Carlin Music Corp. in the U.S. and Canada Administered by Carbert Music Inc.
All Rights for Affirmative Music Administered by Warner-Tamerlane Publishing Corp.

Words and Music by TREVOR HORN, JON ANDERSON, TREVOR RABIN and CHRIS SQUIRE

G/A A Am7 G/A
After my own indecision, they confused me so. My love said
Owner of a lonely heart.
A Am7 G/A A C/A
never question your will at all. In the end you've got to go. Look
Own-
G/A Asus Ab13
before you leap and don't you hesitate at all. No, no.
-er of a lonely heart.
E13 F13 F#13 G13 Ab13 A13 B5 C5 D5 G5
A5 B5 C5 D5 G5 N.C.
Play 4 times
(Instrumental)
A5 B5 C5 Dsus2 G5 A5 B5 C5 Dsus2 G5
Owner of a lonely heart. Owner of a lonely heart. (Much better than a)
A5 B5 C5 Dsus2 G5
owner of a broken heart.
1
A5 B5 C5 Dsus2 G5
Owner of a lonely heart.
2
A5 B5 C5 D5 A5 Am7 G/A A Am7 G/A
owner of a lonely heart. Owner of a lonely heart.
A Am7 G/A A Am7 G/A
Sooner or later each conclusion will decide the lonely heart.
Owner of a lonely heart.
A Am7 G/A A Am/G F
It will excite it, will delight it, will give a better start. Don't de-
Owner of a lonely heart.
Eb/F F Eb/F
ceive your free will at all. Don't deceive your free will at all. Don't de-
(Instrumental)
F Eb/F F Eb/F
Repeat and Fade
ceive your free will at all. Just receive it. Just receive it.

OYE COMO VA

© 1963, 1970 (Renewed 1991, 1998) EMI FULL KEEL MUSIC

Words and Music by
TITO PUENTE

Moderate Latin Rock

Am7 D9 Play 4 times Am7 D9 Play 4 times Am

D Am D Am Am7 D

O - ye Co-mo Va, mi ri - mo,

Am7 D Am D Am/E Am7

bue-no pa go-zar, mu-la - ta.

D Am7 D Am7 D

Am7 D Am7 D Am7

D Am7 D Am7 D

Am7 D9 Am7 D9 Am7 D9

Play 3 times Am D Am D Am

PENNY LANE

Copyright © 1967 Sony/ATV Songs LLC
Copyright Renewed
All Rights Administered by Sony/ATV Music Publishing, 8 Music Square West, Nashville, TN 37203

Words and Music by JOHN LENNON
and PAUL McCARTNEY

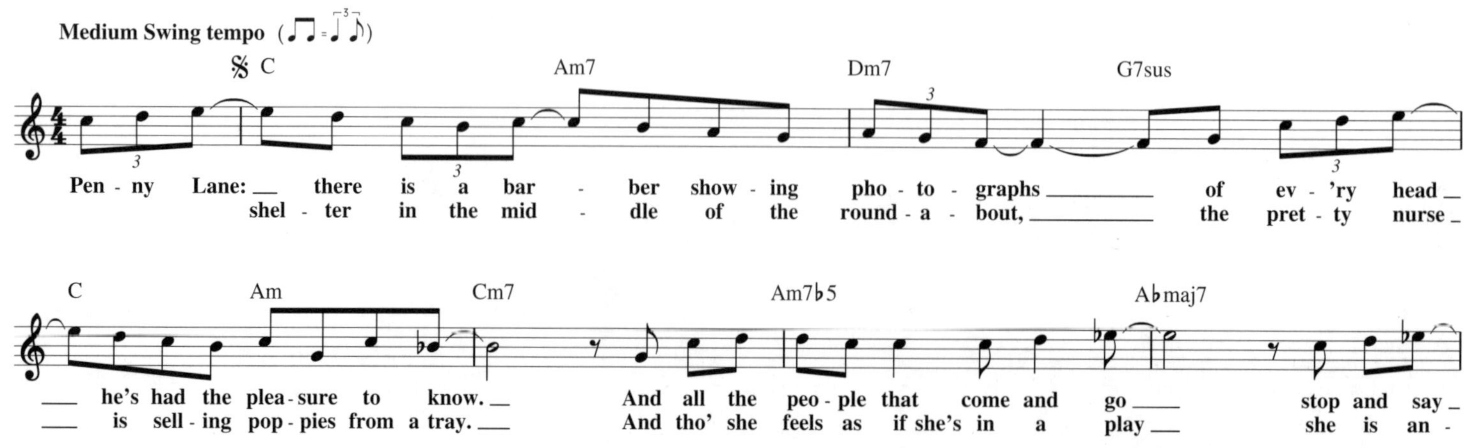

G7sus G7 G7sus G7 C Am7 Dm7 G7sus
___ hel - lo. On the cor - ner is a bank - er with a mo - tor - car; ___ The lit - tle chil -
- y - way. Pen - ny Lane: the bar - ber shaves an - oth - er cus - tom - er; ___ We see the bank -
C Am Cm7 Am7♭5 A♭maj7
- dren laugh at him be - hind his back. And the bank - er nev - er wears a mac ___ in the pour -
- er sit - ting wait - ing for a trim. And then the fire - man rush - es in ___ from the pour -
G7sus G7 F B♭ B♭/D E♭
- ing rain, ver - y strange! ___ Pen - ny Lane ___ is in my ears ___ and in my eyes, ___ (Instrumental)
- ing rain, ver - y strange! ___
B♭ B♭/D E♭ To Coda G
wet
there
be - neath the blue ___ sub - ur - ban skies ___ I sit. And mean - while back in Pen - ny Lane ___
C Am Dm7 G7sus C Am
___ there is a fire - man with an hour ___ glass, ___ and in his pock - et is a por - trait of the
Cm7 Am7♭5 A♭maj7 G7sus G7
Queen. He likes to keep his fire en - gine clean; ___ It's a clean ___ ma - chine!
G7sus G7 C Am Dm7 G C Am
(Instrumental)
Cm Am7♭5 A♭maj7 G7sus
F B♭ B♭/D E♭
Pen - ny Lane ___ is in my ears ___ and in my eyes, ___ (Instrumental)
B♭ B♭/D E♭ G D.S. al Coda
full of fish ___ and fin - ger pies ___ in sum - mer. Mean - while back be - hind the
CODA
G C C/E F
mean - while back... Pen - ny Lane ___ is in my ears ___ and in my eyes, ___ (Instrumental)
C C/E F C
there be - neath the blue ___ sub - ur - ban skies ___ (Instrumental) Pen - ny Lane. ___

PAPERBACK WRITER

Copyright © 1966 Sony/ATV Songs LLC
Copyright Renewed
All Rights Administered by Sony/ATV Music Publishing, 8 Music Square West, Nashville, TN 37203

Words and Music by JOHN LENNON
and PAUL McCARTNEY

Bright Rock
N.C.
Pa - per-back wri - ter, pa - per-back writ - er. (Instrumental)
G7
(End instrumental) Dear _ Sir or Mad-am, will you read my book? It took me
It's a thou - sand pag - es, give or take a few; I'll be
years to write, _ will you take a look? It's based on a nov - el by a man named Lear and I
writ - ing more _ in a week or two. I can make it long - er if you like the style, I can
C
G7
need a job ___ so I want to be a pa - per-back writ - er, ___ pa - per-back writ - er. ___
change it 'round _ and I want to be a pa - per-back writ - er, ___ pa - per-back writ - er. ___
It's the dirt - y sto - ry of a dirt - y man, _ and his cling - ing wife _ does - n't
If you real - ly like it you can have the rights, _ it could make a mil - lion for you
un - der-stand. His son is work - ing for the Dai - ly Mail; _ it's a stead - y job ___ but he
o - ver-night. If you must re - turn _ it you can send it here, _ but I need a break _ and I
C
G7
N.C.
wants to be a pa - per-back writ - er, ___ pa - per-back writ - er. ___
want to be a pa - per-back writ - er, ___ pa - per-back writ - er. ___ Pa - per-back
writ - er, pa - per-back writ - er. (Instrumental)
G7
Repeat and Fade
(End instrumental) Pa - per-back writ - er. ___

PARANOID

© Copyright 1970 (Renewed) Westminster Music Ltd., London, England
TRO - Essex Music International, Inc., New York, controls all publication rights for the U.S.A. and Canada

Words and Music by ANTHONY IOMMI, JOHN OSBOURNE, WILLIAM WARD and TERENCE BUTLER

PHILADELPHIA FREEDOM

Copyright © 1975 by Big Pig Music Ltd.
All Rights for the United States Administered by Intersong U.S.A., Inc.

Words and Music by ELTON JOHN
and BERNIE TAUPIN

CODA
Eb Dm7 Cm7
don't you know I love - ove - ove you. Don't you know I
Eb Dm7 Cm7 Eb/F Bb
love - ove - ove you, yes I do. (Phil - a - del - phi - a free - dom) I
Eb Dm7 Cm7 Eb/F Bb
Repeat and Fade
love - ove - ove you, yes I do. (Phil - a - del - phi - a free - dom) Don't you know that I

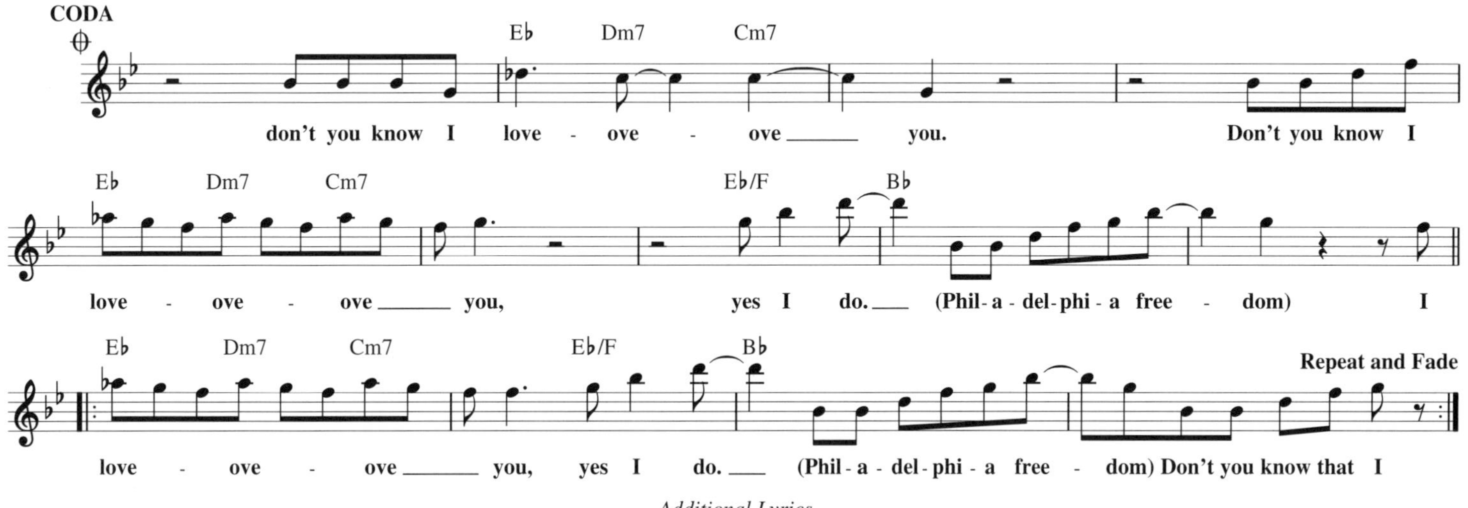

Additional Lyrics

2. If you choose to, you can live your life alone
Some people choose the city,
Some others choose the good old family home
I like living easy without family ties
'Til the whippoorwill of freedom zapped me
Right between the eyes.
Chorus

POWER TO THE PEOPLE

© 1971 (Renewed 1999) LENONO.MUSIC
All Rights Controlled and Administered by EMI BLACKWOOD MUSIC INC.

Words and Music by
JOHN LENNON

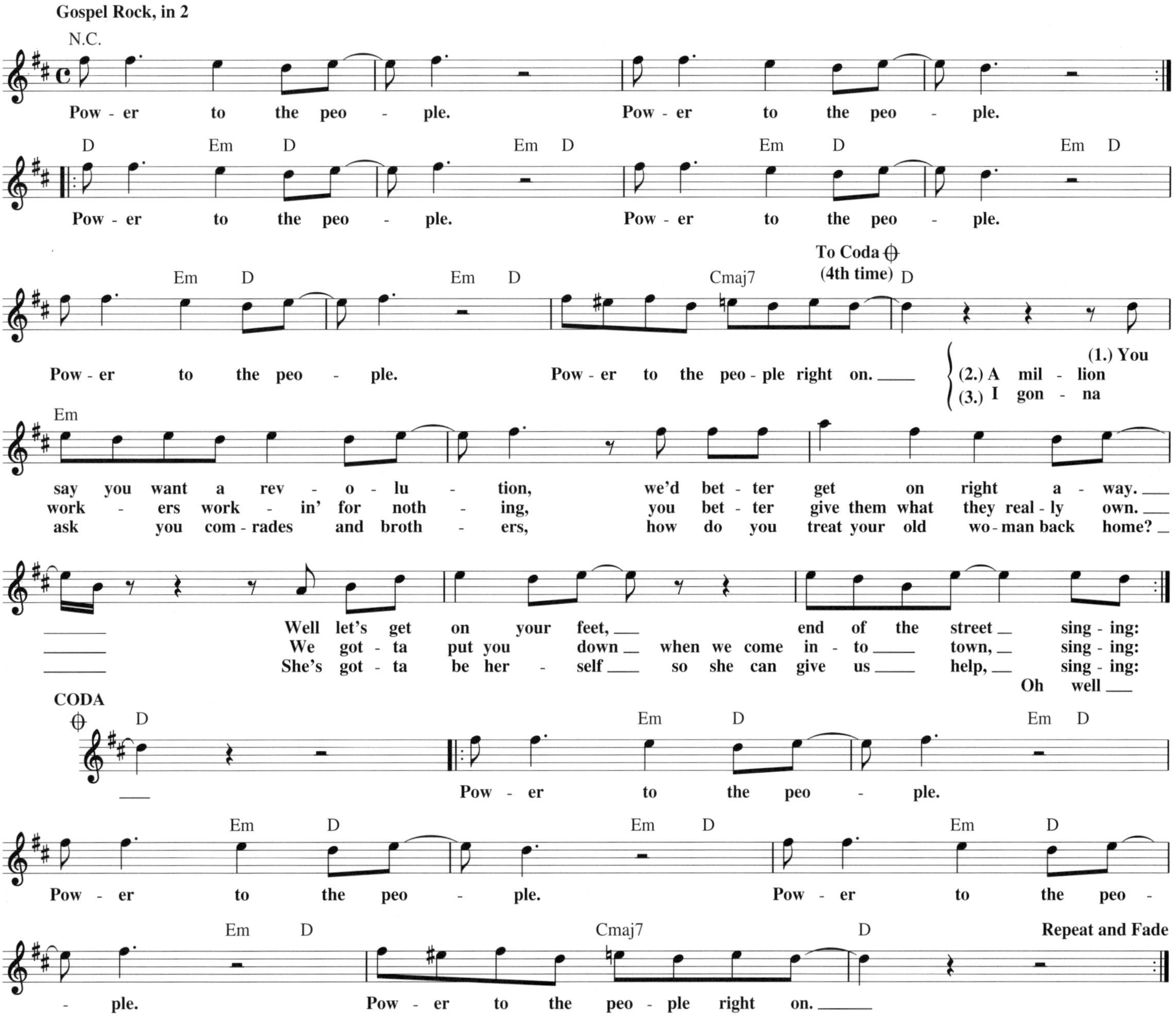

Gospel Rock, in 2
N.C.
Pow - er to the peo - ple. Pow - er to the peo - ple.
D Em D Em D Em D Em D
Pow - er to the peo - ple. Pow - er to the peo - ple.
Em D Em D Cmaj7
To Coda (4th time) D
Pow - er to the peo - ple. Pow - er to the peo - ple right on.
(1.) You
(2.) A mil - lion
(3.) I gon - na
Em
say you want a rev - o - lu - tion, we'd bet - ter get on right a - way.
work - ers work - in' for noth - ing, you bet - ter give them what they real - ly own.
ask you com - rades and broth - ers, how do you treat your old wo - man back home?
Well let's get on your feet, end of the street sing - ing:
We got - ta put you down when we come in - to town, sing - ing:
She's got - ta be her - self so she can give us help, sing - ing:
Oh well
CODA
D Em D Em D
Pow - er to the peo - ple.
Em D Em D Em D
Pow - er to the peo - ple. Pow - er to the peo -
Em D Cmaj7 D
Repeat and Fade
- ple. Pow - er to the peo - ple right on.

PIANO MAN

© 1973 (Renewed 2001), 1974 JOEL SONGS

Words and Music by
BILLY JOEL

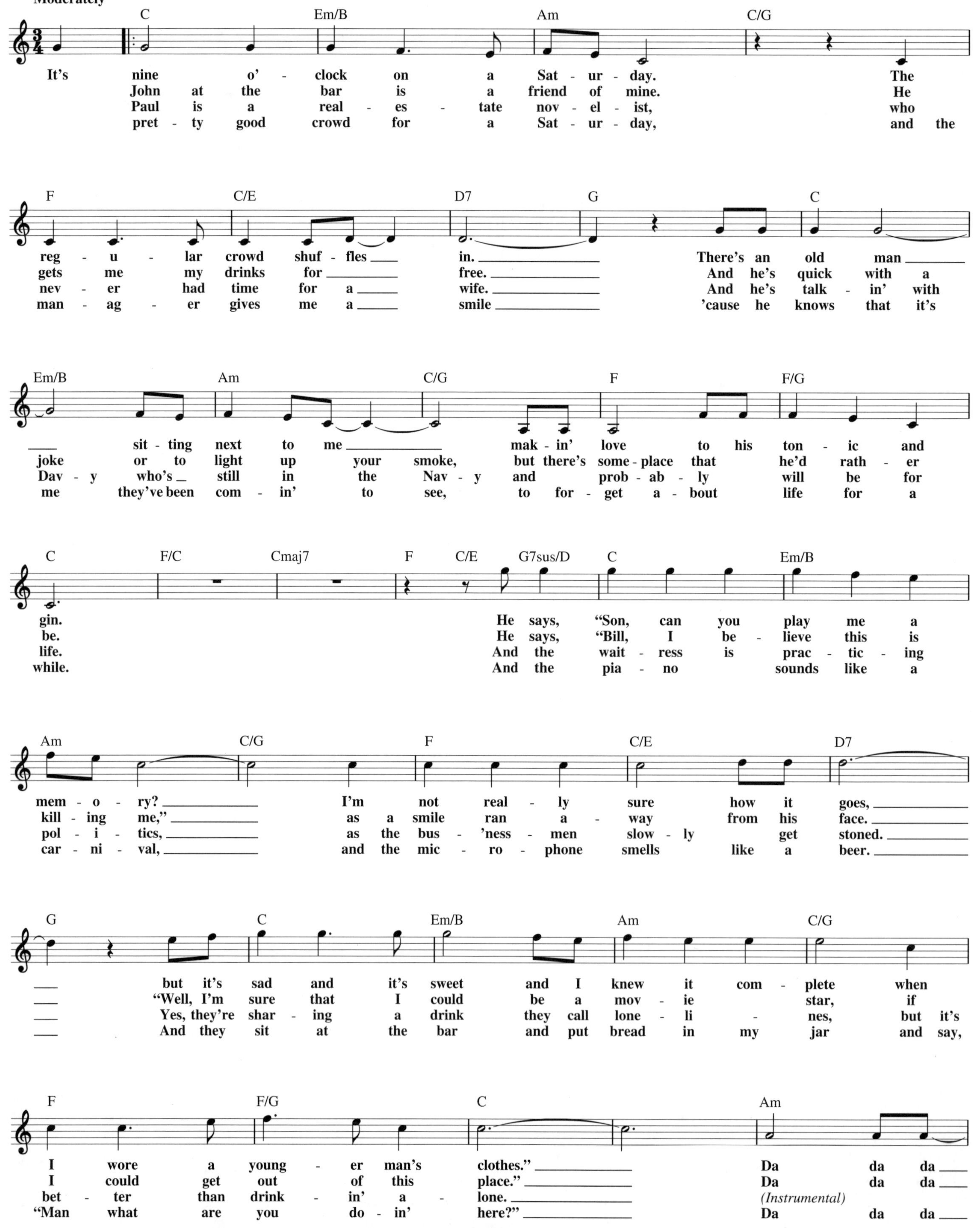

Am/G D7/F♯ F Am Am/G
de de da da da de de
de de da da da de de
de de da da da de de
D6/F♯ D7 G G/F C/E
da da da
da da da
(End instrumental)
da da da
G7/D C Em/B Am C/G
Sing us a song, you're the pia - no man.
F C/E D7 G C
Sing us a song to - night. Well, we're all in the
Em/B Am C/G F F/G
mood for a mel - o - dy, and you've got us feel - in' al -
C F/C Cmaj7 G7sus C/G G7sus
1 - 3
4
right.
Now
Now
It's a
C Em/B Am C/G F
(Instrumental)
F/G C F/C Cmaj7 F/C C Dm7/C
C F/C Cmaj7 F C/E G7sus/D C

PIECE OF MY HEART

Copyright © 1967 Sony/ATV Songs LLC, Unichappell Music Inc. and Sloopy II Music
Copyright Renewed
All Rights on behalf of Sony/ATV Songs LLC Administered by Sony/ATV Music Publishing, 8 Music Square West, Nashville, TN 37203

Words and Music by BERT BERNS
and JERRY RAGOVOY

PINK HOUSES

© 1983 EMI FULL KEEL MUSIC

Words and Music by
JOHN MELLENCAMP

POINT OF KNOW RETURN

© 1977 EMI BLACKWOOD MUSIC INC. and DON KIRSHNER MUSIC
All Rights Controlled and Administered by EMI BLACKWOOD MUSIC INC.

Words and Music by STEVE WALSH,
PHIL EHART and ROBERT STEINHARDT

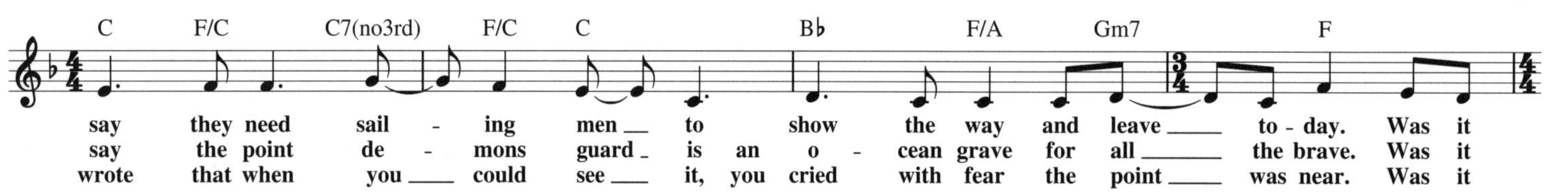

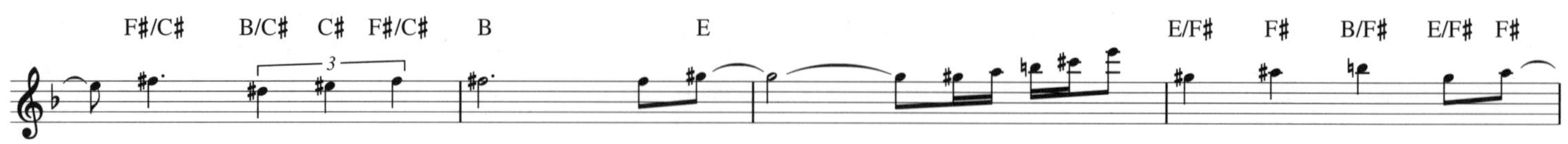

N.C.
G
F
(End instrumental)
Your father, he said he needs
C/E
F
you. Your moth - er, she said she loves
G
F
you. Your broth - ers, they ech - o the words
C/E
C
E♭sus2
"How far to the point of know re - turn,
B♭
C
B♭/F
F
B♭/F
to the point of know re - turn? Well, how long? (Instrumental)
D.S. al Coda
C/F
F
B♭/F
F
B♭/F
C/F
F
How long?" (Instrumental) To -
CODA
B♭/F
F
B♭/F
C/F
F
Dm
C
B♭
How long? (Instrumental) How long to the point of know re - turn?
B♭/F
F
B♭/F
1
C/F
F
2
C/F
F
B♭/F
F
B♭/F
(Instrumental) know re - turn? (Instrumental)
Repeat and Fade
C/F
F
B♭/F
F
B♭/F
C/F
F
How long?" (Instrumental)

THE PUSHER

Copyright © 1964 IRVING MUSIC, INC.
Copyright Renewed

Words and Music by
HOYT AXTON

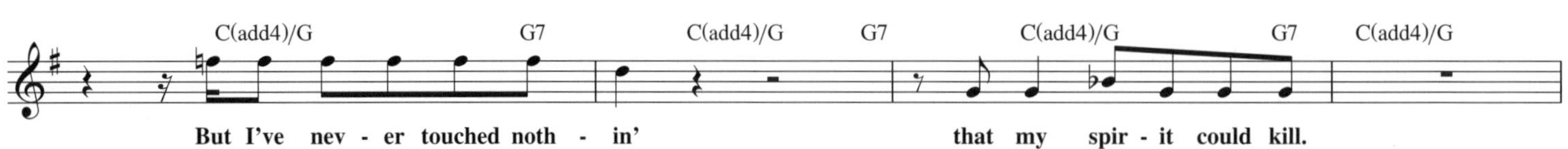

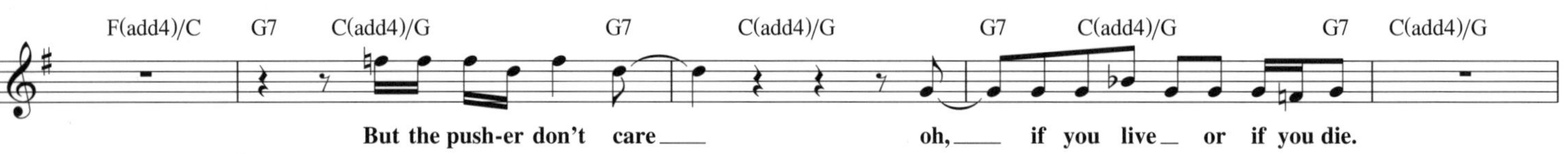

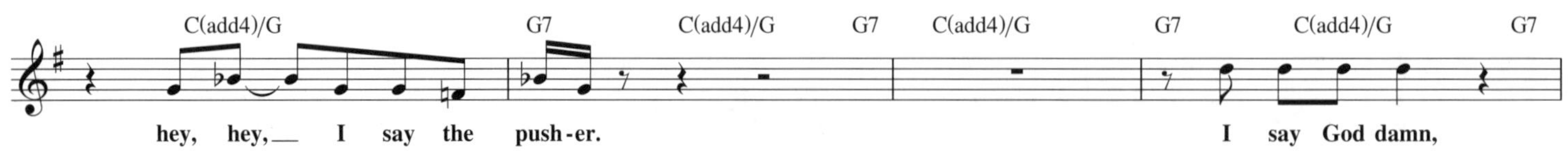

G7 C(add4)/G G7 C(add4)/G G7 C(add4)/G G7 C(add4)/G
Oh, but the push-er is a mon-ster. Good God, he's not a
G7 C(add4)/G G7 C(add4)/G C F(add4)/C C7 F(add4)/C
nat-'ral man. The deal - er for a nick-el, Lord he'll sell you lots of sweet dreams.
C7 F(add4)/C C7 F(add4)/C G7 C(add4)/G G7 C(add4)/G
Ah, but the push-er'll ruin your bod - y. Lord, he'll leave your,
G7 C(add4)/G G7 C(add4)/G G7 C(add4)/G G7 C(add4)/G G7 C(add4)/G G7
he'll leave your mind to scream. God damn, oh, oh, the push-er.
C(add4)/G G7 C(add4)/G G7 C(add4)/G G7 C(add4)/G G7 C(add4)/G G7 C(add4)/G
God damn, God damn, the push-er. I say God damn, God,
To Coda
G7sus C(add4)/G G7 C(add4)/G G7 N.C./B♭ G7 C(add4)/G G7 C(add4)/G
God damn the push-er man. Well, now if
G7 C(add4)/G G7 C(add4)/G G7 C(add4)/G G7 C(add4)/G
I were the pres-i-dent of this land, you know I'd de - clare to-tal war on the push-er man.
G7 C(add4)/G G7 C(add4)/G G7 C(add4)/G
I'd cut him if he stands, then I'd shoot him if he'd run. Then I'd kill him with my Bi - ble
D.S. al Coda
G7 C(add4)/G G7 C(add4)/G G7 C(add4)/G G7 C(add4)/G G7 C(add4)/G
and my raz - or and my gun. God, damn oh, the push-er.
CODA
G7 C(add4)/G G7 C(add4)/G G7 N.C./G

RADAR LOVE

Copyright © 1973 Snamyook
All Rights Administered by Sony/ATV Music Publishing, 8 Music Square West, Nashville, TN 37203
International Copyright Secured All Rights Reserved

Words and Music by GEORGE KOOYMANS
and BARRY HAY

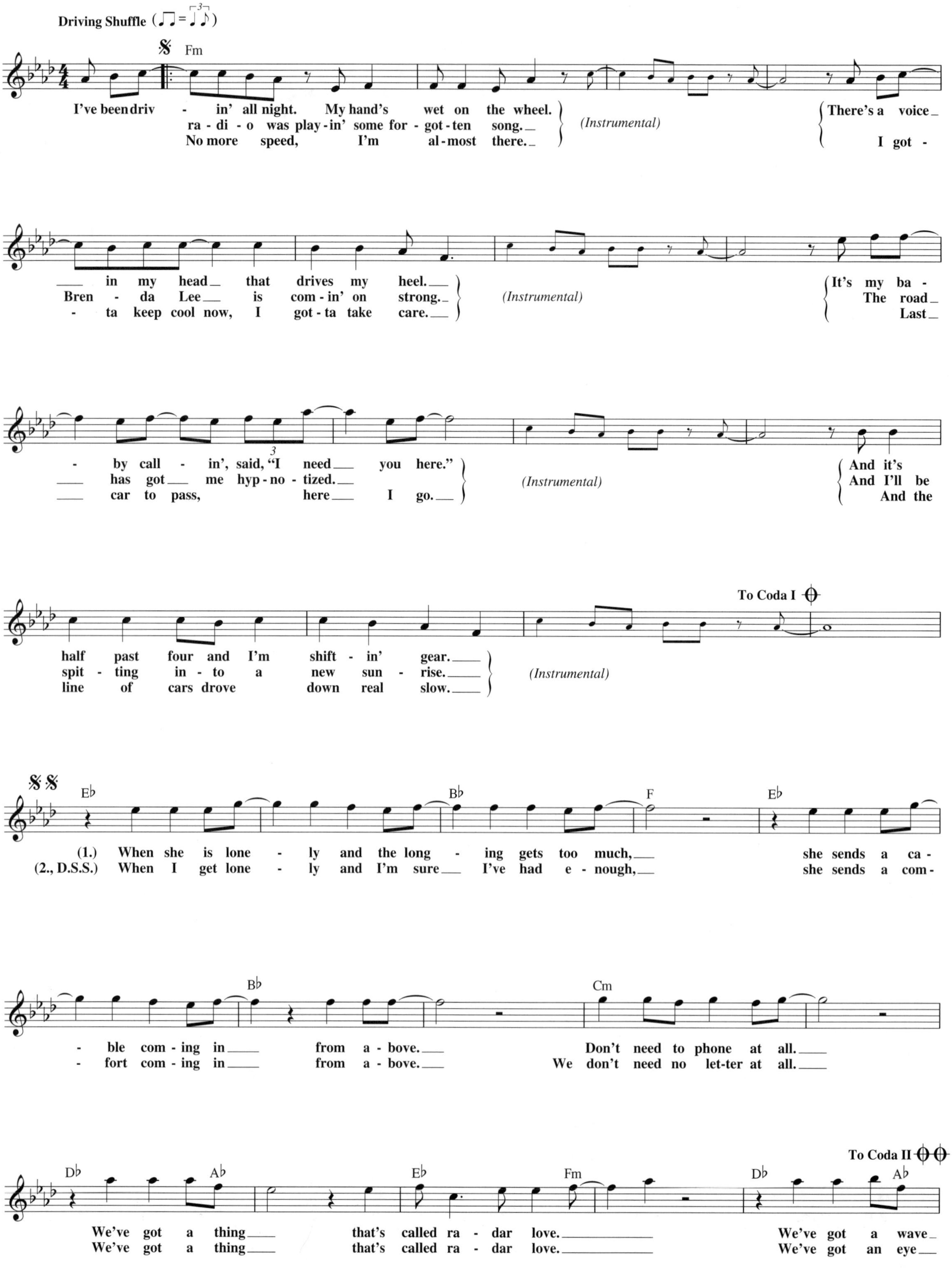

Driving Shuffle

Fm

I've been driv - in' all night. My hand's wet on the wheel.
ra - di - o was play - in' some for - got - ten song.
No more speed, I'm al - most there.
(Instrumental)
There's a voice
I got -

in my head that drives my heel.
Bren - da Lee is com - in' on strong.
- ta keep cool now, I got - ta take care.
(Instrumental)
It's my ba -
The road
Last

- by call - in', said, "I need you here."
has got me hyp - no - tized.
car to pass, here I go.
(Instrumental)
And it's
And I'll be
And the

To Coda I

half past four and I'm shift - in' gear.
spit - ting in - to a new sun - rise.
line of cars drove down real slow.
(Instrumental)

E♭ B♭ F E♭

(1.) When she is lone - ly and the long - ing gets too much,
(2., D.S.S.) When I get lone - ly and I'm sure I've had e - nough,
she sends a ca -
she sends a com -

B♭ Cm

- ble com - ing in from a - bove. Don't need to phone at all.
- fort com - ing in from a - bove. We don't need no let-ter at all.

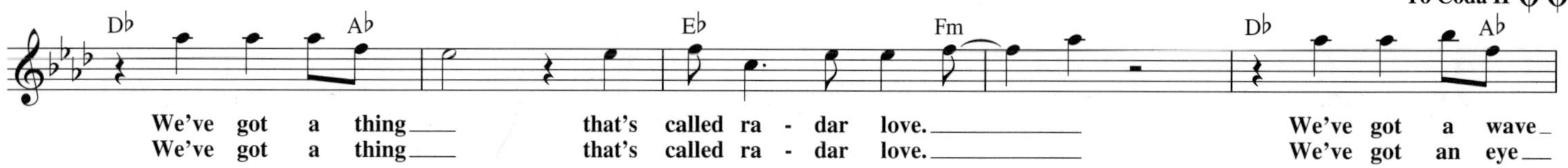

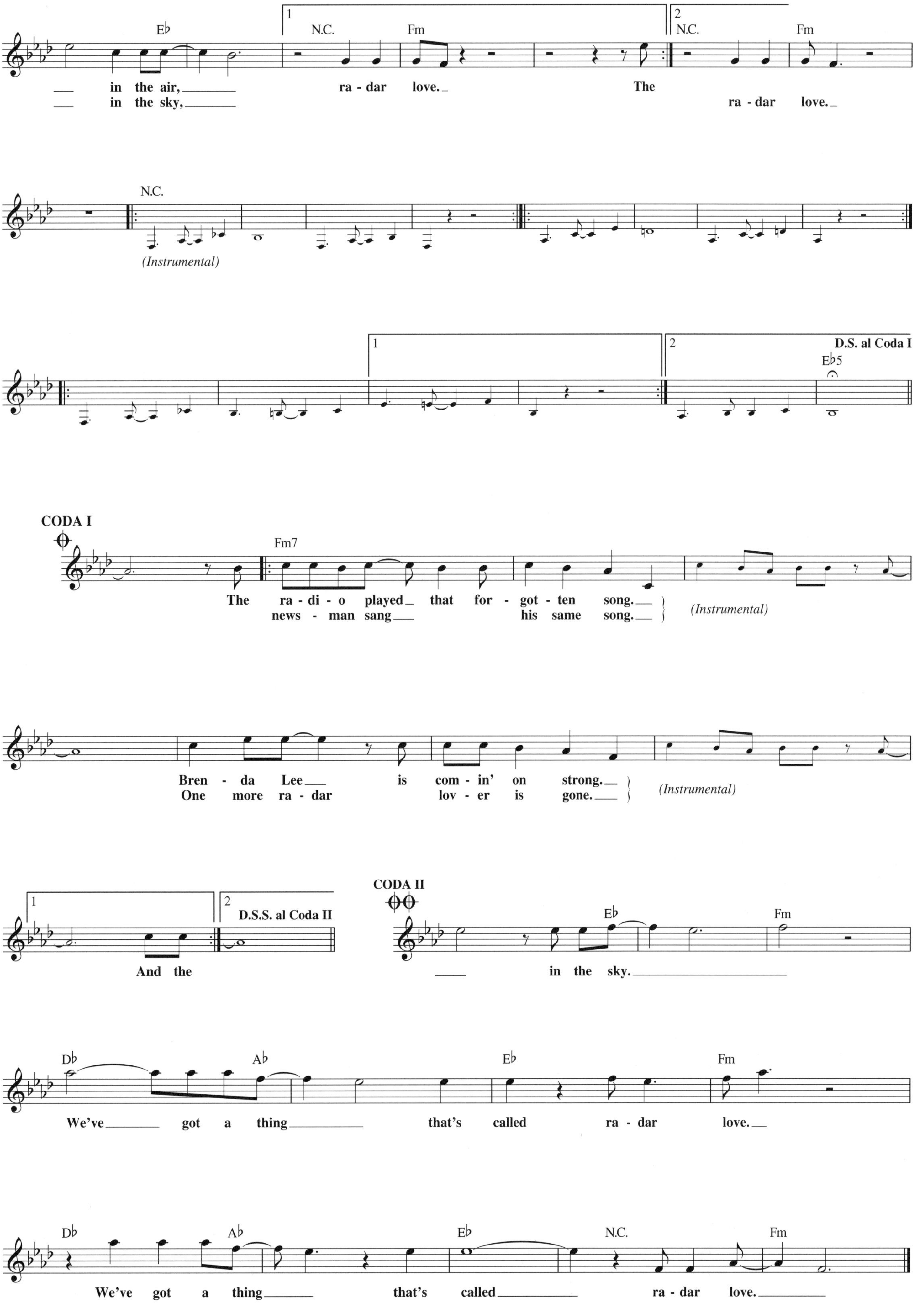

E♭
1
N.C.
Fm
2
N.C.
Fm
in the air,
ra - dar love.
The
in the sky,
ra - dar love.
N.C.
(Instrumental)
1
2
D.S. al Coda I
E♭5
CODA I
Fm7
The ra - di - o played that for - got - ten song.
news - man sang his same song.
(Instrumental)
Bren - da Lee is com - in' on strong.
One more ra - dar lov - er is gone.
(Instrumental)
1
2
D.S.S. al Coda II
And the
CODA II
E♭
Fm
in the sky.
D♭
A♭
E♭
Fm
We've got a thing that's called ra - dar love.
D♭
A♭
E♭
N.C.
Fm
We've got a thing that's called ra - dar love.

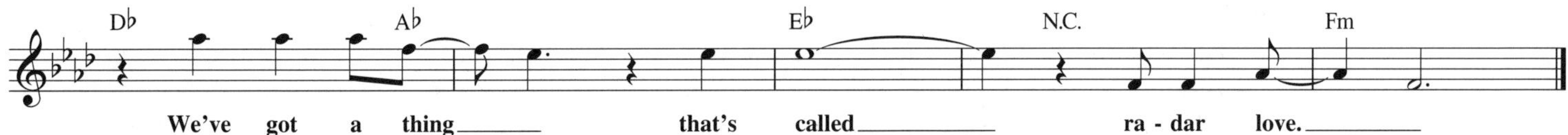

R.O.C.K. IN THE U.S.A.
(A Salute to 60's Rock)

© 1986 EMI FULL KEEL MUSIC

Words and Music by
JOHN MELLENCAMP

RAMBLIN' MAN

Copyright © 1973 by Unichappell Music Inc. and F.R. Betts Music Co.
Copyright Renewed
All Rights Administered by Unichappell Music Inc.

Words and Music by
DICKEY BETTS

REASON TO BELIEVE

Copyright © 1966 (Renewed) Allen Stanton Productions

Words and Music by
TIM HARDIN

REFUGEE

Copyright © 1979 ALMO MUSIC CORP.

Words and Music by TOM PETTY
and MIKE CAMPBELL

REBEL, REBEL

© 1974 EMI MUSIC PUBLISHING LTD., JONES MUSIC AMERICA and MOTH MUSIC
All Rights for EMI MUSIC PUBLISHING LTD. Controlled and Administered by COLGEMS-EMI MUSIC INC.
All Rights for JONES MUSIC AMERICA Administered by ARZO PUBLISHING
All Rights for MOTH MUSIC Administered by CHRYSALIS SONGS

Words and Music by
DAVID BOWIE

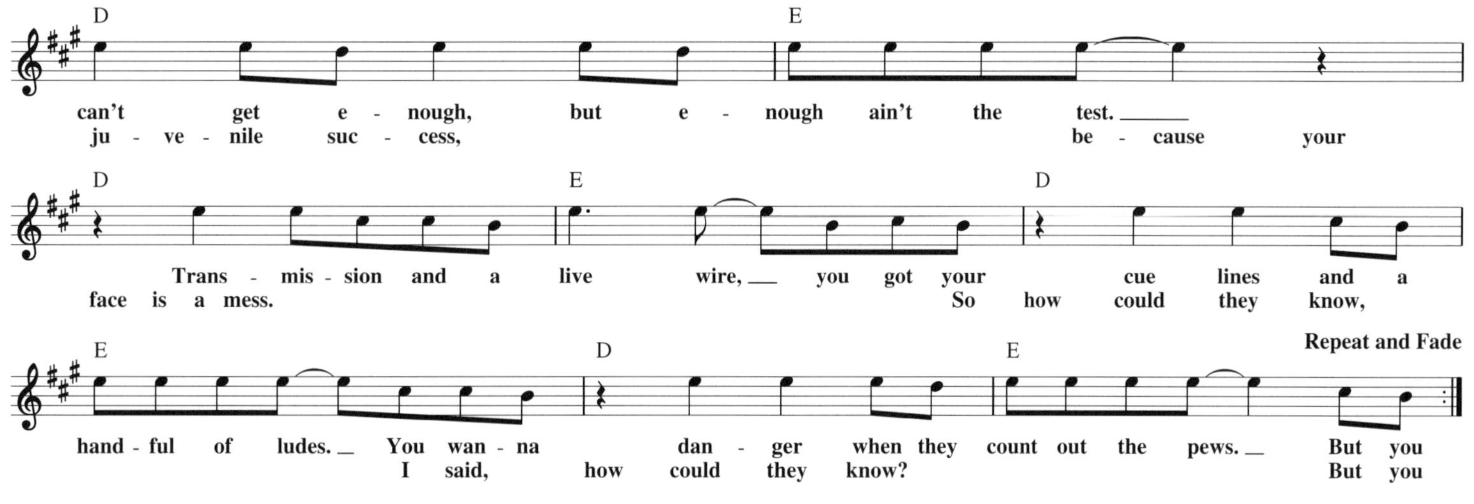

D
E
can't get e - nough, but e - nough ain't the test.
ju - ve - nile suc - cess, be - cause your
D
E
D
Trans - mis - sion and a live wire, you got your cue lines and a
face is a mess. So how could they know,
E
D
E
Repeat and Fade
hand - ful of ludes. You wan - na dan - ger when they count out the pews. But you
I said, how could they know? But you

REVOLUTION

Copyright © 1968 Sony/ATV Songs LLC
Copyright Renewed
All Rights Administered by Sony/ATV Music Publishing, 8 Music Square West, Nashville, TN 37203

Words and Music by JOHN LENNON
and PAUL McCARTNEY

Moderate Rock and Roll Shuffle

C F
You say you want a rev - o - lu - tion, well you know, we all want
say you got a real so - lu - tion, well you know, we'd all love
say you'll change the con - sti - tu - tion, well you know, we all want

C
to change the world. You tell me that it's e - vo - lu - tion, well
to see the plan. You ask me for a con - tri - bu - tion, well
to change your head. You tell me it's the in - sti - tu - tion, well

F G7
you know, we all want to change the world.
you know, we're all do - ing what we can.
you know, you better free your mind in - stead.

Dm G6 Dm
But when you talk a - bout de - struc - tion, don't you know that you can
But if you want mon - ey for peo - ple with minds that hate, all I can tell you is, "Broth - er you
But if you go car - ry - ing pic - tures of Chair - man Mao, you ain't go - ing to make it with any - one

B♭ C A G11 C F6
count me out.
have to wait."
an - y - how.
Don't you know it's gon - na be al - right,

C F6 C F6 1, 2 G11
al - right, al - right. *(Instrumental)*

C/G G11 3 C/G G7♯9 C F C
You
You
Al - right, al - right, al - right, al - right,

F C F G7 C
al - right, al - right, al - right, al - right. *(Instrumental)*

RENEGADE

Copyright © 1978 ALMO MUSIC CORP. and STYGIAN SONGS
All Rights Controlled and Administered by ALMO MUSIC CORP.

Words and Music by
TOMMY SHAW

The jig is up, the news is out, they
fi - nal - ly found me, the ren - e - gade who had it made re - trieved for a boun - ty.
Nev - er more to go a - stray, this will be the end to - day of the want - ed man,
want - ed man.
Repeat and Fade
Guitar solo ad lib.
RIDIN' THE STORM OUT
© 1973 (Renewed 2001) EMI SOSAHA MUSIC INC. and JONATHAN THREE MUSIC
Words and Music by
GARY RICHRATH
Moderately
Rid - in' the storm out, wait - in' for the thaw out on a full
La - dy's be - side me. She's there to guide me. She says
moon night in the Rock - y Moun - tain win - ter.
that all a - lone we've fi - n'lly found our home.
The wine bot - tle's low, watch - ing for the snow. Think -
The wind out - side is fright'ning, but it's kind - er than light - ning life in the cit - y.
- ing a - bout what I've been miss - ing in the cit - y.
A hard life to live, but it gives back what you give.
And I'm
not miss - ing a thing, watch - ing the full moon cross - ing the range.
Rid - in' the storm out. Rid - in' the storm out. Rid - in' the storm out.
Rid - in' the storm out.

RHIANNON

Copyright © 1975, 1977 Welsh Witch Music
All Rights Administered by Sony/ATV Music Publishing, 8 Music Square West, Nashville, TN 37203

Words and Music by
STEVIE NICKS

N.C.
Hey! Hey! Hey! Ha! Hey! Hey! Hey! Hey! Hey! Hey!
Hey! Hey! Hey! Hey! Hey! Hey! Hey! Hey! Hey! Hey!
Repeat and Fade

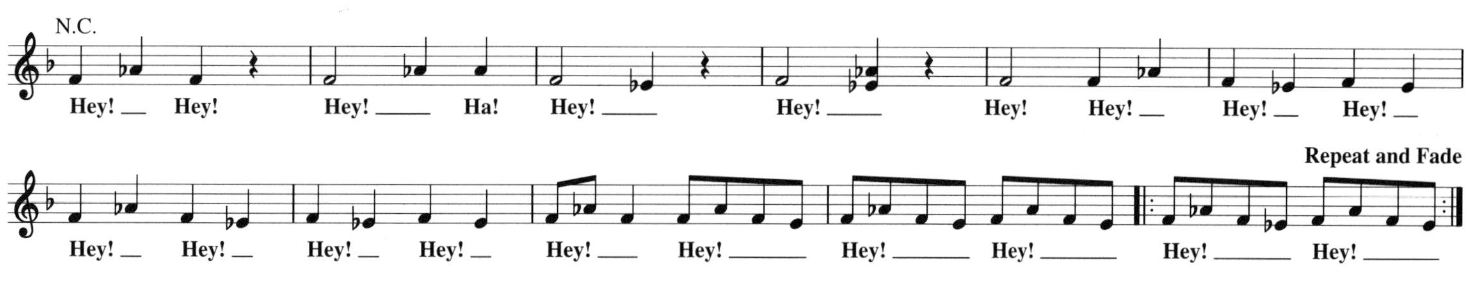

ROCK AND ROLL ALL NITE

Copyright © 1975, 1977 by Cafe Americana and Hori Productions America, Inc.
All Rights for Cafe Americana in the U.S. Administered by Intersong U.S.A., Inc.
All Rights for Hori Productions America, Inc. Administered by
Universal - PolyGram International Publishing, Inc.
All Rights outside the U.S. excluding Japan Controlled by Universal - PolyGram International Publishing, Inc.

Words and Music by PAUL STANLEY
and GENE SIMMONS

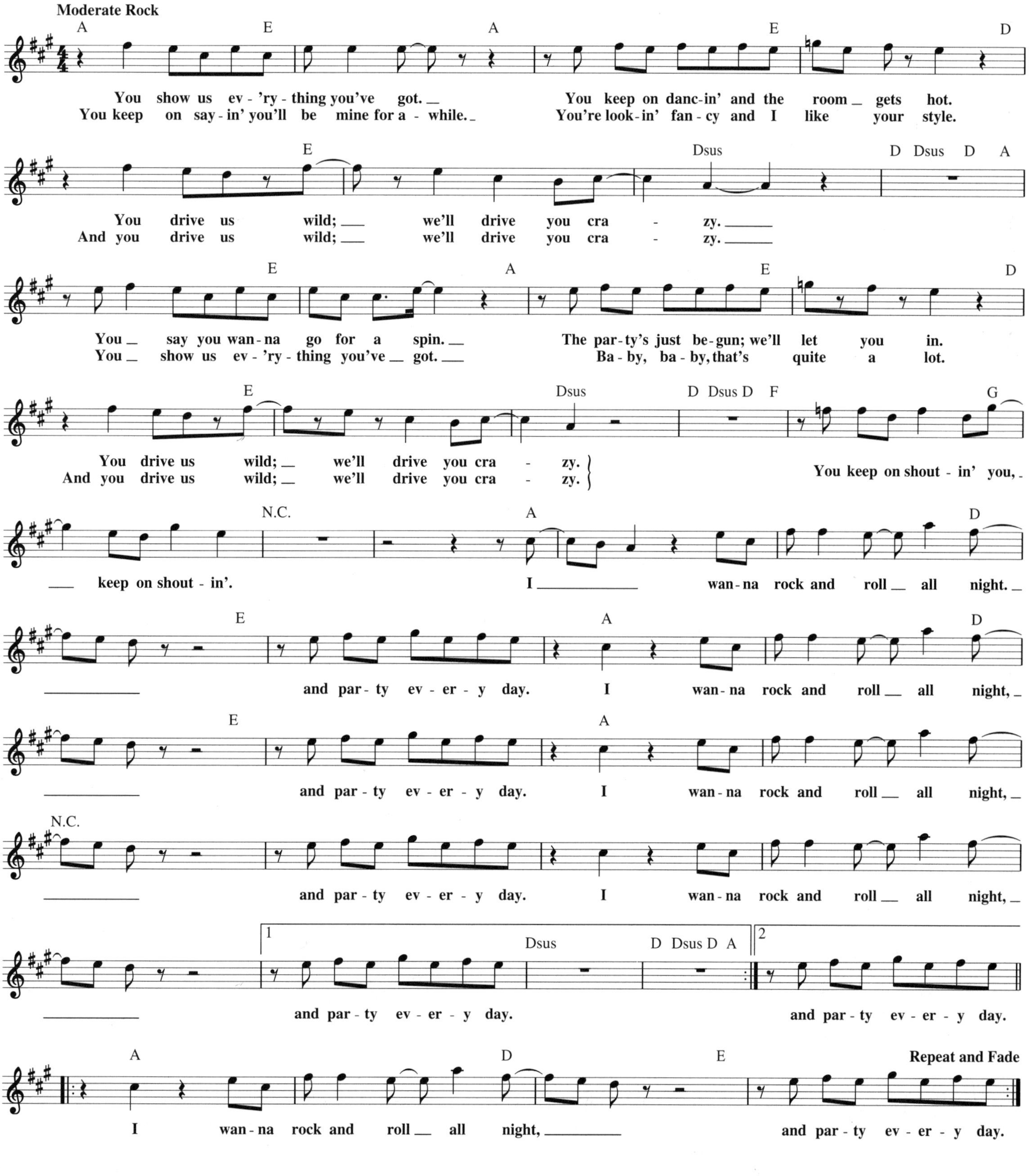

Moderate Rock
A E A E D
You show us ev - 'ry - thing you've got. You keep on danc-in' and the room gets hot.
You keep on say - in' you'll be mine for a - while. You're look-in' fan - cy and I like your style.
E Dsus D Dsus D A
You drive us wild; we'll drive you cra - zy.
And you drive us wild; we'll drive you cra - zy.
E A E D
You say you wan - na go for a spin. The par - ty's just be - gun; we'll let you in.
You show us ev - 'ry - thing you've got. Ba - by, ba - by, that's quite a lot.
E Dsus D Dsus D F G
You drive us wild; we'll drive you cra - zy.
And you drive us wild; we'll drive you cra - zy.
You keep on shout - in' you,
N.C. A D
keep on shout - in'. I wan - na rock and roll all night.
E A D
and par - ty ev - er - y day. I wan - na rock and roll all night,
E A
and par - ty ev - er - y day. I wan - na rock and roll all night,
N.C.
and par - ty ev - er - y day. I wan - na rock and roll all night,
1 Dsus D Dsus D A 2
and par - ty ev - er - y day. and par - ty ev - er - y day.
A D E
Repeat and Fade
I wan - na rock and roll all night, and par - ty ev - er - y day.

ROCKIN' INTO THE NIGHT

Copyright © 1979 by Fittest Music, Ensign Music Corporation, Easy Action Music and WB Music Corp.
All Rights for Fittest Music Controlled and Administered by Ensign Music Corporation
All Rights for Easy Action Music Administered by WB Music Corp.

Words and Music by FRANK SULLIVAN,
JIM PETERIK and ROBERT GARY SMITH

Steady Rock

G D Em C
Cruis - in' down the mo - tor - way, got my girl by my side.

G D Em Bm
We're both a lit - tle anx - ious, ooo we got love on our mind.

C Em D
Wait - ing, an - ti - ci - pat - ing, for the fire - works in the night.

G F C Em
Well, I swear we were do - in' eight - y when we

F Bb F C Bb G Bb
saw those mo - tel lights. And we were rock - in' in - to the night, rock - in' in -

C G Bb
to the night, oo hoo rock - in'. Rock - in' in - to the night, rock - in' in -

C Bb F C Bb G D Em
to the night, yeah... Out on the back street, tak - ing

C G D Em
love where I can, I found a sweet ma - don - na ooo with a

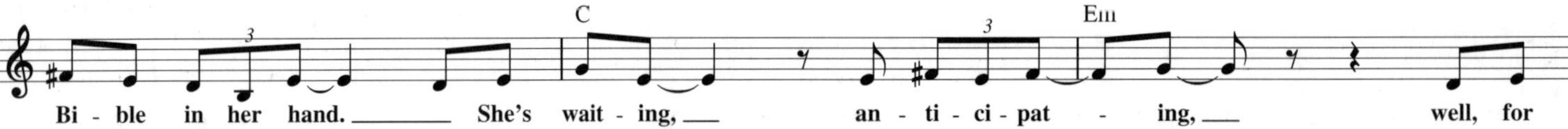

D G F C Em
some-one to save her soul. Well, I ain't no new mes-siah, but I'm
F B♭ F C B♭ G B♭
close e-nough for rock and roll. And we were rock-in' in-to the night, rock-in' in-
1 C 2 C
to the night. We were to the night. And she's
D F B♭ F C B♭ G
pull-in' in yes, she's pull-in' in.
(Instrumental)
D Em C G D Em Bm
C Em D
Wait-ing, an-ti-ci-pat-ing for the fire-works in the night.
G F C Em
Well, I swear we were do-in' eight-y when we
F B♭ F C B♭ G B♭
saw those mo-tel lights. We were rock-in', rock-in' in-to the
C G
night, ooo yeah Rock-in' in-to
B♭ C
Repeat and Fade
the night, rock-in' in-to the night, hoo rock-in'!

ROCK AND ROLL HOOCHIE KOO

Copyright © 1970 by Rick Derringer Music, Inc.
Copyright Renewed
All Rights Administered by Careers-BMG Music Publishing, Inc.

Words and Music by
RICK DERRINGER

ROLL ON DOWN THE HIGHWAY

Copyright © 1974 Sony/ATV Songs LLC
All Rights Administered by Sony/ATV Music Publishing, 8 Music Square West, Nashville, TN 37203

Words and Music by RANDY BACHMAN
and CHARLES TURNER

Driving Rock

D C

We rent-ed a truck and a sem - i to go trav - el down the long and wind - ing road.
Look at the sign, we're in the wrong place. Move out, boys, and let's get read - y to race.

B♭ A7sus A7

Look on the map, I think we've been there be - fore. Close out the door, let's roll once more.
Four fif - ty - four com - ing o - ver the hill. The man on pa - trol is gon - na give us a bill.

D C

Cop's on the cor - ner look, he's start - ing to write. I don't need no tick - et, so I screamed out of sight.
Time's real short, you know the dis - tance is long. I'd like to have a jet, but it's not in the song.

B♭ A7sus A7

Drove so fast that my eyes can't see. Look in the mirror; is he still fol - low - ing me? Let it roll
Climb back in the cab, cross your fin - gers for luck. We got - ta keep mov - ing if we're gon - na make a buck. Let it roll

D G D G

(Instrumental) down the high - way. (Instrumental) Let it roll

D G D B♭ 1 C D

(Instrumental) down the high - way. Roll, roll. (Instrumental)

G/D D G/D D G/D D G/D D

(End instrumental)

2 C D G/D D B♭ 1, 2 C 3 C

(Instrumental)

D C B♭

(1.-3.) (Instrumental solo)
(4.) Let it roll. Let it roll.

Play 4 times 𝄋

A7sus A7 D D G

Let it roll. (1., 2.) (Instrumental solo) (Instrumental)
(3., 4.) Let it roll. down the high -

To Coda ⊕

D G D G D B♭

- way. (Instrumental) Let it roll (Instrumental) down the high - way. Roll,

1 C 2 C D N.C.

roll. Let it roll roll, roll. (Instrumental)

D.S. al Coda

D

Let it roll

CODA

⊕ C D

roll, roll.

ROXANNE

© 1978 G. M. SUMNER
Published by MAGNETIC PUBLISHING LTD. and Administered by
EMI BLACKWOOD MUSIC INC. in the USA and Canada

Written and Composed by
STING

RUN TO YOU

Copyright © 1984 IRVING MUSIC, INC., ADAMS COMMUNICATIONS, INC.,
ALMO MUSIC CORP. and TESTATYME MUSIC
All Rights for ADAMS COMMUNICATIONS, INC. Controlled and Administered by IRVING MUSIC, INC.
All Rights for TESTATYME MUSIC Controlled and Administered by ALMO MUSIC CORP.

Words and Music by BRYAN ADAMS
and JIM VALLANCE

SAY YOU LOVE ME

Copyright © 1976 by Careers-BMG Music Publishing, Inc.

Words and Music by
CHRISTINE McVIE

Brightly

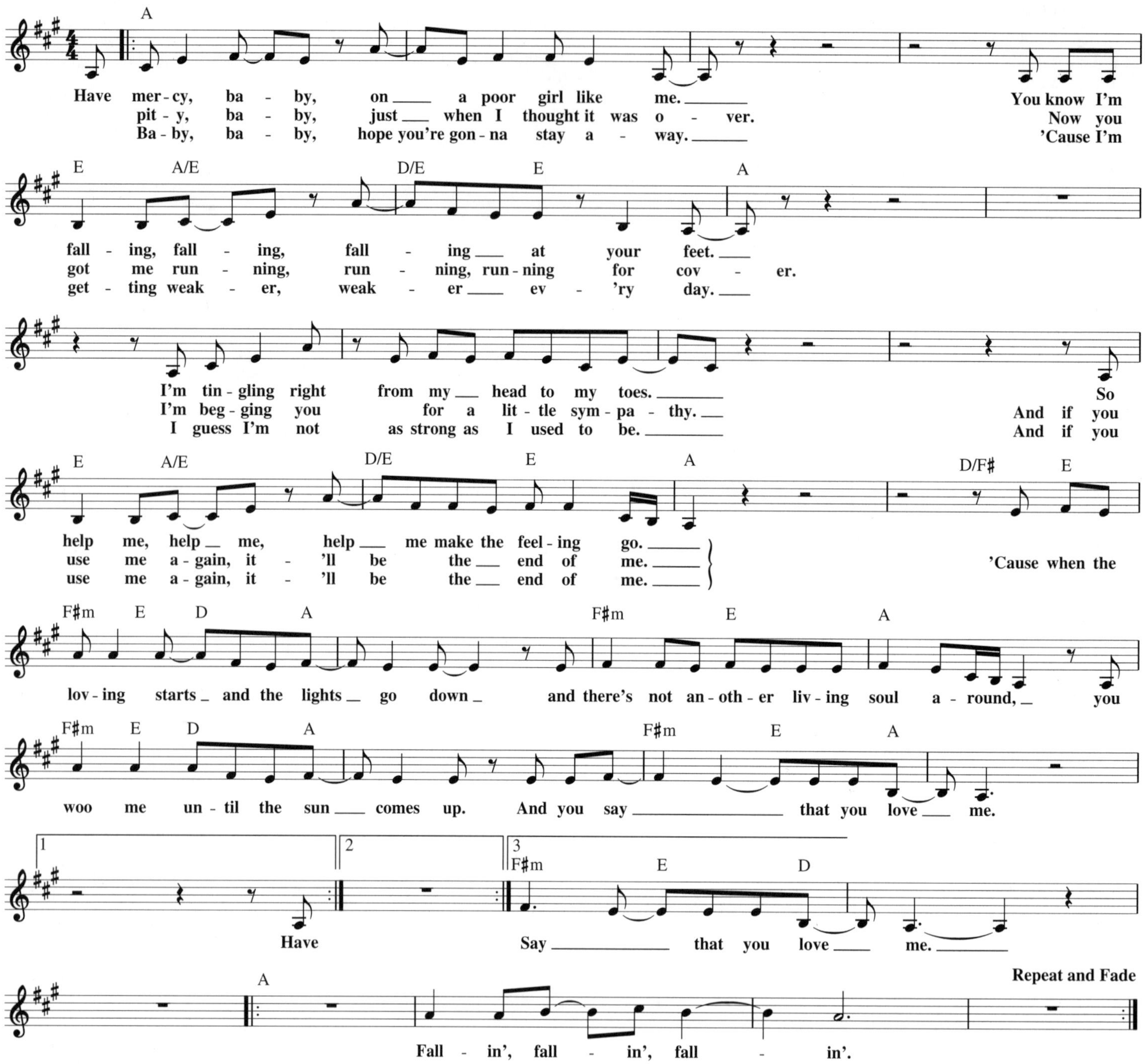

A

Have mer - cy, ba - by, on ___ a poor girl like me. ___ You know I'm
pit - y, ba - by, just ___ when I thought it was o - ver. Now you
Ba - by, ba - by, hope you're gon - na stay a - way. ___ 'Cause I'm

E A/E D/E E A

fall - ing, fall - ing, fall - ing ___ at your feet. ___
got me run - ning, run - ning, run - ning for cov - er.
get - ting weak - er, weak - er ___ ev - 'ry day. ___

I'm tin - gling right from my ___ head to my toes. ___ So
I'm beg - ging you for a lit - tle sym - pa - thy. ___ And if you
I guess I'm not as strong as I used to be. ___ And if you

E A/E D/E E A D/F# E

help me, help ___ me, help ___ me make the feel - ing go. ___
use me a - gain, it - 'll be the ___ end of me. ___
use me a - gain, it - 'll be the ___ end of me. ___
'Cause when the

F#m E D A F#m E A

lov - ing starts ___ and the lights ___ go down ___ and there's not an - oth - er liv - ing soul a - round, ___ you

F#m E D A F#m E A

woo me un - til the sun ___ comes up. And you say ___ that you love ___ me.

1 2 3 F#m E D

Have Say ___ that you love ___ me. ___

A Repeat and Fade

Fall - in', fall - in', fall - in'.

SHAKEDOWN

from the Paramount Motion Picture BEVERLY HILLS COP II

Copyright © 1987 by Famous Music Corporation, Kilauea Music,
Gear Publishing Company and Swindle Music, Inc.
All Rights for Kilauea Music and Gear Publishing Company
Controlled and Administered by Famous Music Corporation

Words and Music by KEITH FORSEY,
HAROLD FALTERMEYER and BOB SEGER

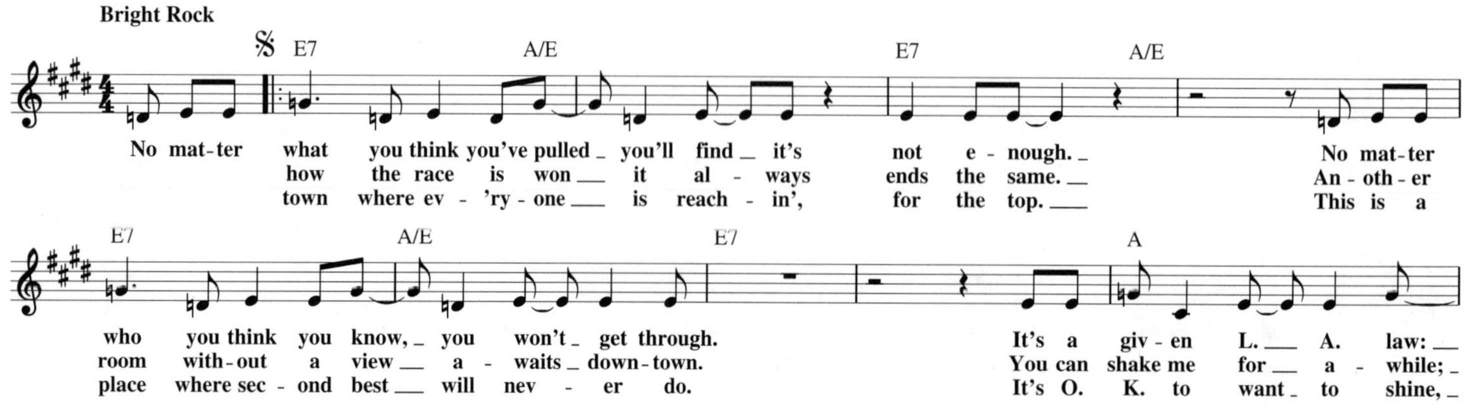
Bright Rock
E7 A/E E7 A/E
No mat - ter what you think you've pulled you'll find it's not e - nough. No mat - ter
how the race is won it al - ways ends the same. An - oth - er
town where ev - 'ry - one is reach - in', for the top. This is a
E7 A/E E7 A
who you think you know, you won't get through. It's a giv - en L. A. law:
room with - out a view a - waits down - town. You can shake me for a - while;
place where sec - ond best will nev - er do. It's O. K. to want to shine,

D/A A7sus G/A D/A E7 A/E
some-one's fas-ter on the draw. No mat-ter where you hide I'm com-in' af-ter you.
live it up in style. No mat-ter what you do I'm going to take you down.
but once you step a-cross that line, no mat-ter where you hide I'm com-in' af-ter you.
To Coda
1
E7 A/E E7
(Instrumental)
No mat-ter
2
E7
Shake-down, break-down, take-down; eve-ry-bod-y wants in-to the crowd-ed light.
G A E7
Break-down, take-down; you're bust-ed. Let down your
D E7 D E7 D
guard, hon-ey, just a-bout the time you think that it's al-right. Break-down, take-down; you're bust-
E7 A/E E7 A/E E7
-ed.
(Instrumental)
A/E E7 A/E E7
D.S. al Coda
This is the
CODA
E7
Shake-down; break-down, take-down; eve-ry-bod-y wants in-to the
crowd-ed light. Break-down, take-down; you're bust-ed.
G A E7 D E7
Shake-down, break-down;
Let down your guard,
hon-ey, just a-bout the time you think that
Repeat and Fade
D E7 D E7 G A
it's al-right. Break-down, take-down; you're bust-ed.

SHATTERED

© 1978 EMI MUSIC PUBLISHING LTD.
All Rights for the U.S. and Canada Controlled and Administered by COLGEMS-EMI MUSIC INC.

Words and Music by MICK JAGGER
and KEITH RICHARDS

E5 B5 E5 B5
What does it mat - ter? does it mat - ter?
Uh huh, does it mat - ter? Uh huh, I'm a - shat - tered.
E5 B5 E5 B5
Mm. I'm, shat - tered. Huh! Sung: Sha - doo - bee. Spoken: Shat - tered.
E5 B5 E5
Sung: Sha - doo - bee. Shat - tered. Shat - tered. Spoken: Don't you know the crime rate's go - in'
Tough, tough, tough, tough, tough, tough, tough!
B5 E5 B5
up, up, up, up, up? To live in this town you must be
We got rats on the West Side, bed - bugs up - town.
E5 B5 E5
What a mess! This town's in tat - ters. I been shat - tered. Uh
My brain's been bat - tered, splat - tered all o - ver Man - hat - tan.
B5 E5 B5 E5
huh. What say? Sung: Sha - doo - bee. Shat - tered. Sha - doo - bee.
B5 E5 B5 E5
Spoken: Uh, huh. This town's full of mon - ey grab - bers. Go a -
head! Bite the Big Ap - ple. Don't mind the mag - gots! Uh huh.
B5 E5 B5
Shat - tered. Sha - doo - bee. My brain's been bat - tered!
E5 B5 E5
My fam - 'ly come a - round 'n' flat - ter, flat - ter, flat - ter, flat - ter, flat - ter, flat - ter, flat - ter.
B5 E5 B5 E5
Pile it up! Pile it up! Pile it high on the plat - ter!

SHE CAME IN THROUGH THE BATHROOM WINDOW

Copyright © 1969 Sony/ATV Songs LLC
Copyright Renewed
All Rights Administered by Sony/ATV Music Publishing, 8 Music Square West, Nashville, TN 37203

Words and Music by JOHN LENNON
and PAUL McCARTNEY

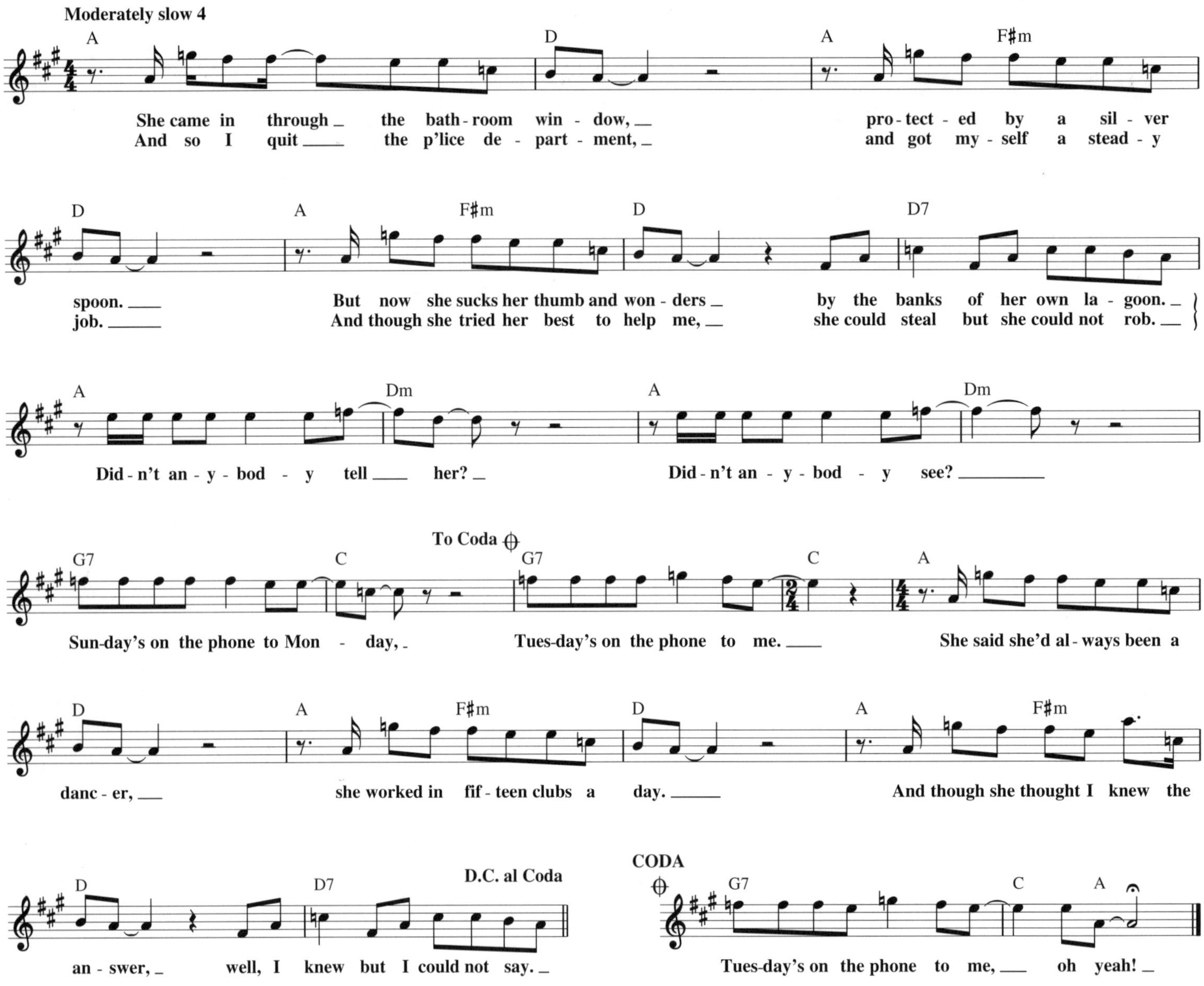

Moderately slow 4

A D A F♯m

She came in through the bath-room win-dow, pro-tect-ed by a sil-ver
And so I quit the p'lice de-part-ment, and got my-self a stead-y

D A F♯m D D7

spoon. But now she sucks her thumb and won-ders by the banks of her own la-goon.
job. And though she tried her best to help me, she could steal but she could not rob.

A Dm A Dm

Did-n't an-y-bod-y tell her? Did-n't an-y-bod-y see?

To Coda ⊕

G7 C G7 C A

Sun-day's on the phone to Mon-day, Tues-day's on the phone to me. She said she'd al-ways been a

D A F♯m D A F♯m

danc-er, she worked in fif-teen clubs a day. And though she thought I knew the

D D7 D.C. al Coda

an-swer, well, I knew but I could not say.

CODA

⊕ G7 C A

Tues-day's on the phone to me, oh yeah!

SHE'S ALWAYS A WOMAN

© 1977, 1978 IMPULSIVE MUSIC

Words and Music by
BILLY JOEL

Eb Bb Eb Ab Abmaj7
love, she can take you or leave you she can ask for the truth but she'll nev - er be -
Ab6 Ab Bb7 Eb Bb7 G
lieve you. And she'll take what you give her as long as it's free yeah, she
Cm Cm/Bb Ab6 Bb7 Eb Ebsus Eb Eb/D Cm Cm/Bb F7/A F7
steals like a thief but She's Al - ways A Wom - an to me. Oh she takes care of her -
Bb Bb/A Gm Eb Ab Ab/G Fm Bb7 Eb Ab/Eb Eb
self she can wait if she wants, she's a - head of her time.
Ebm Ebm/Db Cdim Ab Db Db/C Bbm Gb6 Cb Cb/Bb Adim7 F7
Oh and she nev - er gives out and she nev - er gives in, she just chang - es her
Bb Bb6 Bb7 Eb Bb Eb Eb7
mind.
And she'll prom - ise you more than the gar - den of E - den. Then she'll care - less - ly
She is fre - quent - ly kind and she's sud - den - ly cru - el. She can do as she
Ab Abmaj7 Ab6 Ab Bb7 Eb Bb7 G To Coda
cut you and laugh while you're bleed - in'. But she brings out the best and the worst you can be blame it
pleas - es she's no - bod - y's fool. But she can't be con - vict - ed she's earned her de - gree and the
Cm Cm/Bb Ab6 Bb7 Eb Ebsus Eb Bb
all on your - self 'cause She's Al - ways A Wom - an to me. Hum
D.S. al Coda
Eb Bb G Cm Cm/Bb Ab6 Bb7 Eb Ebsus Eb Eb/D
Hum
CODA
Cm Cm/Bb Ab Eb Fm Bb7
most she will do is throw shad - ows at you but She's Al - ways A Wom - an to
Eb Ebsus Eb Bb Eb Bb7 G Cm Cm/Bb Ab6 Bb7 Eb Ebsus Eb
me. Hum Hum

SHE'S GOT A WAY

© 1971 (Renewed 1999) IMPULSIVE MUSIC

Words and Music by
BILLY JOEL

SHOW ME THE WAY

Copyright © 1975 ALMO MUSIC CORP. and NUAGES ARTISTS MUSIC LTD.
All Rights Administered by ALMO MUSIC CORP.

Words and Music by
PETER FRAMPTON

SHE'S SO COLD

© 1980 EMI MUSIC PUBLISHING LTD.
All Rights for the U.S. and Canada Controlled and Administered by COLGEMS-EMI MUSIC INC.

Words and Music by MICK JAGGER
and KEITH RICHARDS

CODA
G C F G
you was a beau - ty, a sweet, sweet, beau - ty, a sweet, sweet beau - ty, but stone, stone cold. You're so cold, you're so
C F G C
cold, cold, cold. You're so cold, you're so cold. I'm so hot for you, I'm so hot for you,
F G C F G
Repeat and Fade
I'm so hot for you, and you're so cold. I'm the burn - ing bush, I'm the burn - ing fire, I'm the bleed - ing vol - ca - no.

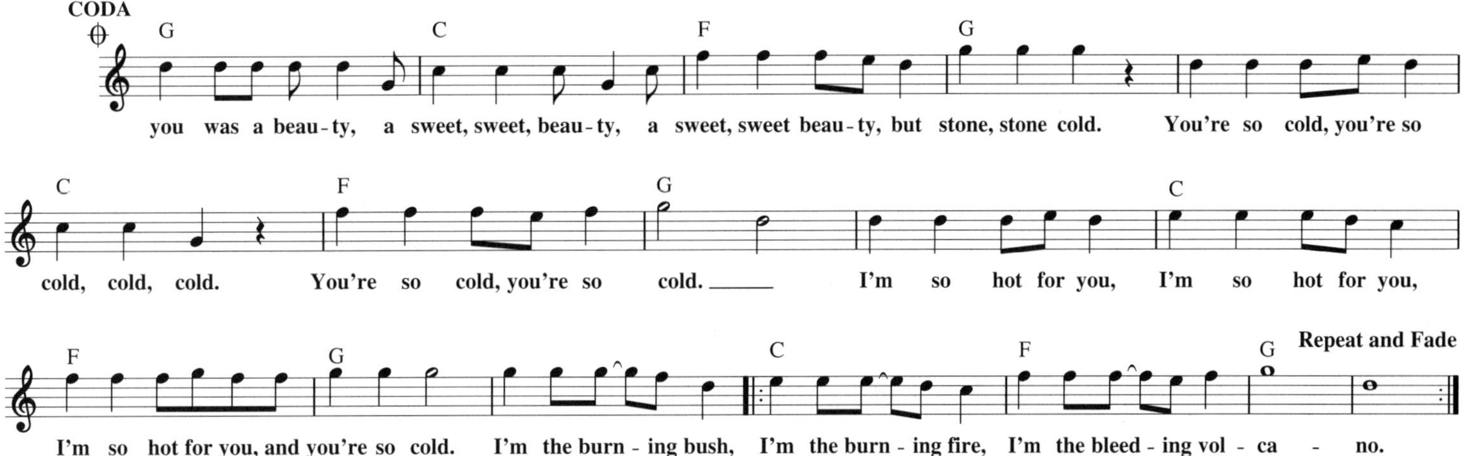

SO YOU WANT TO BE A ROCK AND ROLL STAR

Copyright © 1966; Renewed 1994 Songs Of DreamWorks (BMI) and Sixteen Stars Music (BMI)
Worldwide Rights for Songs Of DreamWorks Administered by Cherry River Music Co.

Words and Music by ROGER McGUINN
and CHRIS HILLMAN

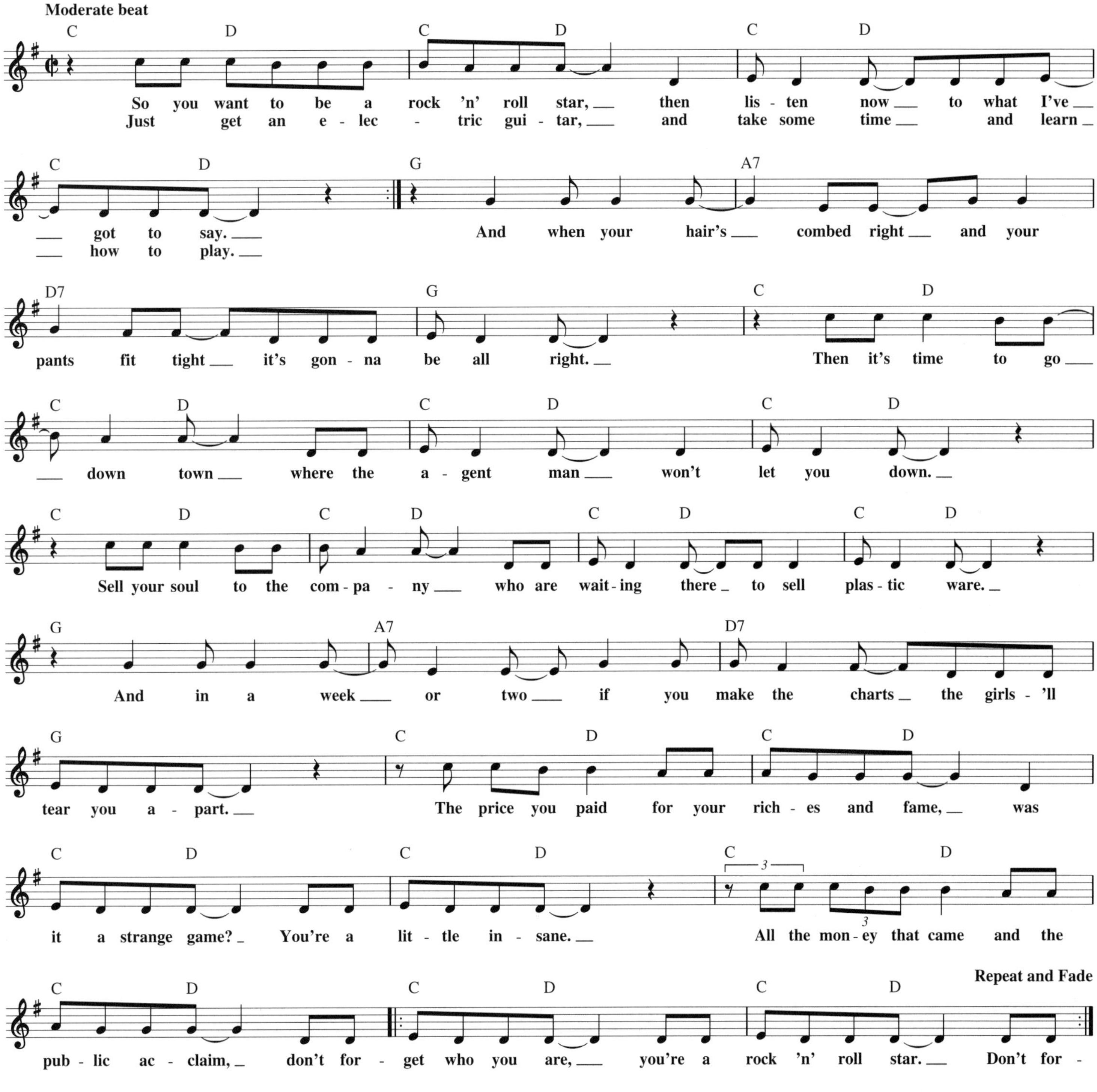

Moderate beat
C D C D C D
So you want to be a rock 'n' roll star, then lis - ten now to what I've
Just get an e - lec - tric gui - tar, and take some time and learn
C D G A7
got to say. And when your hair's combed right and your
how to play.
D7 G C D
pants fit tight it's gon - na be all right. Then it's time to go
C D C D C D
down town where the a - gent man won't let you down.
C D C D C D C D
Sell your soul to the com - pa - ny who are wait - ing there to sell plas - tic ware.
G A7 D7
And in a week or two if you make the charts the girls - 'll
G C D C D
tear you a - part. The price you paid for your rich - es and fame, was
C D C D C D
it a strange game? You're a lit - tle in - sane. All the mon - ey that came and the
C D C D C D
Repeat and Fade
pub - lic ac - claim, don't for - get who you are, you're a rock 'n' roll star. Don't for -

SIGN OF THE GYPSY QUEEN

Copyright © 1972 IRVING MUSIC OF CANADA LTD.
Copyright Renewed
All Rights Administered by IRVING MUSIC, INC.

Words and Music by
LORENCE HUD

Moderate Rock

Em D(add9) Am C

Light - ning smokes on the hill rise; brought the man with the warn - in' light,
Get my sad - dle and tie it on West - ern Wind, who is fast and strong.
Shad - ows mov - in' with - out a sound from the hold of his sleep - less town.

Em D(add9) Am C

shout - in' loud, "You had bet - ter fly while the dark - ness can help you hide."
Jump on back, he is good and long; we'll re - sist till he reach the dawn.
E - vil seems to be ev - 'ry - where; heed the spir - it that brought de - spair.

Em D(add9) Am C **To Coda**

Trou - bles com - in' with - out con - trol; no one's stay - in' who's got a hope.
Run - nin' seems like the best de - fense; stay - in' just don't make an - y sense.
Trou - bles com - in' with - out con - trol; no one's stay - in' who's got a hope.

Em D(add9) Am C

Hur - ri - cane at the ver - y least, in the words of the Gyp - sy Queen.
No one could ev - er stop it now; show the cards of the gyp - sy town.

N.C. Em D Am C

(Instrumental) Sign of the Gyp - sy Queen; pack your things and leave.

Em D Am C | 1 Em D(add9)

Word of a wom - an who knows: "Take all your gold and you go."

Am C | 2 Em D Am C Em D

Am C N.C. Em(add9) | 1-7 | 8 **D.C. al Coda**

Instrumental solo, half-time feel *Solo ends*

CODA

Em D(add9) Am C

Hur - ri - cane at the ver - y least. in the words of the Gyp - sy Queen.

N.C. Em D Am

(Instrumental) *Half-time feel ends* Sign of the Gyp - sy Queen; pack your

C Em D Am C **Repeat and Fade**

things and leave. Word of a wom - an who knows; "Take all your gold and you go.".

SO INTO YOU

Copyright © 1977 Sony/ATV Songs LLC
All Rights Administered by Sony/ATV Music Publishing, 8 Music Square West, Nashville, TN 37203

Words and Music by BUDDY BUIE,
DEAN DAUGHTRY and ROBERT NIX

SMOKE ON THE WATER
© 1972 (Renewed 2000) B. FELDMAN & CO. LTD. trading as HEC MUSIC
All Rights for the United States and Canada Controlled and Administered by GLENWOOD MUSIC CORP.
Words and Music by RITCHIE BLACKMORE, IAN GILLAN, ROGER GLOVER, JON LORD and IAN PAICE
Moderate Rock
N.C.(G5)
(C5) (Bb5)
1–5 (G5)
6 (G5)
(Instrumental)
(End instrumental) We
G5 F5 G5
all came out to Mon - treux on the Lake Ge - ne - va shore - line
They burned down the gam - bling house, it died with an aw - ful sound.
We end - ed up at the Grand Ho - tel, it was emp - ty, cold and bare. But with the
F5 G5
to make rec - ords with the mo - bile, we did - n't have much time.
A funk - y Claude was run - ning in and out, pull - ing kids out the ground.
Roll in Truck Stones thing just out - side, mak - ing our mu - sic there. With a
F5 G5
But Frank Zap - pa and the Moth - ers were at the best place a - round.
When it all was o - ver, we had to find an - oth - er place.
few red lights, a few old beds we made a place to sweat.
F5 G5
But some stu - pid with a flare gun burned the place to the ground.
But Swiss time was run - ning out. it seemed that we would lose the race.
No mat - ter what we get out of this, I know I know we'll nev - er for - get.
C Ab5 G5 C5 Ab5
Smoke on the wa - ter, a fire in the sky. Smoke on the wa - ter.
1, 2
N.C.(G5) (C5) (Bb5) (G5) (C5) (Bb5) (G5)
(Instrumental)
(End instrumental)
3
N.C.(G5) (C5) (Bb5) (G5)
D.C. and Fade
(C5) (Bb5) (G5)
(Instrumental)
(SHE'S) SOME KIND OF WONDERFUL
Copyright © 1967 by Dandelion Music Company
Copyright Renewed
Words and Music by JOHN ELLISON
Moderate Rock Shuffle
D
I don't need a whole lot's of mon - ey. I don't need
her in my arms you know she
a big fine car. I got ev - 'ry - thing that a
sets my soul on fire. Ooh when my ba - by kiss -
man could want. I got more then I could ask for.
es me my heart be - comes filled with de - sire. When she

G7
I, I don't _ have to run a - round. I don't have ___ to stay out all night.
wraps her lov - in' arms ___ a - round ___ me it 'bout drives me out of my mind. _
D
'Cause I got me a sweet a sweet lov - in' wo - man and she knows _
Yeah, ___ when my ba - by kiss - es me _ chills ___
A
___ just how to treat me right. ___
___ run up and down ___ my spine. ___
Well my ba - by, she's al - right.
G7
Well, my ba - by she's clean out of sight. Don't you know that she's, know that she is,
D G D G
she's some kind of won - der - ful. She's some kind of won - der - ful. Yeah, she is,
D G 1 D
she's, she's some kind of won - der - ful. Yeah, yeah yeah yeah. ___ When I hold _
2 D
yeah. ___ Now is there an - y - bod - y ___ got a sweet _ lit - tle wo-man
like mine? There's got to be some - bod - y ___ got a, got a sweet _ lit - tle wo-man
like mine. Yeah. Now can I get a wit - ness? Can I get a
Bm D6 Bm
wit - ness? Well, can I get a wit - ness? Can I get a wit - ness? Can I get a
D6 Bm
wit - ness? Can I get a wit - ness I'm talk - in', talk - in' 'bout my
D G7 D
Repeat and Fade
ba - by. She's some kind of won-der - ful. Talk-in' 'bout my ba - by. She's some kind of won-der - ful. Talk-in' _ 'bout my

SOMEBODY TO LOVE

© 1976 QUEEN MUSIC LTD.
All Rights Controlled and Administered by BEECHWOOD MUSIC CORP.

Words and Music by
FREDDIE MERCURY

Moderate 4

𝄋

Ab Eb/G Fm Ab Bb Eb7

Each morn - ing I get up, I die a lit - tle, can't bare - ly stand on my feet. Take a

(D.S.) *(Instrumental)*

Ab Eb/G Fm Bb7 Eb7

look in the mir - ror and cry. Lord, what you're do - ing to me. I have

To Coda ⊕

Ab Bb7 Eb Bb7/D Eb Db

spent all my years in be - liev - ing you, but I just can't get no re - lief, Lord.

down on my knees and I start to pray 'till the tears run down from my eyes, Lord.

(Instrumental continues) *(End instrumental)*

Ab Eb7/G Fm7 Dbmaj7

Some - bod - y, some - bod - y, can an - y - bod - y find me

1

Eb(N.C.) Ab Ab/G Fm Db

some - bod - y to love? *(Instrumental)*

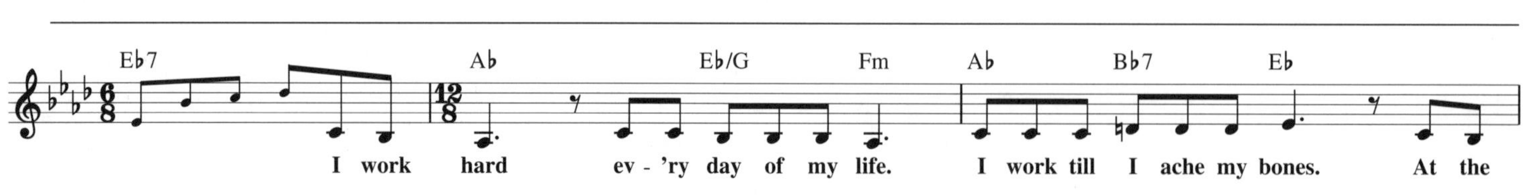
Eb7 Ab Eb/G Fm Ab Bb7 Eb
I work hard ev - 'ry day of my life. I work till I ache my bones. At the

Ab Eb/G Fm Bb7 Eb7
end I take home my hard earned pay all on my own. I get

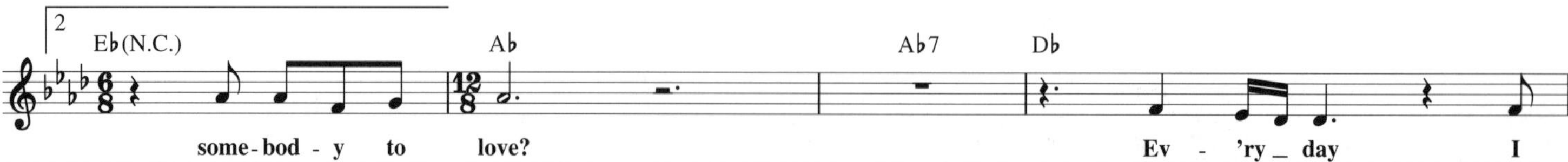
2
Eb(N.C.) Ab Ab7 Db
some - bod - y to love? Ev - 'ry day I

Gb
4 4
try and I try and I try, but ev - 'ry - bod - y wants to put me down, they

Gbm
say I'm go - in' cra - zy.
Bb7
They say I got a lot of wat - er in my brain, got
no com-mon sense. I got no - bod-y left to be - lieve.
Eb7
Ab/Eb
Yeah, yeah, yeah, yeah.
D.S. al Coda
CODA
Ab
Ooh, some - bod - y, some - bod - y, can an - y - bod - y find me
Eb7/G
Fm7
Dbmaj7
Eb(N.C.)
Eb7
some - bod - y to love?
Ab/G
(Instrumental)
Fm
Got no feel, I got no rhy - thm, I just keep los - ing my beat. I'm
Eb7/G
O. K., I'm al - right, ain't gon - na face no de - feat. I just
Eb/G
got - ta get out of this pris - on cell, one day I'm gon - na be free, Lord.
Eb
Bb7/D
Db
Repeat ad lib.
Find me some - bod - y to love. Some - bod - y, some - bod - y, some - bod - y, some - bod - y,
some - bod - y, find me some - bod - y, find me some - bod - y to love. Can
Eb/Ab
Db/Ab
an - y - bod - y find me some - bod - y to
N.C.
love? Find me some - bod - y to
1,2
3
love! Find me love! Find me, find me, find me, find me.
Ab(N.C.)

SOMEBODY TO LOVE

Copyright © 1967 IRVING MUSIC, INC.
Copyright Renewed

Words and Music by
DARBY SLICK

SORRY SEEMS TO BE THE HARDEST WORD

Copyright © 1976 by Big Pig Music Ltd.
All Rights for the United States Administered by Intersong U.S.A., Inc.

Words and Music by ELTON JOHN
and BERNIE TAUPIN

SOMEONE SAVED MY LIFE TONIGHT

Copyright © 1975 by Big Pig Music Ltd.
All Rights for the United States Administered by Intersong U.S.A., Inc.

Words and Music by ELTON JOHN
and BERNIE TAUPIN

Em C/G Em
Some-one saved my life _ to-night, _ some-one saved my life _ to-night, _ some-one saved my life _ to-night, _
C Em C/G
Some-one saved my life _ to-night, _ some-one saved my life _ to-night, _ so save your strength _ and run the field, you
A7 D.S. al Coda
play a-lone. _
CODA
G C Repeat and Fade
Some-one saved, some-one saved, some-one saved my life _ to-night. _
SOMETHING
© 1969 HARRISONGS LTD.
Copyright Renewed 1998
Words and Music by
GEORGE HARRISON
Slowly
F Eb G7/D C Cmaj7 C7
(Instrumental)
Some-thing in _ the way _ she moves, _ at-tracts _ me like _ no oth-er lov -
Some-thing in _ her smile _ she knows, _ that I _ don't need _ no oth-er lov -
Some-thing in _ her way _ she knows, _ and all _ I have _ to do is think _
F C/E D7 G Am7 G7/B
- er. Some-thing in _ the way _ she woos _ me. _
- er. Some-thing in _ her style _ that shows _ me. _
_ of her. Some-thing in _ the things _ she shows _ me. _
I
Am Am/G# Am/G D7/F# To Coda 1 F Eb G7/D 2 F Eb G7/D
don't want to leave _ her now, you know I be-lieve _ and how. _ (Instrumental) (Instrumental)
A C#m/G# F#m F#m/E D G
You're ask-ing me _ will my _ love grow, I don't know _ I _ don't
A C#m/G# F#m F#m/E D G C D.S. al Coda
know. You stick a-round _ now, it may show, I don't know _ I _ don't know.
CODA
F Eb G7/D A F Eb G7/D C
(Instrumental)

SPACE ODDITY

© Copyright 1969 (Renewed) Onward Music Ltd., London, England
TRO - Essex Music International, Inc., New York, controls all publication rights for the U.S.A. and Canada

Words and Music by
DAVID BOWIE

Slowly
C/G Em C/G
Ground Con - trol to Ma - jor Tom. Ground Con - trol to Ma - jor Tom.
Em Am Am/G D/A
Take your pro - tein pills and put your hel - met on.
C/G Em C/G
Ground Con - trol to Ma - jor Tom. Com - menc - ing count - down, en - gines
Em Am Am/G D/A
on. Check ig - ni - tion and may God's love be with you.
N.C. C/G
(Instrumental)
This is Ground Con - trol to Ma - jor Tom,
This is Ma - jor Tom to Ground Con - trol,
E7 F Fm C/G
you've real - ly made the grade. And the pa - pers want to know whose shirts you wear
I'm step - ping though the door. And I'm float - ing in a most pe - cu - liar way.
F 1 Fm C/G F 2 Fm C/G
Now it's time to leave the cap - sule if you dare.
And the stars look ver - y dif - fer - ent to - day.
3
F Fmaj7/C Em7 Fmaj7/C
For here am I sit - ting in a tin can, far a - bove the world
float - ing 'round my moon.

Em7 B♭ Am G
Plan - et Earth is blue, and there's noth - ing I can
To Coda
F C F G A C F G A
do. (Instrumental)
Fmaj7/C Em7 A
C D E
C/G E7 F
Though I'm past one hun - dred thou - sand miles, I'm feel - ing ver - y still And I
Fm C/G F Fm C/G
think my space - ship knows which way to go. Tell my wife I love her ver - y much. She knows.
F G E7 Am Am/G
Ground Con - trol to Ma - jor Tom, your cir - cuit's dead, there's some - thing wrong. Can you
D/A C/G G
D.S. al Coda
hear me Ma - jor Tom? Can you hear me Ma - jor Tom? Can you hear me Ma - jor Tom? Can you..
CODA
Fmaj7/C Em7 A C D E
Repeat and Fade
Guitar solo ad lib.

SPINNING WHEEL

© 1968 (Renewed 1996) EMI BLACKWOOD MUSIC INC. and BAY MUSIC LTD.
All Rights Controlled and Administered by EMI BLACKWOOD MUSIC INC.

Words and Music by
DAVID CLAYTON THOMAS

STAND BACK

Words and Music by
STEVIE NICKS

Copyright © 1983 Welsh Witch Music and Controversy Music
All Rights on behalf of Welsh Witch Music Administered by Sony/ATV Music Publishing,
8 Music Square West, Nashville, TN 37203
All Rights on behalf of Controversy Music Administered by WB Music Corp.

START ME UP

© 1981 EMI MUSIC PUBLISHING LTD.
All Rights for the U.S. and Canada Controlled and Administered by COLGEMS-EMI MUSIC INC.

Words and Music by MICK JAGGER
and KEITH RICHARDS

STATESBORO BLUES

Copyright © 1929 by Peer International Corporation
Copyright Renewed

Words and Music by
WILLY McTELL

Moderate Shuffle

D7 G7 D7

(1., 5.) Wake up, ma - ma, turn your lamp down low.
(2., 4.) *(See additional lyrics)*

G7 D7

Wake up, ma - ma, turn your lamp down low. Ya

A7 G7 D7 To Coda

got no nerve, ba - by to turn Un - cle John from your door.

1,3 A7 | 2 A7 | D7 G7 D7 G7

(Instrumental)

D7 A7 G7 D7 | 1 A7 | 2 A7

(3.) Well, my
(End instrumental)

D7 N.C. D7 N.C.

ma - ma died and left me, my pa - pa died and left me. I

D7 N.C. D7

ain't good look - in', ba - by, but I'm some - one sweet and kind.

G7 D7

I'm goin' to the coun - try, ba - by, do you wan - na go?

A7 G7

Spoken: If you can't make it, baby, *Sung:* your sis - ter Lu - cille said she

D7 A7 D.C al Coda (with repeats) CODA C#13 D13

wan - na go.
Spoken: Well, I sho' nuff tell ya...

Additional Lyrics

2. I woke up this mornin', and I had them Statesboro blues.
I woke up this mornin', and I had them Statesboro blues.
Well, I looked over in the corner, baby.
Your grandpa seem to have them, too.

4. I love that woman better than any woman I've ever seen.
Well, I love that woman better than any woman I've ever seen.
Well, she treat me like a king, yeah, yeah, yeah.
I treat her like a doggone queen.

STRAIGHT FROM THE HEART

© 1981 EMI BLACKWOOD MUSIC INC., PANGOLA PUBLISHING COMPANY and MILENE MUSIC, INC.
All Rights for PANGOLA PUBLISHING COMPANY Controlled and Administered by EMI BLACKWOOD MUSIC INC.

Words and Music by DICKEY BETTS
and JOHNNY COBB

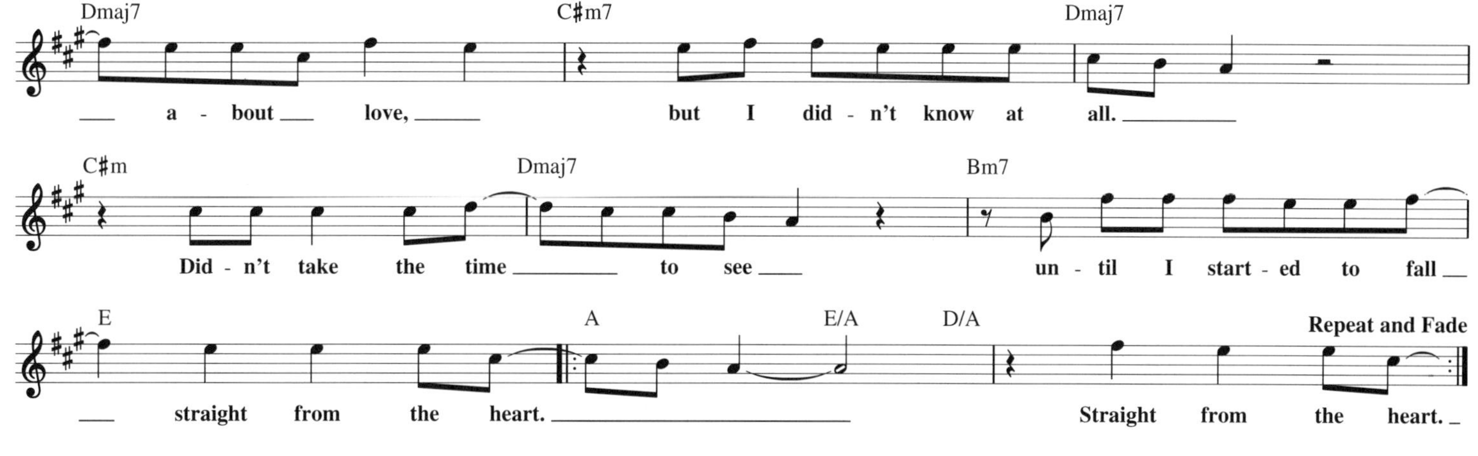

STRAWBERRY FIELDS FOREVER

Copyright © 1967 Sony/ATV Songs LLC
Copyright Renewed
All Rights Administered by Sony/ATV Music Publishing, 8 Music Square West Nashville, TN 37203

Words and Music by JOHN LENNON
and PAUL McCARTNEY

Slowly

A5 Em7 F#7

Let me take you down 'cause I'm go - in' to Straw-ber - ry Fields. Noth - ing is

D E F# Dmaj7 A

real, and noth-ing to get hung a-bout. Straw-ber - ry Fields for - ev - er.

E G#m/D# E7/D Bm7/F# C#7/E# F#m F#m7/E D

Liv - ing is eas - y with eyes closed, mis - un - der - stand - ing all you see.
No one I think is in my tree, I mean it must be high or low.
Al - ways know, some - times think it's me, but you know I know when it's a dream.

E7 A F#m D E

It's get - ting hard to be some - one but it all works out; it does - n't mat - ter much to
That is, you know you can't tune in but it's all right, that is, I think it's not too
I think a "No" will be a "Yes," but it's all wrong, that is, I think I dis - a -

D A Em7

me. / bad. / gree. Let me take you down 'cause I'm go - ing to Straw - ber - ry Fields.

C#dim D E F#

Noth - ing is real, and noth - ing to get hung - a - bout...

1 Dmaj7 A — 2 Dmaj7 A F#m

Straw-ber - ry Fields for - ev - er. Straw-ber - ry Fields for - ev - er,

Dmaj7 A Dmaj7 E D A

Straw-ber - ry Fields for - ev - er, Straw-ber - ry Fields for - ev - er.

SUITE: JUDY BLUE EYES

Copyright © 1970 Gold Hill Music
Copyright Renewed
All Rights Administered by Sony/ATV Music Publishing, 8 Music Square West, Nashville, TN 37203

Words and Music by
STEPHEN STILLS

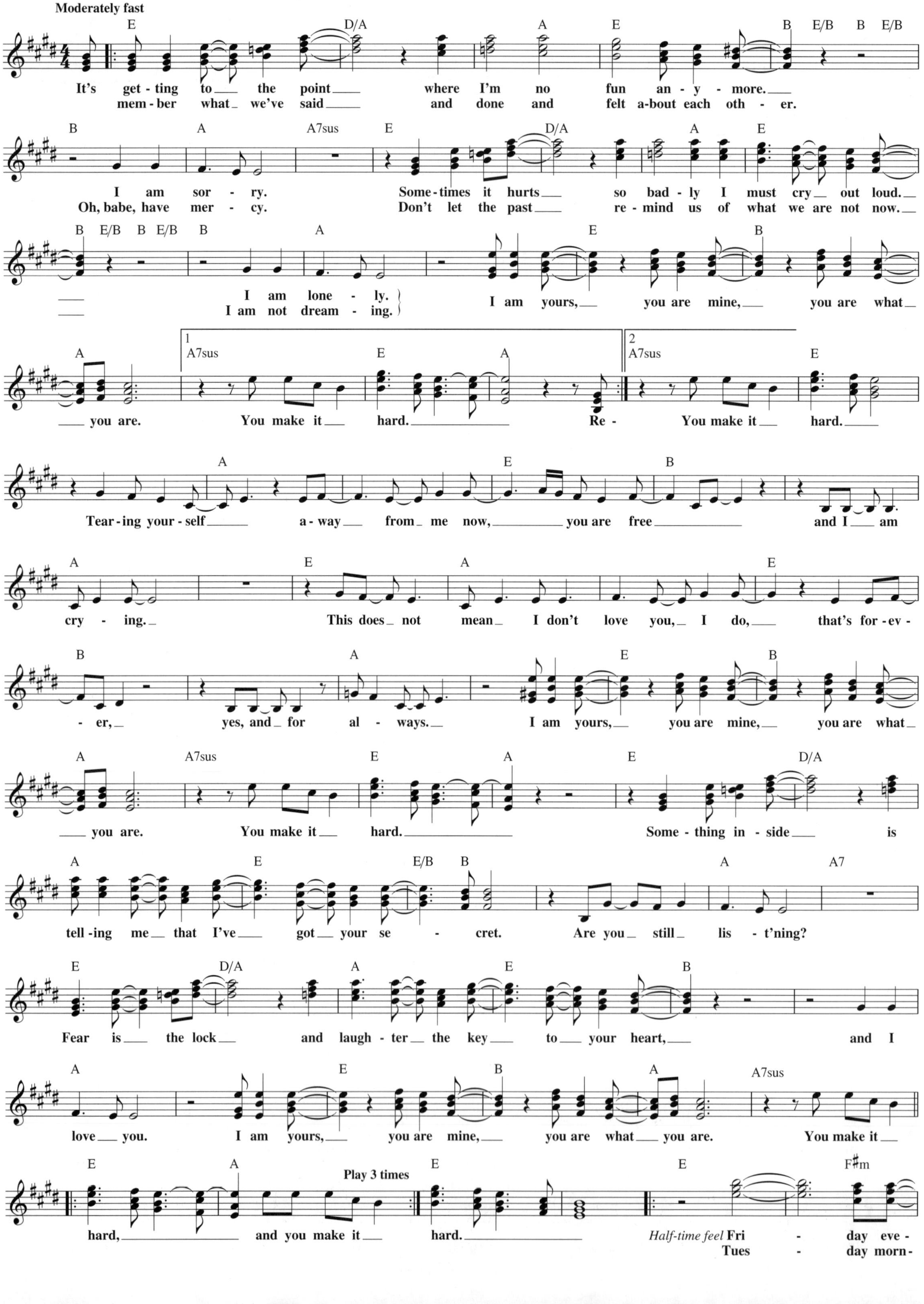
Moderately fast
E D/A A E B E/B B E/B
It's get - ting to the point where I'm no fun an - y - more.
mem - ber what we've said and done and felt a - bout each oth - er.
B A A7sus E D/A A E
I am sor - ry. Some - times it hurts so bad - ly I must cry out loud.
Oh, babe, have mer - cy. Don't let the past re - mind us of what we are not now.
B E/B B E/B B A E B
I am lone - ly.
I am not dream - ing.
I am yours, you are mine, you are what
A 1 A7sus E A 2 A7sus E
you are. You make it hard. Re - You make it hard.
A E B
Tear - ing your - self a - way from me now, you are free and I am
A E A E
cry - ing. This does not mean I don't love you, I do, that's for - ev -
B A E B
er, yes, and for al - ways. I am yours, you are mine, you are what
A A7sus E A E D/A
you are. You make it hard. Some - thing in - side is
A E E/B B A A7
tell - ing me that I've got your se - cret. Are you still lis - t'ning?
E D/A A E B
Fear is the lock and laugh - ter the key to your heart, and I
A E B A A7sus
love you. I am yours, you are mine, you are what you are. You make it
E A E E F#m
Play 3 times
hard, and you make it hard.
Half-time feel Fri - day eve -
Tues - day morn -

E F♯m E F♯m/A E/A A A7
- ning, Sun - day in the af - ter - noon.
- ing, please be gone, I'm tired of you.
A E E5 E5
What have you got to lose? (Instrumental) (Instrumental)
D A D
Can I tell it like it is? But lis - ten to me ba - by. It's my heart
G/A A A7 E
that's a - suf - f'rin'. It's a - dy - in'. And that's what I have to lose. (Instrumental)
E5 E F♯m E
I've got an an - swer. I'm
Will you come see me Thurs -
F♯m E F♯m/A E/A A A7sus A E
go - ing to fly a - way.
- days and Sat - ur - days?
What have I got to lose?
E5 E5 D/E
(Instrumental) (Instrumental) Half time feel ends
Chest - nut - brown ca - nar -
Voic - es of the an -
Lac - y, lilt - ing lyr -
E A/E E7 D/E
- y, ru - by throat - ed spar - row, sing a song, don't be long,
- gels, ring a - round the moon - light, ask - ing me, said she so free,
- ic, los - ing love, la - ment - ing, change my life, make it right,
F♯m/E E A Bm
thrill me to the mar - row.
"How can you catch the spar - row?"
be my la - dy.
Do do do do do, do
F♯m D E A Bm F♯m D E F♯m D E
do do do do do, do do do do do, do do do do. do do do. Que lin -
A Bm F♯m D E A Bm F♯m D E A Bm F♯m D E
- da me la trai - ga Cu - ba, la re - i - na de la
sol no tie - ne san - gre a - hi, y que tris - te que no
A Bm F♯m D E A Bm F♯m D E
Mar - Car - i - be. Cie - lo pue - do va - ya. Oh va! Oh va!
A Bm F♯m D E A Bm F♯m D E F♯m D E
Do do do do do, do do do do do, do do do do do, do do do do, do do do.

SUMMER IN THE CITY

Copyright © 1966 by Alley Music Corp., Trio Music Company, Inc. and Mark Sebastian
Copyright Renewed

Words and Music by JOHN SEBASTIAN,
STEVE BOONE and MARK SEBASTIAN

SUMMER OF '69

Copyright © 1984 IRVING MUSIC, INC., ADAMS COMMUNICATIONS, INC.,
ALMO MUSIC CORP. and TESTATYME MUSIC
All Rights for ADAMS COMMUNICATIONS, INC. Controlled and Administered by IRVING MUSIC, INC.
All Rights for TESTATYME MUSIC Controlled and Administered by ALMO MUSIC CORP.

Words and Music by BRYAN ADAMS
and JIM VALLANCE

SUNSHINE OF YOUR LOVE

Copyright © 1968, 1973 by Dratleaf Ltd.
Copyright Renewed
All Rights Administered by Unichappell Music Inc.

Words and Music by JACK BRUCE,
PETE BROWN and ERIC CLAPTON

SUNSHINE SUPERMAN

Copyright © 1966 by Donovan (Music) Ltd.
Copyright Renewed
All Rights Administered by Peer International Corporation

Words and Music by
DONOVAN LEITCH

SURRENDER

© 1978 SCREEN GEMS-EMI MUSIC INC. and ADULT MUSIC
All Rights Controlled and Administered by SCREEN GEMS-EMI MUSIC INC.

Words and Music by
RICK NIELSEN

Db5 Ab5 Gb5
What - ev - er hap - pened to all this sea - son's los - ers of the year?
Db5 Ab5
Ev - 'ry time I got to think - ing,
Gb5 Db5 Gb5
where'd they dis - ap - pear? When I woke up,
Ab5 Db5
Mom and Dad are roll - ing on the couch.
Gb5 Ab5 Db5
Roll - ing num - bers, rock and roll - ing, got my Kiss rec - ords out.
Db Bbm7
Mom - my's al - right, Dad - dy's al - right, they
Ab5 Gb5 Db
just seem a lit - tle weird. Sur - ren - der, sur - en -
Bbm7 Ab5 Gb5
- der, but don't give your - self a - way,
ay, ay, ay. A - way.
Db
Gb Db Ab5 Db
A - way.
Sur - ren - der, sur - ren -
Repeat and Fade
Bbm7 Ab5 Gb5
- der, but don't give your - self a - way. Sur - ren -

SUSIE-Q

Copyright © 1957 (Renewed) by Arc Music Corporation (BMI)

Words and Music by DALE HAWKINS, STAN LEWIS and ELEANOR BROADWATER

With a beat
Eb
Oh, Su - sie Q, oh, Su - sie Q, oh, Su - sie
Ab7 Eb
Q, how I love you, my Su - sie Q. I like the way you walk,
Ab7
I like the way you talk. I like the way you walk, I like the way you
B7 Bb7 1 Eb N.C. 2 Eb
talk, my Su - sie Q. Oh, Su - sie Q.

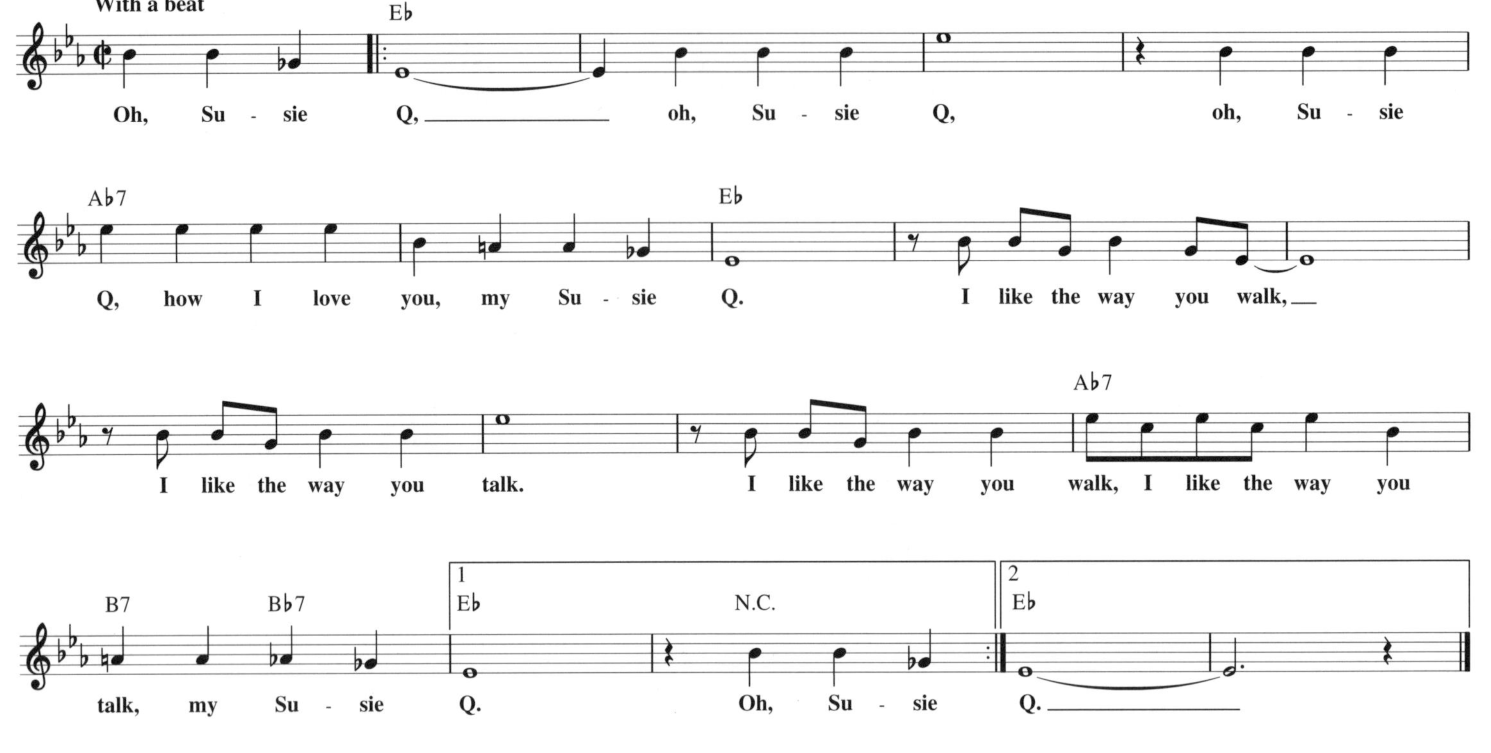

SWEET DREAMS (ARE MADE OF THIS)

Copyright © 1983 by BMG Music Publishing Limited
All Rights for the U.S. Administered by BMG Songs, Inc.

Words and Music by DAVID A. STEWART and ANNIE LENNOX

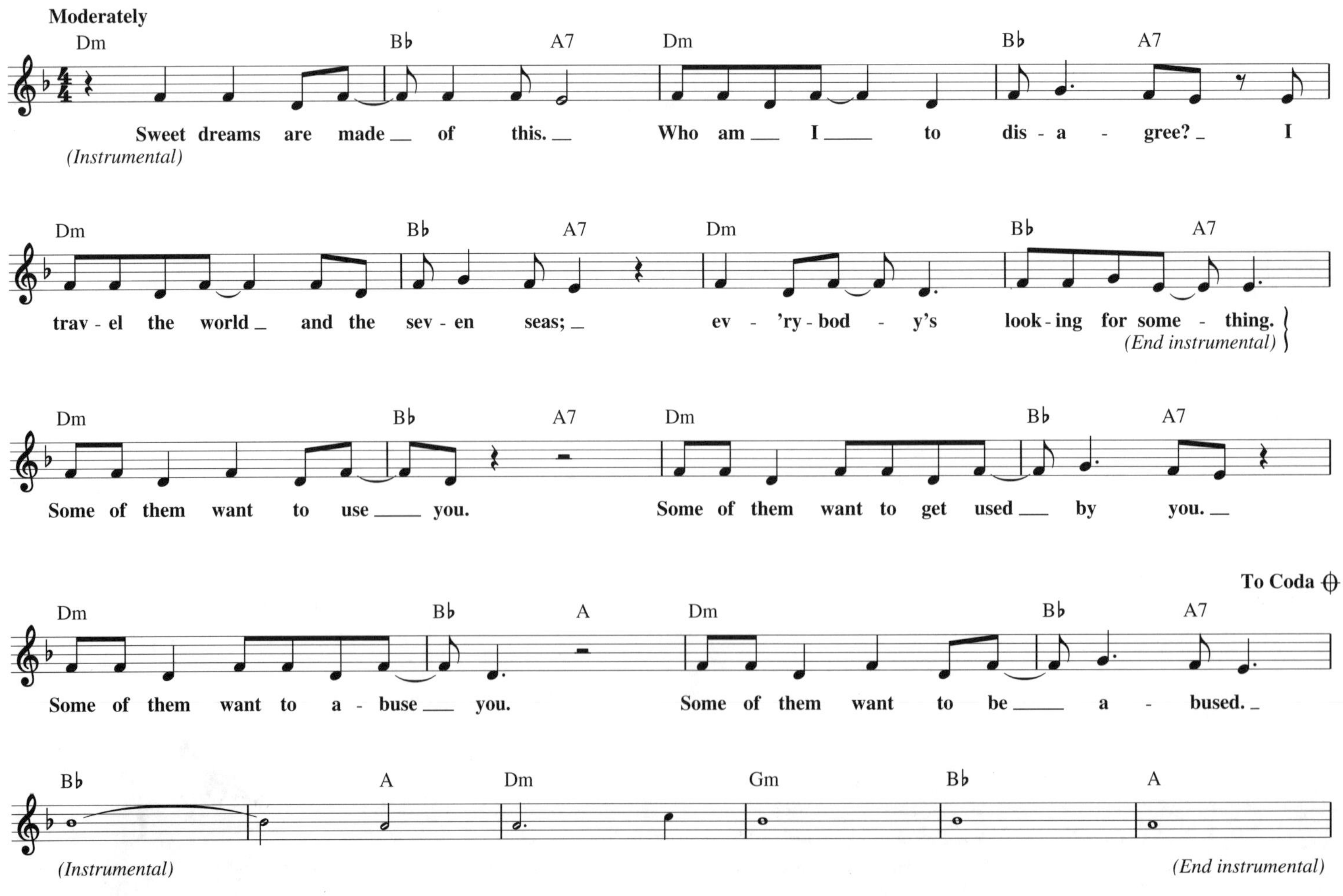

Moderately
Dm Bb A7 Dm Bb A7
Sweet dreams are made of this. Who am I to dis - a - gree? I
(Instrumental)
Dm Bb A7 Dm Bb A7
trav - el the world and the sev - en seas; ev - 'ry - bod - y's look - ing for some - thing.
(End instrumental)
Dm Bb A7 Dm Bb A7
Some of them want to use you. Some of them want to get used by you.
To Coda
Dm Bb A Dm Bb A7
Some of them want to a - buse you. Some of them want to be a - bused.
Bb A Dm Gm Bb A
(Instrumental)
(End instrumental)

Dm Bb A7 Dm Bb A7
Sweet dreams are made of this. Who am I to dis - a - gree? I

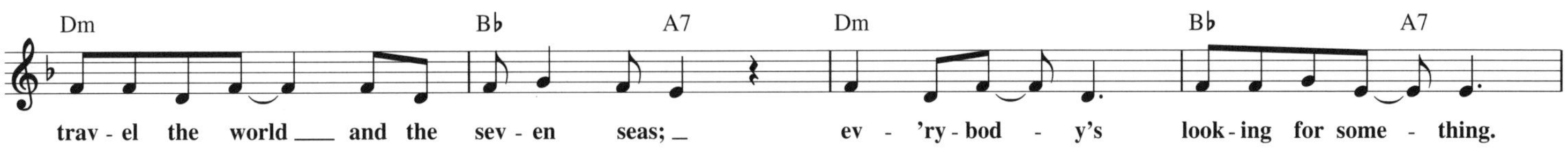
Dm Bb A7 Dm Bb A7
trav - el the world and the sev - en seas; ev - 'ry - bod - y's look - ing for some - thing.

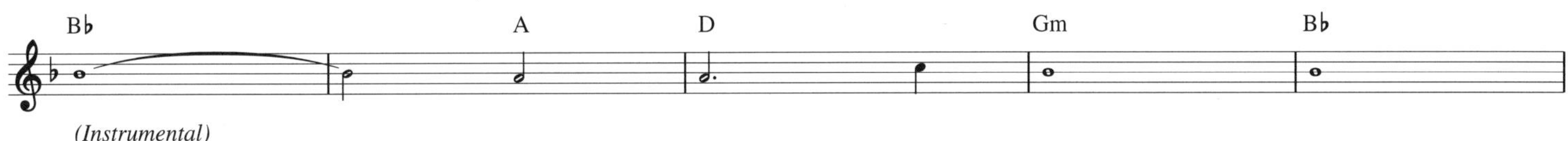
Bb A D Gm Bb
(Instrumental)

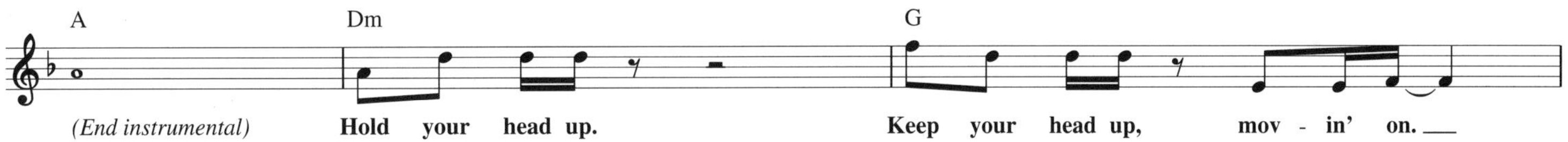
A Dm G
(End instrumental)
Hold your head up. Keep your head up, mov - in' on.

Dm G Dm
Hold your head up, mov - in' on. Keep your head up, mov - in' on. Hold your head up, mov - in' on.

D.C. al Coda
G Dm7 G
Keep your head up, mov - in' on. Hold your head up, mov - in' on. Keep your head up.

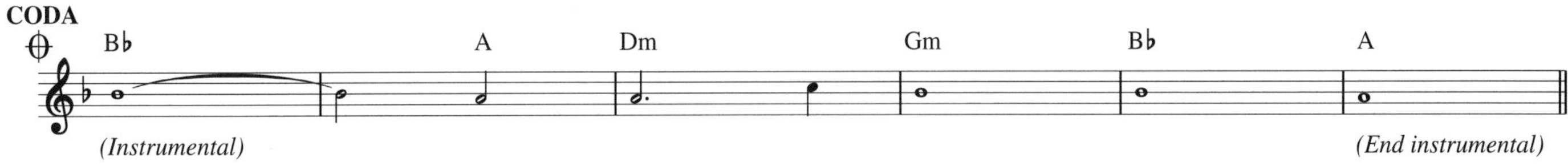
CODA
Bb A Dm Gm Bb A
(Instrumental)
(End instrumental)

Dm Bb A7 Dm Bb A7
Sweet dreams are made of this. Who am I to dis - a - gree? I

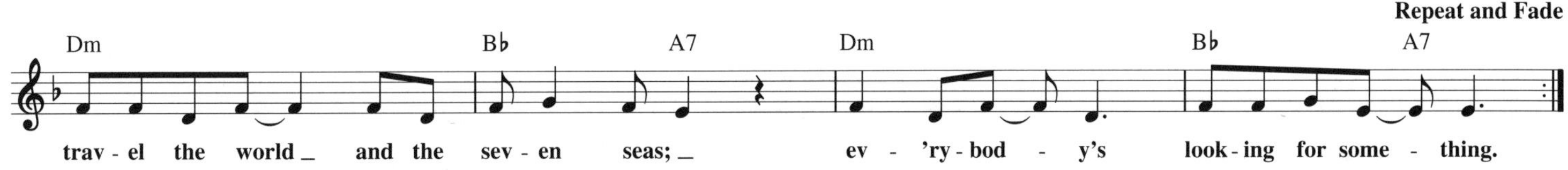
Repeat and Fade
Dm Bb A7 Dm Bb A7
trav - el the world and the sev - en seas; ev - 'ry - bod - y's look - ing for some - thing.

SUSSUDIO

© 1984 PHILIP COLLINS LTD. and HIT & RUN MUSIC (PUBLISHING) LTD.
All Rights Controlled and Administered by EMI APRIL MUSIC INC.

Words and Music by
PHIL COLLINS

SWEET EMOTION

Copyright © 1975 Daksel LLC
All Rights Administered by Sony/ATV Music Publishing, 8 Music Square West, Nashville, TN 37203

Words and Music by STEVEN TYLER
and TOM HAMILTON

SWEET TALKIN' WOMAN

© 1977, 1978 EMI APRIL MUSIC INC.

Words and Music by
JEFF LYNNE

TAKE THE LONG WAY HOME

Copyright © 1979 ALMO MUSIC CORP. and DELICATE MUSIC
All Rights Controlled and Administered by ALMO MUSIC CORP.

Words and Music by RICK DAVIES
and ROGER HODGSON

Moderately

Cm7 Bb/C F/C C

So you think you're a Ro - me - o ___ play - ing a part in a pic - ture show, well take the
When lone - ly days turn to lone - ly nights ___ you take a trip to the cit - y lights, and take the

Bb/C C Cm7 Bb/C

long way home, take the long way home. If you're the joke of the neigh - bor - hood, ___
long way home, take the long way home. You nev - er see what you want to see, ___

F/C C Bb/C C

why should you care if you're feel - ing good, well take the long way home, take the long way home.
for - ev - er play - ing to the gal - ler - y, you take the long way home, take the long way home.

Em7 Em7/D Am Em/G

But there are times that you feel you're part ___ of the scen - er - y, ___ all ___ the
And when you're up on the stage it's so ___ un - be - liev - a - ble, ___ un - for -
Well, does it feel that your life's be - come ___ a ca - tas - tro - phe? ___ Oh, ___ it

F Bb F/A G Em7

green - er - y ___ is com-in' down, ___ boy. And then your wife seems to think you're part ___ of the
get - ta - ble ___ how they a - dore ___ you. But then your wife seems to think you're los - ing your
has to be ___ for you to grow, ___ boy. When you look through the years and see ___ what you

Am Em/G F Bb F/A To Coda

furn - i - ture, ___ oh ___ it's pe - cu - li - ar, ___ she used to be ___ so
san - i - ty, ___ oh ___ it's ca - lam - i - ty, ___ oh is there no ___ way
could have been, ___ oh ___ what you might have been ___ if you had had ___ more

1. G7 2. G7 Eb Bb F C Bb/C 1. C 2. C D.S. al Coda

nice. out? Oh! ___ *Instrumental ad lib.*

CODA

G7 Cm7 Bb/C

time. So, when the day comes to set - tle down ___

F/C C Bb/C

well, who's to blame if you're not a - round? You took the long way home, you took the

Ab/C 1. F/C 2. F/C

long way home. You took the long way home, you took the long way home, you took the

Bb/C F/C F6/C Cmaj9 Play 3 times

long way home, you took the long way home. Ah, ___ ah. ___

Bb/C Ab/C 1. F/C 2. F/C Bb/C

Long way home, ___ long way home, ___ long way home. ___ long way home, ___ long way home. ___

TAKIN' CARE OF BUSINESS

Copyright © 1974 Sony/ATV Songs LLC
All Rights Administered by Sony/ATV Music Publishing, 8 Music Square West, Nashville, TN 37203

Words and Music by
RANDY BACHMAN

D
Dmaj7
G/A
one like I had __ with you. These eyes __
Dmaj7
Gmaj7/A
Dmaj7
are cry - in'. These eyes have seen a lot of love, but they're nev-er gon-na see an-oth-er one like I had _ with
E
Emaj7
A/B
Emaj7
Amaj7/B
you. These eyes __ are cry - in'. These eyes have
Emaj7
seen a lot of love, but they're nev - er gon - na see an - oth - er one like I had __ with
F#
G
D.S. al Coda
you. These
CODA
C
C(add2)
__ it. __
TONIGHT'S THE NIGHT
(Gonna Be Alright)
© 1976 ROD STEWART
All Rights Controlled and Administered by EMI APRIL MUSIC INC.
Words and Music by
ROD STEWART
Moderately slow Rock beat
C
Fmaj7
C
Fmaj7
Stay a - way _ from my win-dow; stay a - way _ from my back door too. __
C
Fmaj7
C
Fmaj7
Dis-con-nect the tel - e - phone _ line; _ re-lax, ba - by, and draw that blind. _
B♭maj7
G7
F/A
G/B
C
Fmaj7
C
(Instrumental)
Kick off your shoes and sit right down _ and loos-en up __ that
Come on, an - gel, my heart's on fire; __ don't de - ny __ your
Don't say a word, my vir-gin child; _ just let your in - hi -
Fmaj7
C
Fmaj7
C
pret-ty French_gown. _ Let me pour_ you a good long drink; _ ooh, ba - by, don't you
man's de - sire. __ You'd be a __ fool to stop this tide; __ spread yours wings and let me
bi-tions run _ wild. __ The se - cret _ is a - bout to un-fold up - stairs __ be-fore the
Fmaj7
C
Fmaj7
C
hes - i - tate. __
come in - side. __
night's too old. __
'Cause to - night's _ the night; __ it's gon-na be __ al -
Am
Dm
F
C
right. 'Cause I __ love you, girl; ain't no - bod - y gon - na stop us now. __
1, 2
G
3
G
C
Fmaj7
Repeat and Fade
(Instrumental)
(Instrumental)

TEARS IN HEAVEN

Copyright © 1992 by E.C. Music Ltd. and Blue Sky Rider Songs
All Rights for E.C. Music Ltd. Administered by Unichappell Music Inc.
All Rights for Blue Sky Rider Songs Administered by Irving Music, Inc.

Words and Music by ERIC CLAPTON
and WILL JENNINGS

THIRTY DAYS IN THE HOLE

Copyright © 1972 ALMO MUSIC CORP. and EMI UNITED PARTNERSHIP LTD.
Copyright Renewed
Rights for EMI UNITED PARTNERSHIP LTD. Assigned to EMI CATALOGUE PARTNERSHIP
All Rights for EMI CATALOGUE PARTNERSHIP in the U.S. and Canada
Controlled and Administered by EMI U CATALOG INC.

Words and Music by
STEVE MARRIOTT

TIME FOR ME TO FLY

Copyright © 1978 Fate Music (ASCAP)

Words and Music by
KEVIN CRONIN

TIME IN A BOTTLE

Copyright © 1971 (Renewed) Time In A Bottle and Croce Publishing (ASCAP)

Words and Music by
JIM CROCE

TUESDAY AFTERNOON
(Forever Afternoon)

© Copyright 1968 (Renewed) and 1970 (Renewed) Tyler Music Ltd., London, England
TRO-Essex Music International, Inc., New York, controls all publication rights for the U.S.A. & Canada

Words and Music by
JUSTIN HAYWARD

TURN ME LOOSE

© 1980 EMI APRIL MUSIC (CANADA) LTD., EMI BLACKWOOD MUSIC (CANADA) LTD., DEAN OF MUSIC and DUKE RENO MUSIC
All Rights in the U.S.A. Controlled and Administered by EMI APRIL MUSIC INC. and EMI BLACKWOOD MUSIC INC.

Words and Music by PAUL DEAN and DUKE RENO

TUMBLING DICE

© 1972 (Renewed 2000) EMI MUSIC PUBLISHING LTD.
All Rights for the U.S. and Canada Controlled and Administered by COLGEMS-EMI MUSIC INC.

Words and Music by MICK JAGGER
and KEITH RICHARDS

Moderate Rock

C F/C C F/C C F/C
Wom - en think I'm tast - y, but they're al - ways try - ing to waste me and make me burn the can - dle right down,

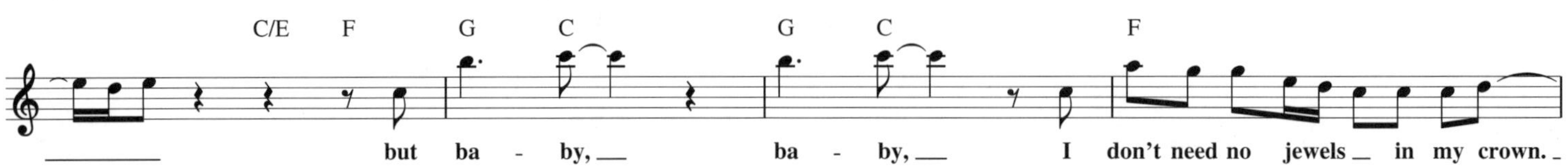
C/E F G C G C F
but ba - by, ba - by, I don't need no jewels in my crown.

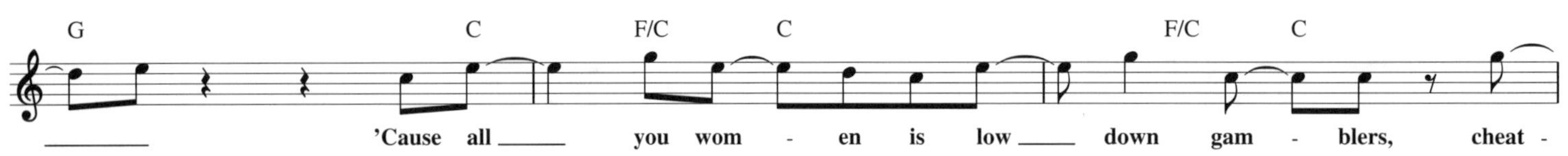
G C F/C C F/C C
'Cause all you wom - en is low down gam - blers, cheat -

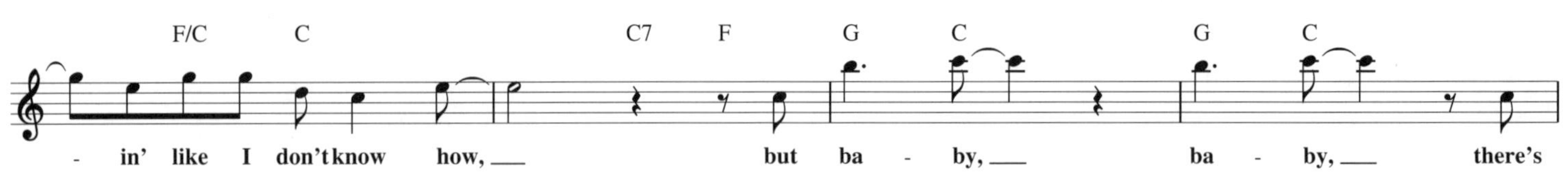
F/C C C7 F G C G C
- in' like I don't know how, but ba - by, ba - by, there's

F G C F/C C
fe - ver in the funk house now. This low down bitch - in' got my

F/C C F/C C C/E F
poor feet a - itch - in', you know, you know the deuce is still wild.

G C G C F N.C.
Ba - by, I can't stay, you got to roll me and call me the tum - blin'

C F/C C F/C C F/C C
dice. Al - ways in a hur - ry, I
F/C C F/C C C7 F
nev - er stop to wor - ry, don't you see the time flash - in' by.
G C G C F
Hon - ey, got no mon - ey, I'm all six - es and sev - ens and nines.
G C F/C C F/C C
Say now, ba - by, I'm the rank out - sid - er, you
F/C C7 F G C G C
can be my part-ner in crime. But ba - by, I can't stay, you got to
F N.C. C F/C C F/C C
roll me and call me the tum - blin', dice. Oh, my,
F/C C F/C C F/C C7 F
my my, I'm the lone crap shoot - er, play - in' the field ev - 'ry night.
G C G C F N.C.
Ba - by, can't stay you got to roll me and call me the tum - blin',
F N.C. F C
Repeat and Fade
dice. Got to roll me. Got to

TWO OUT OF THREE AIN'T BAD

Copyright © 1977 by Edward B. Marks Music Company

Words and Music by
JIM STEINMAN

A D/A A G E
moun-tain of rocks, but there ain't no Coupe de Ville hid - ing at the bot-tom of a Crack-er-jack box.
N.C. C♯m D
(Instrumental) I can't lie. I can't tell you that I'm some-thing I'm not, no
C♯m D
mat-ter how I try. I'll nev-er be a - ble to give you some-thing, some-thing that I just have-n't got.
E A A/C♯ D E7sus
There's on-ly one girl that I will ev-er love, and that was so man-y years a-go.
A A/G♯ F♯m7 D/E
And though I know I'll nev-er get her out of my heart, she nev-er loved me back, ooh
E Esus A A/C♯ D E
I know. I re-mem-ber how she left me on a storm-y night. She kissed me and got out of our bed.
A A/G♯ F♯m7
And though I plead-ed and I begged her not to walk out that door, she
D/E E D/E E
packed her bags and turned right a - way. And she kept on tell - ing me, she
D/E E D/E E A C♯m/G♯ F♯m
kept on tell - ing me, she kept on tell-ing me, "I want you, I need you, but there
D E C♯m F♯m Bm
ain't no way I'm ev - er gon-na love you, now don't be sad, (don't be sad) 'cause
D Fdim7 1 A 2 F♯m Bm
two out of three ain't bad. I bad." Now don't be sad, 'cause
D Fdim7 A A/C♯ D E A
two out of three ain't bad. Ba-by, we can talk all night, but that ain't get-ting us no - where.

TWIST AND SHOUT

Copyright © 1960, 1964 Sony/ATV Songs LLC, Unichappell Music Inc. and Sloopy II Music
Copyright Renewed
All Rights on behalf of Sony/ATV Songs LLC Administered by Sony/ATV Music Publishing, 8 Music Square West, Nashville, TN 37203

Words and Music by BERT RUSSELL
and PHIL MEDLEY

VICTIM OF LOVE

© 1976 EMI APRIL MUSIC INC., LONG RUN MUSIC and FINGERS MUSIC

Words and Music by JOHN DAVID SOUTHER,
DON HENLEY, GLENN FREY and DON FELDER

Moderate Rock

Gm C Gm

What kind of love __ have you got? __ You should be home, _ but you're not. __
Some peo - ple nev - er come clean. __ I think you know _ what I mean. _

B♭ A Gm C

__ A room full of noise __ and dan-ger-ous boys
__ You're walk - in' the wire, __ pain and de - sire,

Gm C Gm

still make you thirst - y and hot. __ I heard a - bout you __ and that man. _
look - in' for love __ in be - tween. __ Tell me your se - crets; I'll tell __

C Gm B♭ A

__ There's just one thing I don't __ un - der - stand. __ You
__ you mine. This ain't no time __ to be cool. __ And

Gm C

say he's a li - ar, and he put out your fire. __ How come you
tell all your girl - friends, your "been a - round the world" friends that

Gm C Gm F Gm7 F/A 𝄋 B♭

still got his gun __ in your hand? __ Vic - tim of love, __ I see a
talk is for los - ers and fools. __ Vic - tim of love, __ I see a
Vic - tim of love, __ you're just a

Gm C B♭ F Gm7 F/A

bro - ken heart. __ You got your sto - ries to tell. __
bro - ken heart. __ I could be wrong, _ but I'm not. __
vic - tim of love. __ I could be wrong, _ but I'm not. __

B♭ B♭/A Gm

Vic - tim of love __ it's such an eas - y part. __ And
Vic - tim of love __ we're not so far __ a - part __ Show me,
Vic - tim of love __ now you're a vic - tim of __ love.

E♭maj7 F — To Coda 𝄌 — 1. Gm — 2. Gm F Gm7 F/A — D.S. al Coda

you know how to play it so well. __
what kind of love __ have you got? _
What kind of love __ have you got? _

CODA 𝄌

Gm E♭maj7 F Gm

What kind of love __ have you got? __

E♭maj7 F Gm

What kind of love __ have you got? __

WALK THIS WAY

Copyright © 1975 Daksel LLC
All Rights Administered by Sony/ATV Music Publishing, 8 Music Square West, Nashville, TN 37203

Words and Music by STEVEN TYLER
and JOE PERRY

C
Play 3 times
A5
To Coda
(Instrumental)
like this!
N.C.
Play 3 times
A5
D.S. al Coda
CODA
N.C.
Repeat and Fade
WE WILL ROCK YOU
© 1977 QUEEN MUSIC LTD.
All Rights Controlled and Administered by BEECHWOOD MUSIC CORP.
Words and Music by
BRIAN MAY
Moderately
Clap Hands
Repeat 4 times
N.C.
Hand clap simile throughout song
Bud - dy you're a boy make a big noise play - in' in the street gon - na be a big man some day you got mud on yo' face you big dis - grace
Bud - dy you're a young man, hard man shout - in' in the street gon - na take on the world some day you got mud on yo' face you big dis - grace
Bud - dy you're an old man, poor man plead - in' with your eyes gon - na make you some peace some day you got mud on your face you big dis - grace. Some -
kick - in' your can all o - ver the place sing - in'
wav - in' your ban - ner all o - ver the place sing - in'
bod - y bet - ter put you back in - to your place sing - in'
we will We Will Rock You,
1, 2
we will We Will Rock You.
3
we will We Will Rock You,
We will We Will Rock You.
We will We Will Rock You.
C
A
(Instrumental)
D
A
D
A
Asus
D
A
Asus
A
Play 3 times

WAITING ON A FRIEND

© 1981 EMI MUSIC PUBLISHING LTD.
All Rights for the U.S. and Canada Controlled and Administered by COLGEMS-EMI MUSIC INC.

Words and Music by MICK JAGGER and KEITH RICHARDS

WE ARE THE CHAMPIONS

© 1977 QUEEN MUSIC LTD.
All Rights Controlled and Administered by BEECHWOOD MUSIC CORP.

Words and Music by
FREDDIE MERCURY

WE CAN WORK IT OUT

Copyright © 1965 Sony/ATV Songs LLC
Copyright Renewed
All Rights Administered by Sony/ATV Music Publishing, 8 Music Square West, Nashville, TN 37203

Words and Music by JOHN LENNON
and PAUL McCARTNEY

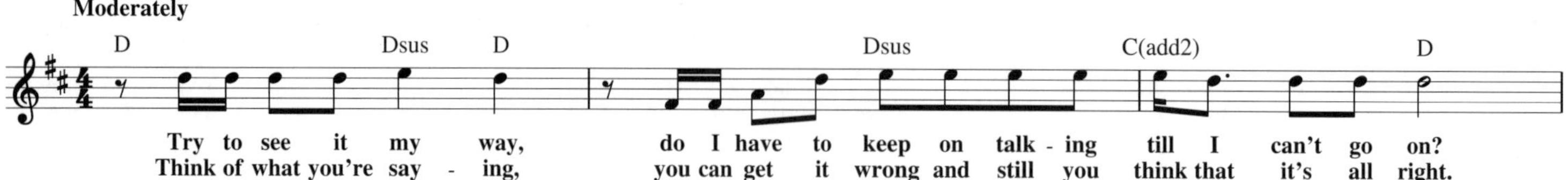
Moderately
D Dsus D Dsus C(add2) D
Try to see it my way, do I have to keep on talk - ing till I can't go on?
Think of what you're say - ing, you can get it wrong and still you think that it's all right.

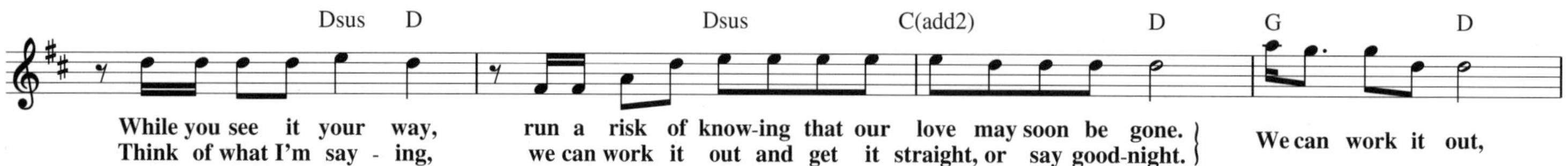
Dsus D Dsus C(add2) D G D
While you see it your way, run a risk of know-ing that our love may soon be gone.
Think of what I'm say - ing, we can work it out and get it straight, or say good-night.
We can work it out,

G Asus A Bm Bm/A Gmaj7
we can work it out. Life is ver - y short and there's no time

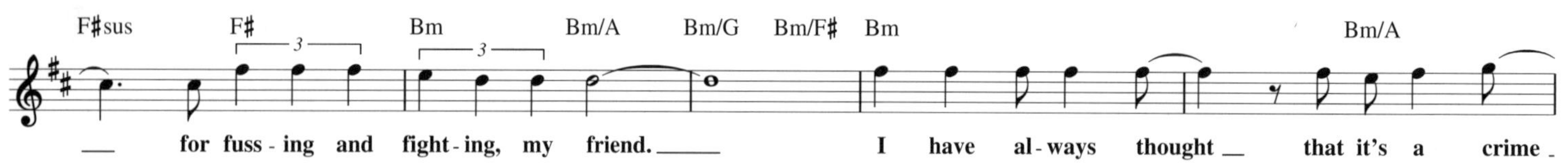
F#sus F# Bm Bm/A Bm/G Bm/F# Bm Bm/A
for fuss - ing and fight - ing, my friend. I have al - ways thought that it's a crime

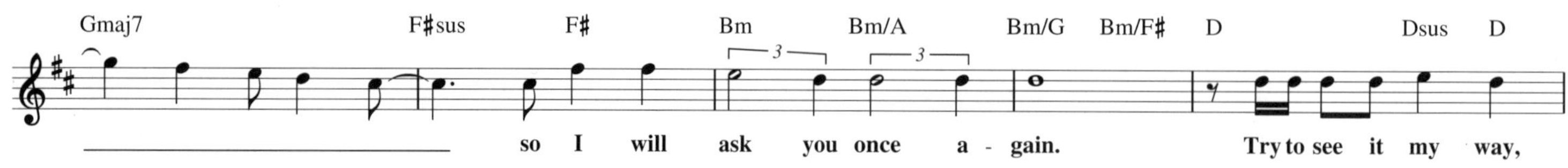
Gmaj7 F#sus F# Bm Bm/A Bm/G Bm/F# D Dsus D
so I will ask you once a - gain. Try to see it my way,

Dsus C(add2) D Dsus D Dsus
on-ly time will tell if I am right or I am wrong. While you see it your way there's a chance that we might fall a -

C(add2) D G D G Asus A D G6/D D
part be-fore too long. We can work it out, we can work it out.
(Instrumental)

WE GOTTA GET OUT OF THIS PLACE

© 1965 (Renewed 1993) SCREEN GEMS-EMI MUSIC INC.

Words and Music by BARRY MANN
and CYNTHIA WEIL

WHATEVER GETS YOU THROUGH THE NIGHT

© 1974 LENONO.MUSIC
All Rights Controlled and Administered by EMI BLACKWOOD MUSIC INC.

Words and Music by
JOHN LENNON

WHEEL IN THE SKY

© 1978, 1980 TRIO MUSIC COMPANY, INC., WEED HIGH NIGHTMARE MUSIC and LACEY BOULEVARD MUSIC

Words and Music by ROBERT FLEISCHMAN, NEAL SCHON and DIANE VALORY

Moderate Rock

Dm

Win-ter is here a - gain oh Lord; have-n't been home in a year or more.
I been try - in' to make it home; got to make it be - fore too long.

C Bb Dm

I hope she holds on a lit - tle long - er.
Ooo I can't take this ver-y much long - er
(Instrumental)

Sent a let - ter on a long sum-mer day made of sil - ver, not of clay.
I'm stand-in' in the sleet and rain. Don't think I'll nev - er gon-na make it home a - gain.

C Bb Dm

Ooo I've been run - nin' down this dust - y road.
The morn - in' sun is ris - in' it's kiss-in' the day.
Ooo the

𝄋 Dm F C Dm F C

wheel in the sky keeps on turn - in'. I don't know where I'll be to - mor - row.

Dm F C G/B C Gm/Bb **To Coda** 𝄌

(1.,2.) Wheel in the sky keeps on turn - in'.
(3.) Wheel in the sky keeps me yearn - in'.
Whoa.

1. Dm *(Instrumental)*

2. G/B C Gm/Bb N.C.

Now, now, now, now, now, for to - mor-row.

Dm *(Instrumental)* *Guitar solo ad lib.* C **Play 3 times**

Bb C Dm C Bb **D.S. al Coda**

Oh, the

CODA

Dm *(Instrumental)*

Oh, the

Dm F

wheel in the sky keeps on
Wheel in the sky keeps on

C Dm F C **Play 4 times** Bb **Repeat and Fade**

turn - in'. I don't know where I'll be to - mor - row.
turn - in'. I don't know, I don't know I don't know.
(Instrumental)

WHILE MY GUITAR GENTLY WEEPS

© 1968 HARRISONGS LTD.
Copyright Renewed 1997

Words and Music by
GEORGE HARRISON

To Coda
D E7 Am Am/G F#m7b5
For ev - 'ry mis - take we must sure - ly be learn -
Look
Fmaj7 Am G C E D.S. al Coda
- ing; Still my gui - tar gen - tly weeps.
CODA
Am Am/G F#m7b5 Fmaj7 Am
at you all. Still my gui - tar
G C E7 Am Am/G F#m7b5
gen - tly weeps.
(Instrumental)
Fmaj7 Am Am/G D E7 Repeat and Fade
WHITE ROOM
Copyright © 1968 by Dratleaf Ltd.
Copyright Renewed
All Rights Administered by Unichappell Music Inc.
Words and Music by JACK BRUCE
and PETE BROWN
Moderate Rock
Dm F/C G/B Bb C Dm F G Bb C
In a white room with black cur - tains, near the sta - tion. Black-roof
no strings could se - cure you at the sta - tion. Plat-form
par - ty she was kind - ness in the hard crowd. Con - so -
coun - try, no gold pave - ments, tired star - lings. Sil - ver
tick - et, rest - less die - sels, good - bye win - dows. I walked
la - tion from the old wound now for - got - ten. Yel - low
hors - es, run - down moon - beams in your dark eyes. Dawn-light smiles on your
in - to such a sad time at the sta - tion. As I walked out, felt my
ti - gers crouched in jun - gles in her dark eyes. She's just dress - ing good-bye
G/B Bb C Dm F G Bb C G Bb
leav - ing, my con - tent - ment. I'll wait in this place where the sun nev - er
own need just be - gin - ning. I'll wait in the queue when the trains come
win - dows, tired star - lings. I'll sleep in this place with the lone - ly
A C G Bb C 1, 2 D N.C.
shines, wait in this place
back, lie with you
crowd, lie in the dark
where the shad - ows run from them - selves.
You said
At the
3 D Gm F Dm C D.C. and Fade Am7
selves. Ah, ah, ah, ah. Ah.

WHITE RABBIT

Copyright © 1966 IRVING MUSIC, INC.
Copyright Renewed

Words and Music by
GRACE SLICK

Moderately
Am
B♭
One pill makes you larg - er and one pill makes you small. And the
you go chas - ing rab - bits and you know you're going to fall. Tell 'em all

Am
B♭
C
ones that moth - er gives you don't do an - y - thing at all. Go ask A - lice
who got a smok - in' cat - er - pil - lar has giv - en you the call. Call A - lice

E♭
F
C
1
2
G
when she's ten feet tall. And if
when she was just small. When men on the

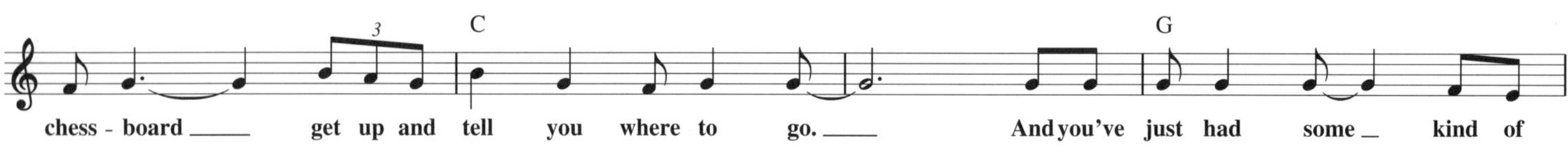
C
G
3
chess - board get up and tell you where to go. And you've just had some kind of

C
Am
mush - room, and your mind is mov - ing low, go ask A - lice, I think she'll know.

B♭
When log - ic and pro - por - tion have fall - en slop - py dead, and the

Am
B♭
C
White Knight is talk - ing back - wards, and the Red Queen's lost her head, re - mem - ber

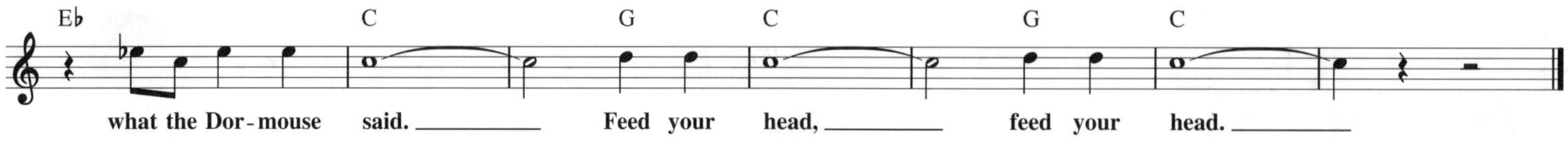
E♭
C
G
C
G
C
what the Dor - mouse said. Feed your head, feed your head.

A WHITER SHADE OF PALE

© Copyright 1967 (Renewed) Onward Music Ltd., London, England
TRO - Essex Music, Inc., New York, controls all publication rights for the U.S.A. and Canada

Words and Music by KEITH REID
and GARY BROOKER

WILD THING

© 1965 (Renewed 1993) EMI BLACKWOOD MUSIC INC.

Words and Music by
CHIP TAYLOR

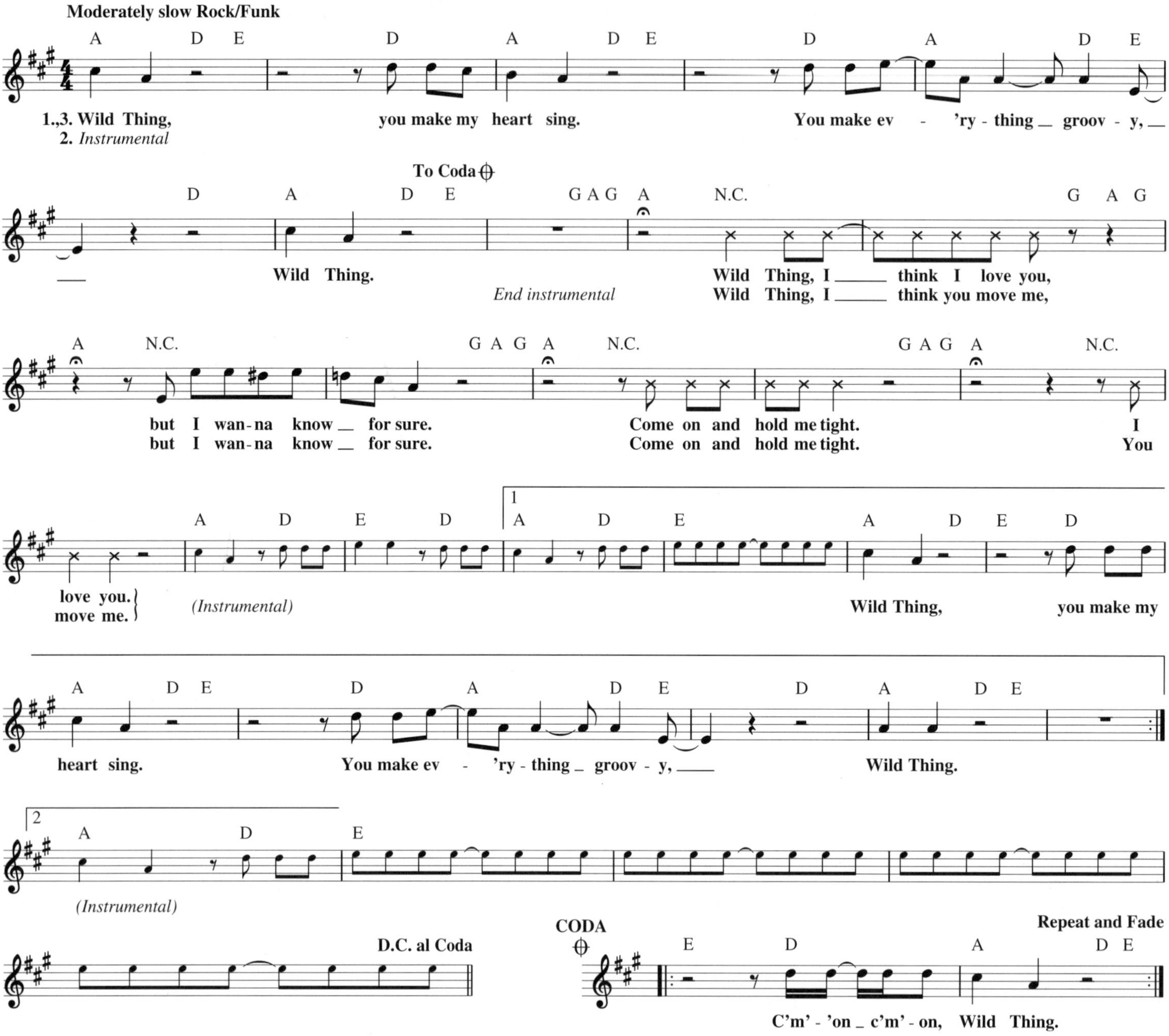

Moderately slow Rock/Funk

A D E D A D E D A D E

1.,3. Wild Thing, you make my heart sing. You make ev - 'ry - thing groov - y,

2. *Instrumental*

To Coda

D A D E G A G A A N.C. G A G

Wild Thing. *End instrumental* Wild Thing, I think I love you,

Wild Thing, I think you move me,

A N.C. G A G A A N.C. G A G A A N.C.

but I wan-na know for sure. Come on and hold me tight. I

but I wan-na know for sure. Come on and hold me tight. You

A D E D 1 A D E A D E D

love you. / move me. *(Instrumental)* Wild Thing, you make my

A D E D A D E D A D E

heart sing. You make ev - 'ry - thing groov - y, Wild Thing.

2 A D E

(Instrumental)

D.C. al Coda

CODA

Repeat and Fade

E D A D E

C'm' - 'on c'm' - on, Wild Thing.

WILLIE AND THE HAND JIVE

© 1958 (Renewed 1986) ELDORADO MUSIC CO. (BMI)/Administered by BUG MUSIC

Words and Music by
JOHNNY OTIS

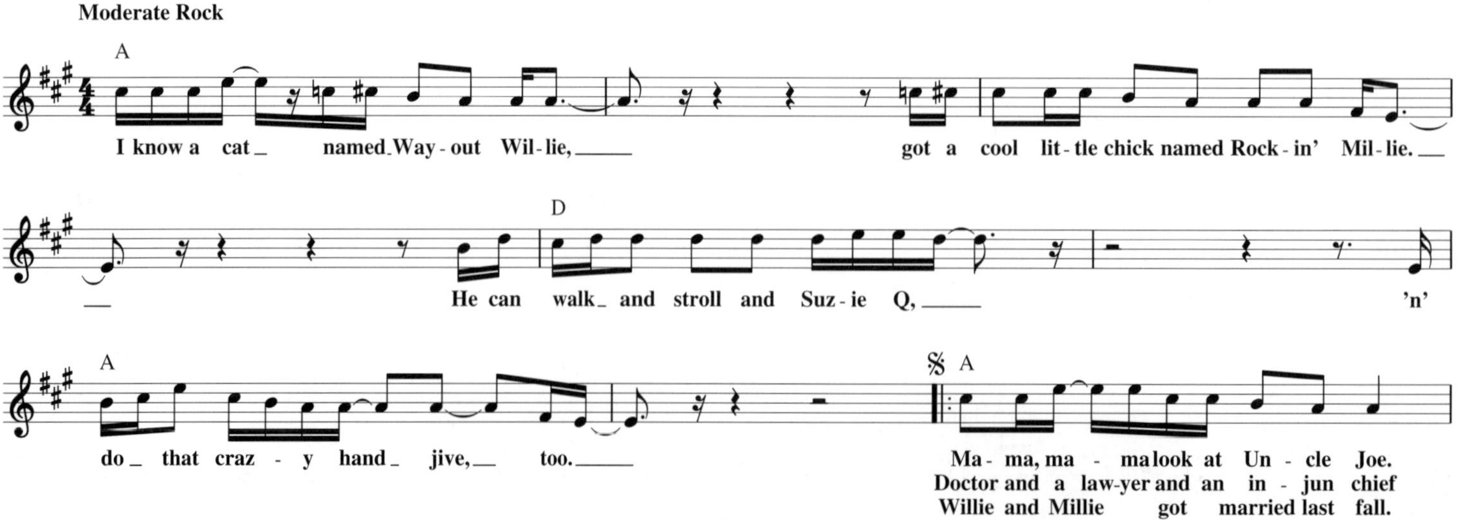

He's a do - in' the hand _ jive with sis - ter Flo.
a - they all dig that crazy beat.
They had a Little Willie Jun - ior and that ain't all. Well, the
D D7 A
Grand-ma gave ba - by sis - ter a dime, to do that hand _ jive one more time. _
Way - out Willie give 'em _ all a treat when he hit that hand _ jive with his feet. _
kids got crazy and it's _ plain to see, a - doin' the hand _ jive on T.V.
D A
Hand _ jive, hand _ jive, _ hand
E A 1-3 4
D.S. and Fade
jive, do _ that cra - zy hand jive, ah. _
WINDY
Copyright © 1967 IRVING MUSIC, INC.
Copyright Renewed
Words and Music by
RUTHANN FRIEDMAN
Moderately
F Eb Bb F Eb Bb C
Who's peek - in' out from un - der a stair - way, call - ing a name that's light - er than air?
Who's trip - pin' down the streets _ of the cit - y, smil - in' at ev - 'ry - bod - y she sees?
Instrumental solo
F Eb Bb F/C F Eb Bb6 F N.C./C
Who's bend - in' down to give ___ me a rain - bow?
Who's reach - ing out to cap - ture a mo - ment?
Ev - 'ry - one knows it's Wind - y.
End solo
N.C./C Gm7 C7 F N.C. Gm7 C N.C.
And Wind - y has storm - y ___ eyes ___ that flash _ at the sound of ___ lies. ___ And Wind - y has
Gm C7 F C 1
wings to ___ fly ___ a - bove the clouds, _ a - bove the clouds, _ a - bove the clouds, _ a - bove the clouds. _
D.C.
(no repeat)
2
a - bove the clouds, _ a - bove the clouds, _ a - bove the clouds. _
F Eb Bb F Eb Bb C
Who's trip - pin' down the streets _ of the cit - y, smil - in' at ev - 'ry - bod - y she sees?
Repeat and Fade
F Eb Bb F Eb Bb6 F
Who's reach - ing out to cap - ture a mo - ment? Ev - 'ry - one knows it's Wind - y.

WONDERFUL TONIGHT

Copyright © 1977 by Eric Patrick Clapton
All Rights for the U.S. Administered by Unichappell Music Inc.

Words and Music by
ERIC CLAPTON

WOULDN'T IT BE NICE

Copyright © 1966 IRVING MUSIC, INC.
Copyright Renewed

Words and Music by BRIAN WILSON,
TONY ASHER and MIKE LOVE

YOU MAKE LOVIN' FUN

Copyright © 1977 by Careers-BMG Music Publishing, Inc.

Words and Music by
CHRISTINE McVIE

G
was - n't hurt - ing an - y one, and we all
but I made it home a - live, so you said
I said, "Take me as I am," 'cause you might
that it's all be - cause of you, and you would -
E
Asus/E
1, 3
A7
D/A
A7
en - joyed the week - end for a change.
that on - ly proves that I'm in -
en - joy some mad - ness for a - while.
- n't want me an - y oth - er
D
A
2, 4, 5
A
N.C.
E
I've been strand - sane.
Now think way.
End instrumental
(2., 5.) You may be right.
(4.) You may be right.
N.C.
A
N.C.
I may be cra - zy; but it just
I may be cra - zy; but it just
E
D
F#m7
may be a lun - a - tic you're look - ing for.
may be a lun - a - tic you're look - ing for.
A
N.C.
E
N.C.
Turn out the light, don't try to save
It's too late to fight, it's too late to change
A
N.C.
D
me. You may be wrong for all I know
me. You may be wrong for all I know
To Coda
Asus/E
A
1
A7
D/A
A7
D/A
A7
but you may be right.
but you may be right.
(Instrumental)
D/A
A7
D/A
A
D.C.
2
A7
D/A
A7
D/A
D.C. al Coda
(End instrumental)
Well re - mem -
(Instrumental)
CODA
A7sus
D/A
A7
D/A
A7
D/A
A7
Repeat and Fade
D/A
A7
(Instrumental)
You may be wrong but you may be right.

YOU AIN'T SEEN NOTHIN' YET

Copyright © 1974 Sony/ATV Songs LLC
All Rights Administered by Sony/ATV Music Publishing, 8 Music Square West, Nashville, TN 37203

Words and Music by
RANDY BACHMAN

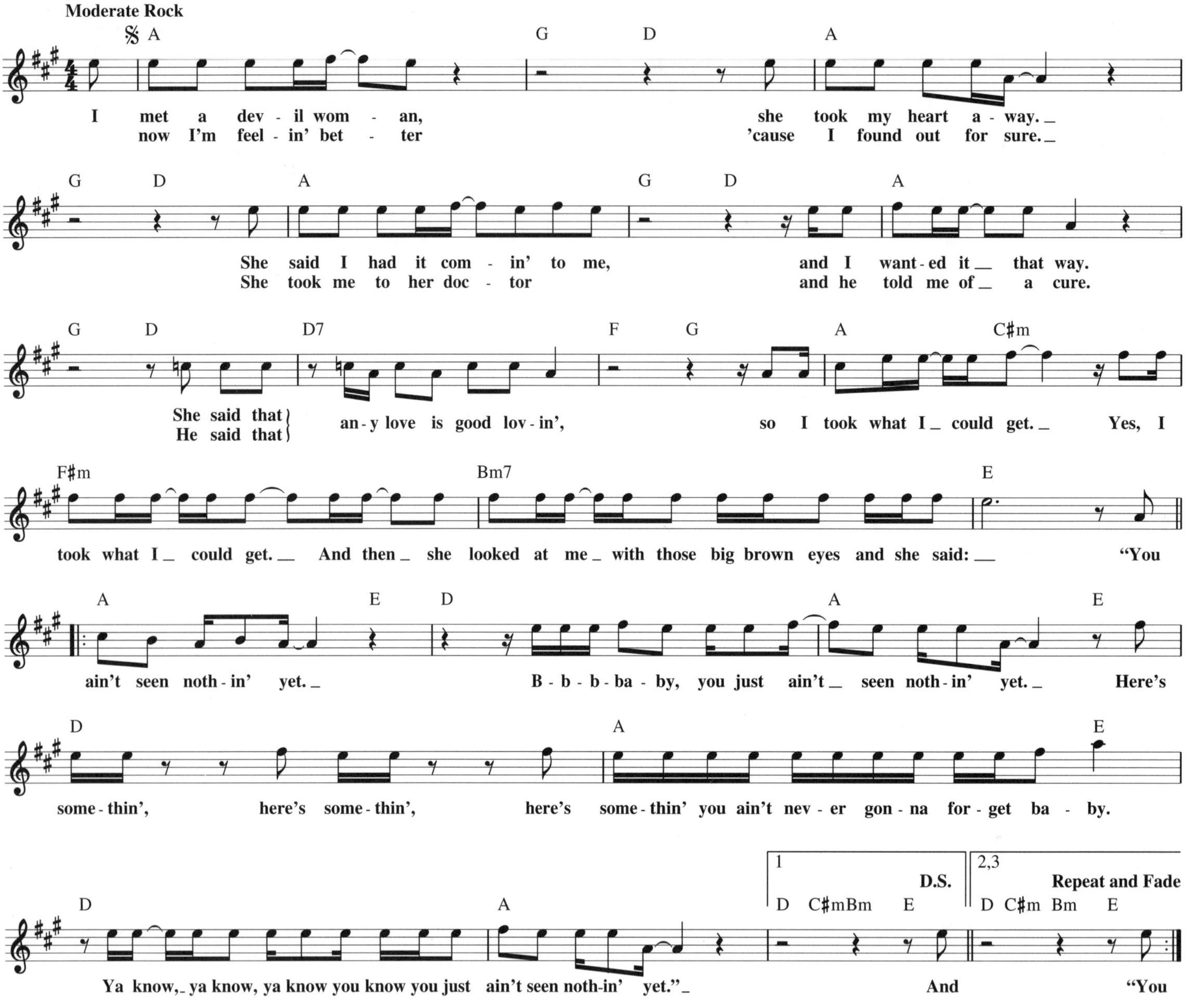

Moderate Rock

A G D A
I met a dev - il wom - an, she took my heart a - way.
now I'm feel - in' bet - ter 'cause I found out for sure.

G D A G D A
She said I had it com - in' to me, and I want - ed it that way.
She took me to her doc - tor and he told me of a cure.

G D D7 F G A C♯m
She said that / He said that any love is good lov - in', so I took what I could get. Yes, I

F♯m Bm7 E
took what I could get. And then she looked at me with those big brown eyes and she said: "You

A E D A E
ain't seen noth - in' yet. B - b - b - ba - by, you just ain't seen noth - in' yet. Here's

D A E
some - thin', here's some - thin', here's some - thin' you ain't nev - er gon - na for - get ba - by.

D A
Ya know, ya know, ya know you know you just ain't seen noth - in' yet."

1. D.S. D C♯m Bm E — And
2,3. Repeat and Fade D C♯m Bm E — "You

YOU WEAR IT WELL

© 1972 (Renewed 2000) EMI FULL KEEL MUSIC, ROD STEWART and CHAPPELL & CO.
All Rights for ROD STEWART Controlled and Administered by EMI APRIL MUSIC INC.

Words and Music by ROD STEWART
and MARTIN QUITTENTON

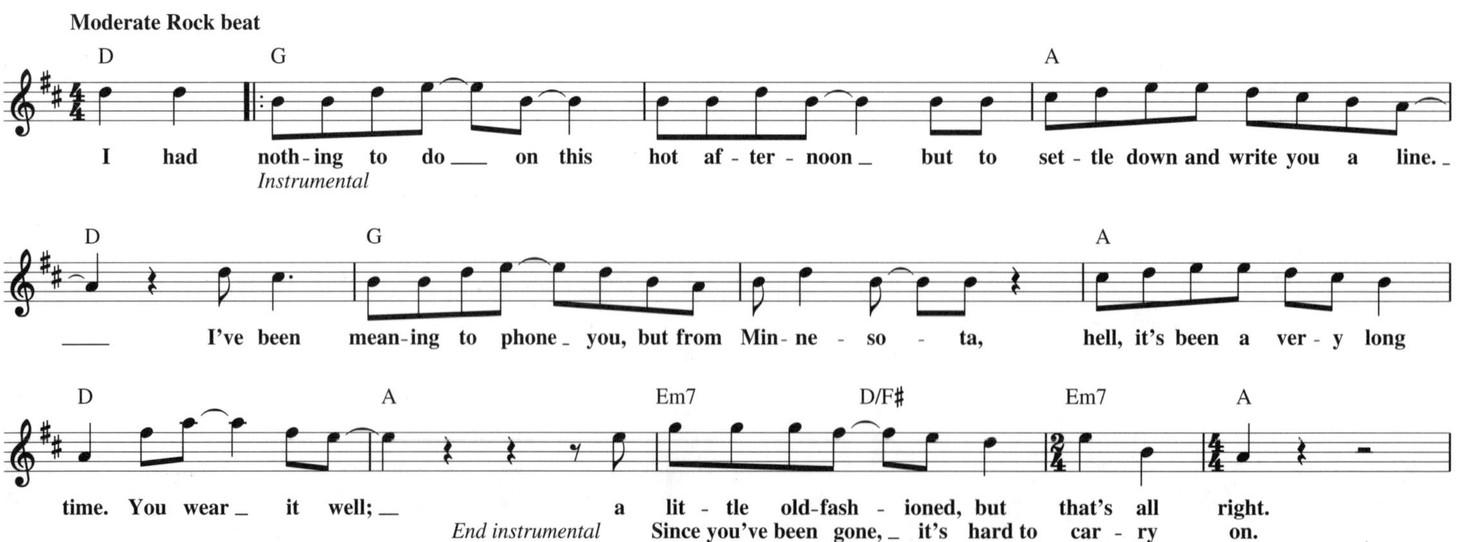

Well, I sup-pose you're think-in' how Bet-ty is sink - in', or he would-n't get in touch _ with me. ___
I'm gon-na write a-bout the birth - day gown that I bought in town, ___ and you sat down and cried on the stairs. _
___ Though I ain't beg-gin' or los-in' my head, _ I sure do want you to know _
___ You knew it did-n't cost the earth, _ but, for what it's worth, _ you made me feel a mil - lion-aire. _
___ that you wear it well; _ ver-y the la - dy in the fan so fine. Oh, my.
___ And you wear it well. _ Mad-ame O-nas - sis got noth-in' on you. No, no.
Re-mem-ber their base-ment par - ties, your broth-ers ca-vort - ing, the all day rock-and-roll
And when my cof-fee is cold _ and I'm get - tin' told _ that I got-ta get back _ to
show. The home - sick blues and the rad - i - cal views _ have-n't left a mark ___ on
work, so when the sun goes low and you're home all a - lone, _ think of me and try not to
you. You wear it well; ___ a lit - tle out of time, _ but I don't
laugh, and I'll wear it well. ___ I don't ob - ject if you call col -
mind. But I ain't for - get-tin' that you were once mine, but I'll be -
lect. 'Cause I ain't for - get-tin' that you were once mine. But I
lieve it with-out e-ven try'n'. _ Now I'm eat-tin' my heart _ out, try'n' to get a let-ter through.
feel it with-out e-ven try'n'. _ Now I'm eat-tin' my heart _ out,
try'n' to get back _ to you.
(Instrumental)
Repeat and Fade
D G A Em7 D/F# N.C. Asus

YOU GIVE LOVE A BAD NAME

© 1986 EMI APRIL MUSIC INC., DESMOBILE MUSIC CO., INC., UNIVERSAL - POLYGRAM INTERNATIONAL PUBLISHING, INC., BON JOVI PUBLISHING and NEW JERSEY UNDERGROUND MUSIC INC.
All Rights for DESMOBILE MUSIC CO., INC. Controlled and Administered by EMI APRIL MUSIC INC.

Words and Music by DESMOND CHILD, JON BON JOVI and RICHIE SAMBORA

E D♯m7 C♯m7 B
Breez - in' through the cli - en - tele, spin - ning yarns that were so lyr - i - cal,
big - bos - omed la - dy with the Dutch ac - cent who tried to change my point of view, her
E D♯m7 C♯m7 1 B E
I real - ly must con - fess right here the at - trac - tion was pure - ly phys - i - cal.
(Instrumental)
ad lib. lines were well re - hearsed, but my heart cried out for
D♯m7 C♯m7 B 2 E A D
(End instrumental) you. You're in my heart; you're in my
A A/C♯ D A A/C♯ D
soul. You'd be my breath should I grow old. You are my lov - er; you're my best
A D C♯m Bm7 A Adim7 E
friend. You're in my soul.
My love for you is im - meas -
You're an es - say in glam - our. Please
D♯m7 C♯m7 B E
- ur - a - ble; my re - spect for you im - mense. You're age - less, time - less,
par - don the gram - mar, but you're ev - 'ry school - boy's dream. You're Cel - tic u - nit - ed,
D♯m7 C♯m7 B E
lace and fine - ness; you're beau - ty and el - e - gance. You're a rhap - so - dy, a
but ba - by, I've de - cid - ed you're the best team I've ev - er seen. And there have been
D♯m7 C♯m7 B E
com - e - dy; you're a sym - pho - ny and a play. You're ev - 'ry love song
man - y af - fairs and man - y times I've thought to leave. But I bite my lip and
D♯m7 C♯m7 1 E A 2 E A
ev - er writ - ten, but hon - ey, what do you see in me. You're in my heart;
turn a - round, 'cause you're the warm - est thing I've ev - er found. You're in my heart;
D A A/C♯ D A A/C♯
you're in my soul. You'd be my breath should I grow old. You are my lov -
D A D C♯m Bm7 A
- er; you're my best friend. You're in my soul.

YOU'RE MY BEST FRIEND

© 1975 B. FELDMAN & CO., LTD., Trading As TRIDENT MUSIC
All Rights Controlled and Administered by GLENWOOD MUSIC CORP.

Words and Music by
JOHN DEACON

YOU'VE GOT TO HIDE YOUR LOVE AWAY

Copyright © 1965 Sony/ATV Songs LLC
Copyright Renewed
All Rights Administered by Sony/ATV Music Publishing, 8 Music Square West, Nashville, TN 37203

Words and Music by JOHN LENNON
and PAUL McCARTNEY

YOU'VE MADE ME SO VERY HAPPY

© 1967 (Renewed 1995) JOBETE MUSIC CO., INC.
All Rights Controlled and Administered by EMI APRIL MUSIC INC. and
EMI BLACKWOOD MUSIC INC. on behalf of JOBETE MUSIC CO., INC. and
STONE AGATE MUSIC (A Division of JOBETE MUSIC CO., INC.)

Words and Music by BERRY GORDY, FRANK E. WILSON,
BRENDA HOLLOWAY and PATRICE HOLLOWAY

B♭
(Instrumental) I love you so much, it seems ___ (Instrumental) you're e - ven in my dreams. _ I can
F C
hear, ___ ba - by, I ___ can hear you're call - ing me. (Instrumental)
B♭ E♭m7
I'm so in love with you ___ All I ev - er want to do ___ is
Dm7 N.C. E♭m7 Dm7 N.C. Dm(add2)
thank you ba - by, thank you, ba - by! (Instrumental)
E♭m D♭
(End instrumental)
E♭m7
You made me ___ so ___ ver - y hap - py. I'm so glad you
A♭9 D♭maj7 B♭7 E♭m7
came in - to my life. (Instrumental) You made me ___ so ___
G♭m6 Fm7 B♭7♭5
ver - y ___ hap - py. You made _ me so, so ver - y hap - py, ba - by.
E♭m7 A♭7♭5 N.C. G♭(add2)
I'm so glad you came in - to ___ my ___ life.
C♭maj7 G♭(add2) C♭maj7
Mmm, ___ I wan - na thank you, girl!
G♭(add2) C♭maj7 G♭(add2)
Ev - 'ry day of my life ___ I wan - na thank you. ___
C♭maj7 G♭(add2) C♭maj7
You made me so ___ ver - y hap - py. Oh, I wan - na spend my life ___
G♭(add2) C♭maj7 G♭(add2) Repeat and Fade
thank - ing you. ___ Thank you, ba - by! ___ Thank you, ba - by! ___ Thank you,

YOUNG AMERICANS

© 1974 EMI MUSIC PUBLISHING LTD., JONES MUSIC AMERICA and MOTH MUSIC
All Rights for EMI MUSIC PUBLISHING LTD. Controlled and Administered by COLGEMS-EMI MUSIC INC.
All Rights for JONES MUSIC AMERICA Administered by ARZO PUBLISHING
All Rights for MOTH MUSIC Administered by CHRYSALIS SONGS

Words and Music by
DAVID BOWIE

G/A A D Em7
not a myth left from the ghet - to. Well, well, well could ya car - ry a ra - zor in case, just in
G G/A A
case of de - pres - sion? Sit on your hands on the bus of sur - viv - ors, blush - ing at all the Af - ro - Shei - las.
D Em7 G
Ain't that close to love? Well, ain't that pos - ter love? Well, it ain't that Bar - bie doll.
G/A A G6 A6
Her heart's been bro - ken, just like you have. All night,
(All night.)
A D Em7
want the young A - mer - i - can, young A - mer - i - can.
(Young A - mer - i - can, young A - mer - i - can, you want the young
G6 G/A A
A - mer - i - can.) All right, you want the young A - mer - i - can.
D Em7
You ain't a pimp, and you ain't a hust - ler. Pimps got a Cad - i and a la - dy's got a Chrys - ler.
G G/A A
Blacks got re - spect and white got his soul train. Ma - ma's got cramps, and look at your hands, hey.
D Em7
(I heard the news to - day, oh boy.) I got - ta suite and you got de - feat.
G G/A A
Ain't there a man who can say no more. And ain't there a wom - an I can sock on the jaw? And
D Em7
ain't there a child I can hold with - out judg - ing? Ain't there a pen that will write be - fore they die?
G G/A
Ain't you proud that you still got fac - es? Ain't there one damn song that can make me break down and
G6 A6
cry? All night I want the young A - mer - i - can.
D Em7 Repeat and Fade
Young A - mer - i - can, young A - mer - i - can, I want the young A - mer - i - can.

YOUNG TURKS

© 1981 ROD STEWART and EMI FULL KEEL MUSIC
All Rights for ROD STEWART Controlled and Administered by EMI APRIL MUSIC INC.

Words and Music by ROD STEWART, KEVIN SAVIGAR, CARMINE APPICE and DUANE HITCHINGS

Moderate Rock

Fm Fm/A♭ Cm7

Bill - y left his home with a dol - lar in his pock - et and a head full of dreams. He said

Fm Fm/A♭ Cm7 Fm

some - how, some way it's got - ta get bet - ter than this. Pat - ti packed her bags, left a

Fm/A♭ Cm7 Fm

note for her mom - ma, she was just sev - en - teen. There were tears in her eyes when she

Fm/A♭ B♭

kissed her lit - tle sis - ter good - bye. They

𝄋 Fm Fm/A♭ Cm7

held each oth - er tight as they drove on through the night, they were so ex - cit - ed. We got just
dise was closed so they head - ed for the coast in a bliss - ful man - ner. They took a
Instrumental solo
Bill - y wrote a let - ter back home to Pat - ti's par - ents try - in' to ex - plain. He said we're

Fm Fm/A♭ Cm7

one shot of life, let's take it while we're still not a - fraid. Be - cause
two - room a - part - ment that was jump - ing ev - 'ry night of the week.
both real sor - ry that it had to turn out this way. But there

Fm Fm/A♭ Cm7

life is so brief and time is a thief when you're un - de - cid - ed. And like a
Hap - pi - ness was found in each oth - er's arms as ex - pect - ed.
ain't no point in talk - ing when there's no - bod - y list - 'ning so we just ran a - way.

Fm Fm/A♭ B♭ To Coda ⊕ E♭ Cm

fist - ful of sand, it can slip right through your hands. ooh!
Bill - y pierced his ears, drove a pick - up like a lun - a - tic, *Instrumental ends*
Pat - ti gave birth to a ten pound ba - by boy, yeah!
Young hearts, be free to - night.

Gm B♭ E♭ Cm Gm 1, 2 A♭

Time is on your side. Don't let them put you down,

C♭ D♭ E♭ A♭ C♭ B♭

don't let 'em push you a - round, don't let 'em ev - er change your point of view. *(Instrumental)*

E♭/B♭ B♭ E♭/B♭ 3 D.S. al Coda

Par - a -
Spoken: Come on now!

CODA ⊕

E♭ Cm Gm E♭ Cm Gm **Repeat and Fade**

hearts, be free to - night. Time is on your side. Young